THE GIRL IN
THE HAIRY PAW

. . P r o g r a m m e . .

(A) SELECTED SHORT SUBJECTS

(B) OVERTURE

Grauman's Chinese Theatre Orchestra — Al Erickson Directing

(C) SID GRAUMAN'S PROLOGUE

Conceived and Staged by SID GRAUMAN

Leroy Prinz, Assistant to Mr. Grauman

"A SCENE IN THE JUNGLE"

(1) The Voo-Doo Dancer
(2) Return of the Hunters
(3) Gathering of the Tribes
(4) Dance to the Sacred Ape
(5) The Captive
(6) "In the Tree Tops" with Pauline Loretta
(7) Eccentric Dance of the Zulus Dudley Dickerson — Ruttledge and Taylor — The Two Sepias — The Bon Bons — Carl Gibson and Bobby Stevens.
(8) The Safari

(9) Serge Flash — European Wonder
(10) Studies in Ebony — The Cacholats
(11) The Black Ballet
(12) Gloria Gilbert — America's Premiere Danseuse
(13) Entrance of the Queen and Her Court
(14) Jimmy Savo
(15) "Goodbye Africa" — Ensemble with Alma Travers and Marguerite Robinson
(16) Chilton and Thomas — Absolutely Individual
(17) Grand Finale — Ensemble

Chorus of Dusky Maidens and African Choral Ensembles
Colton Cronin, Stage Director
Music and Lyrics by Ben Ellison and Harvey Brooks
Prologue and Picture Costumes by Western Costume Company

RKO-Radio Pictures Presents

"KING KONG"

From an Idea Conceived by MERIAN C. COOPER
Story by MERIAN C. COOPER and EDGAR WALLACE
Directed by ERNEST V. SCHOEDSACK and MERIAN C. COOPER
A Cooper-Schoedsack Production
WILLIS O'BRIEN, Chief Technician
DAVID O. SELZNICK, Executive Producer

. . . . . C A S T . . . . .

Ann Darrow	FAY WRAY
Denham	ROBERT ARMSTRONG
Driscoll	BRUCE CABOT
Englehorn	FRANK REICHER
Weston	SAM HARDY
Native Chief	NOBLE JOHNSON
Second Mate	JAMES FLAVIN
Witch King	STEVE CLEMENTO
Lumpy	VICTOR WONG

THE GIRL IN THE HAIRY PAW

King Kong as Myth, Movie, and Monster

edited by Ronald Gottesman and Harry Geduld

Foreword by Rudy Behlmer

A FLARE BOOK/PUBLISHED BY AVON BOOKS

THE GIRL IN THE HAIRY PAW is an original Flare publication.
It has never before appeared in book form.

AVON BOOKS
A division of
The Hearst Corporation
959 Eighth Avenue
New York, New York 10019

Layout and Design by Anthony Basile

The name and character "KING KONG" is used with the permission of
R.K.O. General, Inc.

First Flare Printing, April, 1976

FLARE TRADEMARK REG. U.S. PAT. OFF. AND FOREIGN COUNTRIES, REGISTERED TRADE-
MARK—MARCA REGISTRADA, HECHO EN U.S.A.

Printed in the U.S.A.

ACKNOWLEDGMENTS

It is a pleasure to acknowledge several kinds of help enthusiastically offered by many people, several of whom became our friends over the long gestation period of this enormous and complex book. In particular we wish to thank Steve Vertlieb and Elliott Stein, who were as generous with their advice and encouragement as they were with their invaluable collections of Kong and Kong-related materials. Eric Krueger tracked down many leads from the Lincoln Center branch of the New York Public Library to the Feldman Library at the American Film Institute in Beverly Hills, California. David Allen was kind enough to provide several items from his own collection and to put us in touch with such gracious professionals as Marcel Delgado and other principals involved in the making of *King Kong*. Professor Gottesman's colleague Eric Forrest went out of his way to supply slides and information on the now famous Kong sculpture in Birmingham, England. Sandi Thomason, another of his Parkside colleagues, was responsible for preparing scores of excellent photographs used in the book. Professor Geduld was assisted over and above the call of duty by friends and fellow-scholars at the library of the University of Maryland-Baltimore County and by members of the staff of the American Film Institute and the Library of Congress. Indiana University's Photographic Service must be thanked for their prompt and characteristically expert work on the enlargement and retouching of material that was not always in the best condition for photographic reproduction. Rudy Behlmer read portions of the manuscript and improved its accuracy in the process. While he lived, Merian C. Cooper took a keen interest in our project, and his widow was kind enough to read and correct portions of the manuscript and to supply photographs of her husband for use in the book. Similarly, Mrs. Darlyne O'Brien graciously supplied photographs of her husband. None of these persons are responsible, of course, for our choice of material or errors and omissions that survive their interest.

Another legion of friends, students, well-wishers, librarians and otherwise interested parties are listed below. To all we are grateful for the many services they rendered. The contributions of at least as many other persons have doubtless been neglected here. We hope that those whose names do not appear will forgive us and consider the outcome worthy of their generosity.

Yve Andino	Kathy Goff	Jerry Ohlinger
Mark Bezanson	Pat Gross	Claude Plum
Binnie Braunstein	Robert Hammond	Phil Quetschke
Ernest Burns	Steven P. Hill	Antonio Raimo
Bill Cagle	Roy Huss	Mike Reid
Dave Crow	Mary Jonaitis	Diane Rosenfeldt
Marcel Delgado	Al LaValley	T. J. Ross
Josh Feigenbaum	Arthur Lennig	Joe Slade
Robert Fiedel	Joseph McBride	Aneta Sperber
Mark Frank	Andy McLean	George Stover
Denise Frenner	Bea Jagiello McLean	Debbie Tinsley
Bruce Gearhart	Jerome Mintz	Madeleine Wright
Bill George, Jr.	Mrs. Darlyne O'Brien	

CONTENTS

FOREWORD

During the spring and summer of 1965 I had occasion to spend a considerable amount of time with King Kong's creator, Merian C. Cooper, in conjunction with an article dealing with his impressive career in motion pictures that I was preparing for *Films in Review*. Cooper at the time was seventy-one and lived in Pacific Palisades, near Los Angeles. He also had an office there, and we met either in his home, office or on occasion for lunch at the Beverly Wilshire Hotel in Beverly Hills.

If Cooper had to his credit only the early expeditionary documentaries *Grass* and *Chang*, he certainly would have a secure place in film history, but add to these achievements his contributions to Cinerama—which went beyond his producing and co-directing the first film in the original three negative process, *This is Cinerama*—and the truly unique *King Kong*, which he produced and directed in association with Ernest B. Schoedsack from his own original conception.

A straightforward man of action, Cooper had prodigious energy and youthful enthusiasm. He was involved in a variety of pursuits throughout his lifetime and claimed more adventures and accomplishments than a score of other important figures rolled into one. A flier in both World Wars and the Polish-Russian war of 1919–1921, wounded and twice a prisoner of war, an early advocate and participant in civilian aviation and one of the original directors of Pan American and Western Airlines, a major catalyst in the promotion and general acceptance of three-color Technicolor, head of production at RKO Studios, John Ford's partner and producer for many years—these are some of the highlights of his kaleidoscopic life.

Cooper was split down the middle in his professional interests, his two great passions being films and aviation. He was able to be heavily involved in both.

Fortunately for me, Cooper never did anything halfway. Once he decided to grant me what was to be at first one interview, and he realized that I wanted to dig into all aspects of his amazing career, he helped me in every way possible. I have always been a stickler for accuracy, and at last I met someone who was my match and then some. Cooper's recall was precise and backed up by all kinds of correspondence, letters of agreement, memos, old newspaper accounts and excerpts from one thing or another. He was a saver who believed in photocopying (before the days of Xerox), following up a meeting with written confirmation, and generally organized procedure.

With regard to film, Cooper was first and always a showman—in the traditional meaning of that word. He was most interested in those aspects of the movies which are the most cinematic: exotic locales, sweep and movement, special effects, advances in color reproduction, and the possibilities of the wide screen. Not a dealer in obscurities, in the complexities of human nature, nor in the contemporary scene, his work was bold or sentimental, but very seldom anything in between.

Marguerite Harrison, the newspaper correspondent, political writer and world traveler, who was in partnership with Cooper and Schoedsack and accompanied them during the filming of their study of the primitive, migratory tribe of Iran for *Grass*, described Cooper perfectly in her autobiography, *There's Always Tomorrow* (1935):

> Short, muscular and thickset, with sparse sandy hair, a sharp pointed nose, eyes like blue China buttons, a pugnacious jaw and an aggressive manner. He was disdainful of all the refinements in life which were "soft" in his opinion. . . . Stubborn as a mule, moody, quick-tempered but generous, and loyal to the point of fanaticism. . . . Merian's turn of mind was essentially dramatic. He was forever striving for startling climaxes and sharp contrasts. . . . He already possessed the flair for the bizarre and the unusual and the vivid imagination which have made him one of the most remarkable directors in the film world, but at that time his ambition was . . . to become a great explorer.

Following *Grass*, Cooper and Schoedsack spent fourteen months in the jungles of what was then Siam, making *Chang*. Cooper first met Schoedsack on his way to Poland in 1919. Cooper told me, "Schoedsack and

I were a good team. Fortunately we could do a lot of each other's jobs and overlap one another in various areas, but I certainly was never in his class as a photographer."

In 1929 after completing production on *The Four Feathers,* Cooper was writing in longhand an 85,000 word monograph on baboons, based on notes made while observing the creatures night and day for months during the filming of portions of *The Four Feathers* in Africa. One day, when the manuscript was almost completed, the maid, who took care of his small apartment in New York City, thinking the pile of rumpled papers was trash, threw away the work. Despite his usual attention to records of his work, Cooper had no carbon copies and never could bring himself to rewrite the tome.

During this same period, Cooper read a book written by a good friend, W. Douglas Burden, who was a trustee of the American Museum of Natural History in New York City. *The Dragon Lizards of Komodo* (Putnam's, 1927) was a factual account of the naturalist-explorer and his wife's visit to the island of Komodo in the East Indies. Here, they succeeded in making the first scientific study of the dragons, the first moving picture record of them in the wild and were responsible for the first captive specimens ever to be brought to America: the Burdens presented two nine-foot carnivorous lizards to the Bronx Zoo.

All of this serves as prologue to the genesis of *King Kong.* Answering a letter from his old friend W. Douglas Burden on June 22, 1964, Cooper said in part:

[Beginning in 1929] I was mentally intrigued with the possibility of photographing and capturing a giant gorilla (or two or three of them) in the hopes of getting one back alive to the United States. But as I began to think over your Komodo Island, I wondered how I could get my Gorilla to face your Dragons. There were no airplanes; by boat it seemed a really tough proposition. Then I began to think. Schoedsack and I, in 1927 and 1928, had gone to Africa to film the African scenes, particularly animals, for the picture *Four Feathers.* We planned to intercut these with Hollywood scenes. As you know, this was the first picture in history where people had gone into the wilderness of Africa to shoot scenes to intercut with Hollywood scenes. . . .

On the sceen in the final picture, the hippos of the Rovuma River, the baboons of the Abyssinian frontier and the Fuzzy Wuzzies of the Northern Sudan were all tied together by careful intercutting so as to seem in one place although it was actually ten months' work stretched over about a thousand miles. Schoedsack and I tied it all together by building an integrating location between Palm Springs and Indio . . . and with studio interiors. Back projection had not yet been fully developed (but it was in the air) so in *Four Feathers* Schoedsack and I did it merely by intercutting. Then one day, after one of my conversations with you, I thought to myself, why not film my Gorilla —either a Kivu Gorilla in the Congo or a Spanish African Gorilla, or both, and then go back to your Komodo Island and film your Dragons and for the purposes of the picture tie them both together in the same way as I had tied together the elements of *Four Feathers.* I also had very firmly in mind to giantize both the Gorilla and your Dragons to make them really huge. However, I always believed in personalizing and focusing attention on *one* main character and from the very beginning I intended to make it the Gigantic Gorilla, no matter what else I surrounded him with.

When you told me that the two Komodo Dragons you brought back to the Bronx Zoo, where they drew great crowds, were eventually killed by civilization, I immediately thought of doing the same thing with my Giant Gorilla. I had already established him in my mind on a prehistoric island with prehistoric monsters, and I now thought of having him destroyed by the most sophisticated thing I could think of in civilization, and in the most fantastic way. My very original concept was to place him on the top of the Empire State Building and have him killed by airplanes. I made considerable investigation on how this could be done technically with a live gorilla so as to be believable and at the same time maintain the ratio of the world's largest animal to the world's biggest building. I thought that by mattes and double printing and the new technique called rear projection it could be done. I was already familiar with the Dunning Process of using a blue background and I personally conceived and initiated development of the photographic process afterwards called "miniature projection." Anyhow, technically and dramatically I was confident it was possible and went ahead and wrote a number of outlines of *King Kong* in the years 1929–30 up in my little apartment on E. 73rd St., in New York City. . . .

In a letter to Cooper written on June 15, 1964, Douglas Burden commented:

I recall your contacting me at the American Museum of Natural History late in 1929. You were seeking information about the different species of gorilla. This was in connection with a picture you were then planning to make in Africa. . . .

Having always been tremendously intrigued by this remarkable creature, the gorilla, I was most interested in your project and invited you out to our house in Bedford Village where, on many occasions, we discussed the whole idea at some length. . . .

I remember, for example, that you were quite intrigued by my description of prehistoric Komodo Island and the dragon lizards that inhabited it. . . . You liked the idea of "King of Komodo." You especially liked the strength of words beginning with K such as Kodak, Kodiak Island, and Komodo. . . . I believe that it was a combination of the King of Komodo phrase in my book and your invention of the name Kong that led to the title you used much later on, *King Kong.* . . . I recall describing to you Komodo as a remote, hard to reach volcanic island, the very elements that you used in the setting of your picture. And I told you that I had taken my young wife there which could possibly have led to your use of a young girl in *King Kong.* . . .

In a night letter to Burden sent June 12, 1964, Cooper stated:

In *King Kong* I made a deliberate combination of you, Schoedsack and me. . . . Your description of Komodo Island fulfilled my dramatic 3-D's— Distance, Difficulty, Danger. . . . My idea of taking Fay Wray along stemmed from your taking Babs [Burden's wife] among the Komodo Dragons. My scene of Kong coming out of the jungle to the mountain top and beating his chest against the sun as he looked over the island below came from your description that you gave me of you and Babs breaking out of the mountain forest on Komodo and looking down at the wonderful view below. . . . Indeed the whole basic story I talked over with you with delight many times in 1929 and 1930 as it developed in my mind. . . .

Going back to Cooper's June 22, 1964 letter to Burden, he says:

My ex-partner, Ernest B. Schoedsack, was still in Sumatra making, on his own, a picture entitled *Rango*, so I presented my idea to Myron and David Selznick, both of whom had gone to New York [in 1931] with the idea of getting a new picture company started for David Selznick to run. Instead of starting a new company of his own . . .

he became the studio head of RKO. At Myron Selznick's suggestion I tried to buy from Irving Thalberg over the phone the rights to *Tarzan,* which he had just purchased for about $20,000. I thought that I might be able to do the backgrounds of two African pictures at once, in both of which I could use the wildlife of Africa. I think Myron Selznick offered Thalberg $50,000 for me, which Thalberg declined. Anyhow . . . I later [October or November of 1931] came on out to Hollywood to talk to David Selznick. I found RKO in a turmoil, as this was in the depression, but Selznick was taking hold with a firm hand. He asked me to help him and I told him I was interested only in my adventure picture, *King Kong*, but nobody in Hollywood in the depression was willing to tie up considerable money in what seemed to them a hazardous trip into foreign wilds. . . .

David O. Selznick wrote to Cooper in 1963 to clarify some legal matters, and in reviewing aspects of their past association said in part:

Growing out of our close friendship and the many discussions we had had in New York, I invited you to come out to see whether you would like to become associated with me in the new work. As I further recall it, you said you would come out but refused salary. Subsequently, I did engage you as my executive assistant, and among other things assigned to you the problem of studying and cutting down the overhead (on which you did a superb job). . . .

RKO had made a considerable investment, as I recall it, under the previous studio administration, in a proposed prehistoric film [*Creation*] utilizing an animation process. I requested you to study the whole thing, and the investment, and to give me your recommendations. You did this and . . . brought in the sketches . . . I do recall that I was overwhelmed and enthusiastic. You told me the outline of the story and I told you to proceed. My recollection is quite clear on this. . . .

Most revealing of all is a memo from Cooper to Selznick, dated December 19, *1931*, which I found in late 1970 in the business records storage building containing Selznick's memos. Cooper later showed me his copy of the original.

Dear Mr. Selznick:
    I have carefully gone over the whole *Creation* setup and its possibilities.

1. I made a short test, solely to see the possibilities of animation. In this test, the animal fight is made on a separate key from the men, so that the men can be removed and the animal fight used in the final picture. This has been done to save loss of time and money if the picture is made. The results of animation show that the animals will always be somewhat mechanical, but if kept in motion and the speed slowed down about tweny-five percent, real effects can be realized.

2. The present story construction and the use of the animals is entirely wrong. The whole secret of successful productions of this type is startling, unusual sensation. But that sensation must be of something new, and must have character. Animals can be made into new, sensational story characters, as well as people. This has been proved on the screen in the use of Bimbo in *Chang*, Rin-Tin-Tin, etc. My idea then is to not only use the prehistoric animals for their novelty value, but also to take them out of their present character of just big beasts running around, and make them into a ferocious menace. The most important thing, however, is that one animal should have a really big character part in the picture. I suggest a prehistoric Giant Gorilla, fifty times as strong as a man—a creature of nightmare horror and drama.

I have prepared and am sending with this report, my conception of this Giant Terror Gorilla, and the kind of scenes in which he should be used. These scenes can be made just as drawn in the attached pictures, by using an animated figure against a projection background, all played against a Dunning foreground, with closeup work of full-sized head mask, and hands and feet. So far as I know, this method has never been done on the screen, and should prove sensational. It is entirely practical.

However, before any large amount of money is spent on this picture, I suggest that we make two scenes with the Giant Gorilla, to see how lifelike and terrible a character it can be made. I will make these tests so that if successful, they can be used in the picture without loss of money or time, just as I have the animation test of the fight between the two prehistoric animals. I am attaching budget for this work. As you will see, a large part of the costs are nonrecurrent, such as the construction of the Giant Gorilla, the stop motion projector, etc.

3. Again let me repeat, the success of this picture will depend on startling, unusual character sensation. The Giant Terror Gorilla should give character sensation . . .

Merian C. Cooper

attached:
1. Four scenes with Giant Gorilla.
2. Budget for gorilla construction and test.

As described elsewhere in this book the test was made and enthusiastically received. *Creation* was abandoned and *King Kong* then went into official production utilizing Willis O'Brien's special dimensional animation techniques. In his letter to Cooper, Selznick comments on writer Edgar Wallace's part in the evolution of the script:

In assigning Edgar Wallace to you and persuading you to use him, I of course had in mind not only—and importantly—his tremendous name in England (as well as in America), but his extraordinary speed and talent. . . .

I have never believed, and don't believe now, that Wallace contributed anything much to *King Kong*. But the circumstances of his death complicated the writing credits, and I think we were in agreement that his name should be used and would indeed be helpful. . . .

In a memo from Cooper to Selznick dated July 20, 1932, Cooper discusses the writing credits on *King Kong*:

The present script of *Kong*, as far as I can remember, hasn't one single idea suggested by Edgar Wallace. If there are any, they are of the slightest.

The book * will be signed by Edgar Wallace and Merian C. Cooper, and I think New York should advertise it as based on a story by Edgar Wallace and Merian C. Cooper, if you want to use Wallace's name.

I don't think it fair to say this is based on a story by Wallace alone, when he did not write it, though I recognize the value of his name, and want to use it.

I think this would be fair to the picture, and fair to me, as well.

Cooper told me in 1964 that *Gulliver's Travels* did not influence the development of incidents for *King Kong* in the least. He only recalled vaguely the Lilliputian episodes, not The Voyage to Brobdingnag, which was cited in conjunction with *Kong's* genealogy

_____
* The novelization of the screenplay by Delos Lovelace.

in a French publication, *Midi-Minuit Fantastique* (October-November, 1962). "My influences were Burden's book, *The Dragon Lizards of Komodo,* the desire to do a Giant Gorilla film, and Willis O'Brien's animation technique." He also at times alluded to the obvious overlay of the "Beauty and the Beast" concept.

Cooper became irate when we discussed those who attached "symbolic" overtones—phallic and otherwise —to various aspects of *Kong.* As far as he was concerned there were no hidden meanings, psychological or cultural implications, profound parallels or anything remotely resembling intellectual "significance" in the film.

"*King Kong* was escapist entertainment pure and simple. A more illogical picture could never have been made."

An extremely intelligent man of integrity, pride and courage, Cooper was promoted to a Brigadier General in the Air Force Reserve in 1950, and in 1952 received an honorary Award from the Academy of Motion Picture Arts and Sciences for his many innovations and contributions to the art of motion pictures.

We kept in contact during the eight years between work on my article and his death on April 21, 1973 following a long and valiant battle against cancer.

I asked him once how he approached the making of his personally produced and directed films and he told me: "You must have the ability to look at something and create on your feet; to see something and turn it to dramatic effect; to think under hardship, danger and risk, and to be independent in your work."

Merian C. Cooper was quite a guy. Difficult in many ways—yes, very difficult at times. But quite a guy.

—Rudy Behlmer

PRODUCTION CREDITS:

Executive Producer
David O. Selznick

Produced and Directed by
Merian C. Cooper
Ernest B. Schoedsack

Screenplay by
James Creelman
Ruth Rose

Music by
Max Steiner

Art directors
Carroll Clark
Al Herman

Sound effects
Murray Spivack

Production assistants
Archie S. Marshek
Walter Daniels

Sound recorder
E.A. Wolcott

From an idea conceived by
Merian C. Cooper

Original story by
Merian C. Cooper
Edgar Wallace

Chief technician
Willis H. O'Brien

Technical staff
E.B. Gibson
Marcel Delgado
Fred Reefe
Orville Goldnor
Carroll Shepphird

Photographers
Edward Linden
Vernon L. Walker
J.O. Taylor

Art technicians
Mario Larrinaga
Byron L. Crabbe

Film editor
Ted Cheesman

CAST OF CHARACTERS

Ann Darrow
Fay Wray

Jack Driscoll
Bruce Cabot

Weston, the theatrical agent
Sam Hardy

Second mate
James Flavin

Charley
Victor Wong

Fruit vendor
Paul Porcasi

Crewman
Dick Curtis

Carl Denham
Robert Armstrong

Captain Englehorn
Frank Reicher

Native chief
Noble Johnson

Witch king
Steve Clemento

Press photographer
Roscoe Ates

Theater patron
Leroy Mason

Los Angeles premiere: Grauman's Chinese Theater, New Roxy's, March 2, 1933.

New York premiere: Radio City Music Hall, and the New Roxy's, March 4, 1933.

PART I

BORN: THE EIGHTH WONDER OF THE WORLD

BORN: KING KONG

INTRODUCTION

"THE EIGHTH WONDER OF THE WORLD"

Harry M. Geduld and Ronald Gottesman

Cop: Well Denham: the airplanes got him.
Denham: Oh no: it wasn't the airplanes. It was beauty killed the beast.

According to Greek myth, the maiden Psyche was so beautiful that she aroused the jealousy of the goddess Aphrodite (Venus). Aphrodite ordered her son, the exquisite boy Eros (Cupid), to make Psyche fall in love with an ugly or monstrous creature, but when Eros beheld the maiden he decided instead to become her lover. He visited Psyche in the dark of night and left her before sunrise, forbidding her ever to look upon him. Out of jealousy, Psyche's sisters told her that her lover was a monster who would devour her. One night, overcome with curiosity rather than fear, Psyche took a lamp and gazed upon the sleeping Eros. Distracted by his unexpected beauty, she let a drop of hot oil fall upon his shoulder—whereupon Eros awoke and fled in anger at her disobedience. The grief-stricken Psyche wandered all over the earth in search of her lover. Aphrodite enslaved her and forced her to undertake superhuman tasks. But ultimately Eros entreated Zeus (Jupiter) to release her from bondage. The lovers were then united and Psyche was made immortal and admitted to Olympus, the home of the gods.

Certain elements of this tale have endured through countless centuries and innumerable variations.[1] From Psyche and Eros to Beauty and the Beast to Ann Darrow and King Kong we find the recurrent motif of the helpless maiden left in the clutches of what she takes to be a ruthless monster—but who instead of devouring her falls in love with her and is transformed, wounded, or destroyed by his love and her beauty.

(Sometimes, as in *King Kong,* the enslavement and the superhuman tasks are imposed not on Beauty but on the Beast.) As Michael Grant notes in his *Myths of the Greeks and Romans* (1962), "The story of Cupid and Psyche is one which, like many folk tales, is profoundly penetrated by the belief in intercourse between men and animals."[2] The myth is perhaps older than man, a race-memory of the bestiality out of which, despite the veneers of our civilization and culture, we have only imperfectly emerged, a reminder, too, of the animalism brought to the sex relationship which is (or can be) softened and sublimated by love.

Scholars have noticed similarities between the Greco-Roman Cupid and Psyche story and the myths of other peoples—such as the Vedic tale of Urvasî and Purûravas and the Norse tale "East of the Sun and West of the Moon" in which the maiden-heroine is forced to cohabit with a white bear. G. W. Cox in his *Mythology of the Aryan Nations* (1870) observed that such myths "spring up on all soils from the seed which the Aryan tribes carried away with them when they left their common home, and every variation may therefore be noted as exhibiting the power of growth inherent in the old mythical ideas. In few cases is there even a plausible ground for saying that any one tale is copied or consciously adopted from another; in none is there any necessity for the assumption."

The earliest form in which the maiden/monster story comes down to us is in the Cupid and Psyche myth as it appears in the fourth through sixth books of the *Metamorphoses* or *Golden Ass* of Apuleius, a Latin writer of the second century A.D., who had evidently derived the tale from a Greek source. The *Metmorphoses* of Apuleius is usually considered to be primarily

---

1 Dedicated students may care to know that an authoritative study of the myth, Zingow's *Psyche und Eros,* was published in 1881, that Jahn and Michaels provided the first separate edition (1883) and Friedlaüter (in *Sittengeschichte Roms.*) the earliest close analysis of the myth as it appears in the Apuleius.

2 This, of course, includes *women* and animals. The "belief" to which Grant refers is implicit in the tale of Beauty and the Beast as well as in *King Kong;* it can be traced to pre-evolutionary concepts in Pythagoras and Ovid concerning the interrelationships of all living species and the notions that metamorphosis is a natural condition of the soul and that transformations from beast into man and man into beast are part of the natural order.

a work of entertainment, though its author evidently had a more serious purpose in writing it, namely the creation of an allegorical work concerning the carnal adventures experienced by the soul in its quest for true, mystical (perhaps Platonic) tranquillity. The Cupid and Psyche story seems to have been central to this allegorical purpose—indeed the very name of the heroine is the Greek word for *soul*. However, in telling the tale, Apuleius allowed his story-teller's art to dominate the philosophy. Untold generations have been delighted by the myth though few seem to have been aware of or concerned with its deeper import. The same holds true of much later treatments of the myth in "Beauty and the Beast" and *King Kong*.

After Apuleius the early literary and artistic treatments of the Cupid and Psyche story show considerable efforts to emphasize the philosophical or moral meanings of the myth. In his *Myths of the Greeks and Romans* Michael Grant notes:

"Plotinus (A.D. 205–269/70) and his Neoplatonists . . . gave a much more thoroughgoing interpretation to Apuleius's story, as symbolical of the human soul's quest for love. . . . The Roman catacombs of Domitilla contain frescoes of Cupid and Psyche gathering flowers, and on pagan and early Christian sarcophagi alike Cupid appears as the soul's hope of future life and posthumous happiness. Sometimes the lovers are seen at work on the vintage, "the true vine" first of Dionysiac funerary art and then of Christianity, from which Psyche plucks the grapes that represent the happy afterlife. . . . [Virgil's] story of Cupid and Psyche was well known to Martianus Capella (C.AD 420) who, in a cumbersome Latin allegory, introduced the marriage of Philology and Mercury, in imitation of the wedding of Apuleius' lovers. At the end of the same century Fulgentius interpreted Psyche as lust . . . [her] wicked sisters as the Flesh and Free Will, and Cupid as both the Earthly and the Heavenly Love. . . . [During] the Renaissance Boccaccio did more than anyone else to make the Cupid and Psyche [of Apuleius] known—adding a long allegorical interpretation. There were many editions of the whole work [of Apuleius] from 1649 onwards, and Raphael decorated the Villa Farnesina with twelve scenes of the story. . . . [The tale was later] retold by La Fontaine (1673) and innumerable playwrights ranging from Molière and Calderon to the platitudinous Thomas Shadwell.

If space permitted we could pursue the perenially fascinating story of Cupid and Psyche through its treatments by the Romantic poets, particularly Keats, and thence into poems by Elizabeth Barrett Browning, William Morris and Robert Bridges, into the prose retelling by Walter Pater in his *Marius the Epicurean* (1885), and so on. However, our primary concern is not with the myth and its retellings but with the variations on it in so far as they illuminate the origins of *King Kong* —our own century's most popular version of the myth's most famous variation: the fairy tale of Beauty and the Beast.

As Jean Decock has noticed in his introduction to Robert Hammond's edition of *Beauty and the Beast:* "From the myth to the fairy tale the trajectory is long. . . ." The many folktale variations on the maiden/ monster or Beauty and the Beast story have been classified and studied by the folklorists—as exemplified in types 425–449 on Stith Thompson's *Motif-Index of Folk Literature* (1955). An early anticipation of the Beauty and the Beast tale is found in the Babylonian *Epic of Gilgamesh* (c.2000 B.C.) in which Enkidu, the wild man of the mountain is "civilized" by a temple prostitute sent to make him realize his humanity. Something closer to the more familiar version is found in Straparola's collection, *Piacevoli Notti* (1550); Straparola's source is not known. Earlier still, the old hag or witch in Chaucer's "Wife of Bath's Tale" provides a feminine counterpart (the Loathly Lady) to the Beast figure (a movie variation on this—with reminiscences of *King Kong*—is to be seen in *The Attack of the 50-foot Woman*, 1958); even earlier, the story of Circe (in *The Odyssey*) who tranforms Odysseus' shipmates into swine serves to indicate that where woman may sometimes turn a beast into a man, her powers can also be used to the contrary effect. Shakespeare in *A Midsummer Night's Dream* (c.1594) presents what is certainly the most celebrated comedic version of the Beauty and the Beast tale in the scene of Titania's infatuation with the ass-headed Bottom. The character of the monster-husband appears in the tale of "*Riquet à la Houppe*" in Charles Perrault's *Contes de Ma Mere L'Oye* (Mother Goose, 1697), but the Beauty and the Beast tale in the form in which it is best-known in the nursery evidently crystallized in Mme Marie Leprince de Beaumont's *Magasin des Enfants, Contes Moraux* (1757), and in this version it provided the basis for Grétry's opera, *Zemire et Azor* (1771) and Cocteau's film, *La Belle et la Bête* (1946).

Jean Decock in his Preface to Robert Hammond's edition of the scenario of Cocteau's movie observes that the "deepest meaning" of the Beauty and the Beast story "forbids even setting eyes on someone of the opposite sex, a secular taboo which gives rise to the theme of the metamorphosis of the beloved as half man, half beast. . . . The moral of the classic fairy tale is clear: love is blind. 'Everything is beautiful in the object of your love.'"

Jung comments thus on the significance of the fairy tale:

In this story, if we unravel the symbolism, we are likely to see that Beauty is any young girl who has entered into an emotional bond with her father, no less binding because of its spiritual nature. . . . By learning to love the Beast she awakens to the power of human love concealed in its animal (and therefore imperfect) but genuinely erotic form. Presumably this [enables] . . . her to accept the erotic component of her original wish, which had to be repressed because of a fear of incest. To leave her father [who, in effect, sacrifices her to the Beast] she had, as it were, to accept the incest-fear, to allow herself to live in its presence in fantasy until she could get to know the animal man and discover her own true response to it as a woman. In this way she redeems herself and her image of the masculine from the forces of repression, bringing to consciousness her capacity to trust her love as something that combines spirit and nature in the best sense of the words." (*Man and His Symbols*, 1962).

It may be objected that Jung's analysis has little or no relevance to *King Kong* for although the film's heroine confronts a monster, her father has no place in the story. But Carl Denham, the director who rescues Ann from starvation and jail and provides her with food, clothing and shelter, becomes a surrogate father: he shows no amorous interest in her and his treatment of the girl in relation to the natives of Skull Island and to Kong (both before and after the monster's capture) smacks as much of sacrifice as of showmanship. The combined monster-husband/lover of the original Psyche and Cupid/Beauty and the Beast narratives has, in *Kong*, been split into two distinct and incompatible type-figures: one entirely bestial and monstrous, the other a bashful, unaggressive hero (Jack Driscoll) who becomes Ann's boyfriend ("I'm scared for you," he tells her. "I'm sort of scared of you, too. Ann, I—I guess I love you.")

In connection with the tale of Beauty and the Beast, Jung also describes the dream of one of his women patients:

I am with several anonymous women. . . . We go downstairs in a strange house, and are confronted suddenly by some grotesque "ape-men" with evil faces. . . . We are completely in their power . . .

The alert reader will have noticed that the fairy story does not identify the Beast as an ape-like creature. In fact, though the maidens of myth, legend and folk tale have traditionally been terrified by monsters and grotesque creatures of many kinds—dragons, demons, frogs, dwarfs, etc.—the monstrous ape or gorilla is comparatively rare and probably of fairly recent origin. Cicero in *De Natura Deorum* quotes a remark by Quintus Ennius (second century B.C.): "The ape, vilest of beasts, how like to us!" But this is obviously a satirical jibe at man (comparable to the title of Wyndham Lewis's satirical novel, *The Apes of God*, 1930) rather than an allusion to the nature of the simian. In the Middle Ages, hairy human beings were sometimes considered to be the offspring of sexual unions between apes and humans. Medieval sailors spread tales of satyr-apes who lusted after women. To Renaissance man, the ape, far from being a creature that terrified maidens, was a docile beast destined to be led about in Hell by women who were old maids when they died. The ape's and specifically the gorilla's reputation as a monster has mainly been acquired—for the most part undeservedly—within the past two centuries.

The gorilla was the last of the primates to be studied by the naturalists. Though a great deal still remains to be learned about the gorilla's habits, it can be said with absolute certainty that it is not an aggressive carnivore with a lustful passion for white girls. However, the fantasy of the lecherous ape dies hard. Geoffrey H. Bourne in *The Ape People* (1971) refers to several accounts of sexual assaults (or attempted sexual assaults) by apes on human females. These are dubious stories but they suggest that of all the apes the baboon has long been considered the most lustful. There is a description, by Daniel P. Mannix in *Those About to Die,* of the Roman practice of using baboons to rape little girls as part of the "entertainment" provided in the gladiatorial arena. In Sir Richard Burton's *A Plain and Literal Translation of the Arabian Nights* (1885) we can find the story of an Abyssinian baboon who attempted to rape a woman on a Cairo street but was intercepted and killed by a soldier. Bourne comments: "If such an accident did occur it was probably a straight-out attack by the animal on the woman which was interpreted as a sexual attack." Bourne also notes: "In the Middle East exhibitions have regularly been staged in which tame monkeys were made to copulate with women on the stage. . . . Bernard Heuvelmans *On the Track of Unknown Animals* (1958) described his experiences of seeing a young tame baboon assaulting women who were sunbathing on a Mediterranean beach and attempting to copulate with them."

Whatever may be the sexual predilections of baboons, the gorilla's interest in the human female seems to be nil. In the same work, Bourne offers verifications of this in an interesting anecdote. "There are reports that Trader Horn knew of a case in which a white man shut up a slave girl with a gorilla, having heard that apes were very attracted to human females. He expected that the gorilla would rape her, but the animal made no physical contact at all. He remained in one corner and the girl cried in the other, so there was no result." [3] Despite the total absence of evidence that gorillas have ever had sexual relations with women or even shown any particular interest in them, the fantasy of the gorilla-rapist persists—an apparently ineradicable popular fallacy.

Naturalists have defined two subspecies of gorilla: the lowland gorilla and the mountain gorilla. These subspecies are so similar that, as George B. Schaller states in *The Year of the Gorilla* (1964) "if only one animal is at hand, even an anthropologist would have difficulty in deciding to which race it belongs. The anatomist A. Schultz has listed thirty-four morphological differences between the two, most of them minor."

The first gorillas known to man were the lowland subspecies (*Gorilla gorilla gorilla*) who mainly inhabit those parts of equatorial West Africa now known as Southern Nigeria, Cameroon, Equatorial Guinea and Gabon. In 470 B.C. the Carthaginian Hanno captured three hairy, arboreal animals—called *gorillai*—during an expedition into the mountains of Sierra Leone. When they were attacked by Hanno's party, these animals tried to resist by throwing stones. According to Pliny, as late as 146 B.C., when the Romans invaded Carthage, they found the preserved skins of two of these captured *gorillai* in the temple of Astarte. Despite the name given to these animals it is possible that they were chimpanzees or baboons and not gorillas. Indeed, nearly two millennia were to pass before the various species of higher primates were to be accurately distinguished. An animal called the Pongo —almost certainly another name for the gorilla—was observed c.1560 by an Englishman named Andrew Battell while he was prisoner of the Portuguese in West Africa. Battell's detailed description of this animal occurs in the enlarged edition (1625) of *Purchas his Pilgrimage* by Samuel Purchas the Elder.

Possibly, as Schaller asserts, Battell was the first European to observe the gorilla. However, credit for this is usually given to two missionaries, Jeffries Wyman and Thomas Savage, who were engaged in work along the Gabon River during the 1840s. Wyman and Savage probably never saw a gorilla, but they collected what they claimed were gorilla skulls and they do seem responsible for establishing the legend of the aggressive gorilla—whom, on the strength of tales they had uncritically collected from the local natives, they described as "exceedingly ferocious and always offensive." The anatomist Richard Owen, to whom Wyman and Savage sent some of their gorilla skulls, embroidered the legend by describing the animals he had never seen as "frightfully formidable apes" who hoist unsuspecting blacks up into the trees, strangle them and then drop their corpses to the ground. In 1856 an American, Paul Du Chaillu, earned his place in history by being the first white man to shoot a gorilla. He appears to have had no compunction about imaginatively transferring his own aggressive instincts to the animal he had so proudly slaughtered. In his *Explorations in Equatorial Africa* (1856), Du Chaillu remarks that the gorilla reminded him of "some hellish dream creature—a being of that hideous order, half-man half-beast, which we find pictured by old artists in some representations of the infernal regions." Schaller notes that Du Chaillu "popularized the gorilla with his accounts, but he was castigated by scientists because his descriptions were regarded as fantasy. This was unfortunate. . . . In spite of the exaggerated descriptions, Du Chaillu's account of gorillas remained as one of the most accurate for a hundred years." Accurate or not, its immense influence on the development of the monstrous gorilla of popular fantasy can hardly be doubted.

Knowledge of the existence and nature of the other subspecies, the mountain gorilla (*Gorilla gorilla beringei*), is very recent. In 1861, Speke and Grant, in search of the source of the Nile, were told by natives about man-like creatures, unable to communicate with human beings, who lived among the mountains west of what is now Rwanda and Burundi. In 1898, an elephant hunter named Grogan discovered the skeleton of a giant ape on the slopes of the Virunga Volcanoes in the Belgian Congo. In the same region, in 1902, Captain von Beringe found an ape skeleton which he sent to Dr. Matschie, a German anatomist, who identified it as that of a gorilla belonging to a hitherto unknown subspecies—now called the mountain gorilla or eastern gorilla; its scientific name commemorates its discoverer. Many mountain gorillas have been located in the Virunga Volcanoes area where Dr. Robert Yerkes undertook much of the research for his authoritative book, *The Great Apes* (1929), a work generally considered to have established the modern, scientific study of primates. In 1929 also, the Virunga region was set aside as a permanent sanctuary for the gorilla, which was on the point of becoming extinct at the hands of hunters and so-called sportsmen. Man had begun to understand the gorilla and to protect him from his most savage enemy: *homo sapiens*. But, ironically, only

---

[3] It is relevant, as Bourne notes (*op.cit.*pp.222-224) that the gorilla has a very short penis "usually only about two inches long" in erection. When not erect it can be as short as two centimeters in a full-grown gorilla.

four years later, Hollywood was to create what has become the best-known image and certainly the most enduring calumny of this unfortunate animal.

In almost every respect—except general appearance—King Kong is a fantasy gorilla. He is supposed to be about fifty feet tall and built proportionately, but, as Geoffrey H. Bourne (*op. cit.*) observes: "it would be impossible for a gorilla or an ape or a human or any other animal to achieve the vast size portrayed by King Kong. . . . This is because of the force of gravity exerted by the earth. The material composing the bones would not be strong enough to permit bones of the size required for such a big animal to exist. Nor would the bones be strong enough to support the weight of muscle necessary to move them. In other words, the mechanical properties of living tissues are such that nothing very much bigger than an elephant could exist on land with the existing force of gravity." Actually, although the gorilla is by far the largest of the apes, it seldom exceeds seven feet in height. Its average weight when full-grown, well-fed and in good health is about 500 pounds; it has an armspread of about eight feet, and a life expectancy of about 35 years. Gorillas are not lonely monsters but gregarious animals. Ivan T. Sanderson in *The Monkey Kingdom* (1957) notes that they "travel about in aggregated family parties usually presided over by a single large male; but double parties have been recorded, and sometimes several families will be seen feeding together at the same place, all mingling and getting along most amiably. . . . During the middle of the day . . . [the young gorillas] lounge about and the adults take naps." This hardly recalls the behavior of the most famous inhabitant of Skull Island.

In a recent newspaper interview, Dian Fossey, an authority on the mountain gorilla, stated that "Gorillas are the most maligned creatures in history." She placed the blame on "*King Kong* and ancient and false myths about the ferocity of the gorillas and 'intrepid white hunters.'" From direct personal experience (five years of living among them in their natural habitat), Miss Fossey insists that "Gorillas, no matter how fierce they look, are gentle, playful, shy and good to each other, more likely to flee than fight. They don't want to eat you. They are vegetarians." (*Milwaukee Journal*, January 21, 1973.) In fact, their diet consists not of dinosaurs, helpless natives or luckless New Yorkers, but of such food as green shoots, seedlings, berries, grain, roots and bark, and such roughage as foliage and young banana skins. Miss Fossey has found gorillas to be "nosey, curious and friendly," and claims that their "breast-beating, hooting and charges are just 'bluffs.' They would attempt to fight only to protect themselves and the group."

Of course, *King Kong* is not natural history. Its depiction of the gorilla—though somewhat more sympathetic—is about as reliable as a Nazi description of the Chief Rabbi. But the fantasy-gorilla, the monster-ape and the lecherous monkey are creatures of considerable lineage—not only through the tales of natives and the accounts of non-observers like Richard Owen and trigger-happy Baron Muchausens like Du Chaillu but also in centuries of art and literature, and more recently in pulp fiction and comic books.

A search through medieval bestiaries, Renaissance paintings, woodcuts, engravings and stained glass, and through early pre-Darwinian illustrated works of natural history, such as Goldsmith's six-volume *History of the Earth and Animated Nature* (1774)—which locates "tygers" in Canada—and Buffon's thirty-six volume *Histoire Naturelle* (1749-88) yields many anticipations of the monster gorilla of fantasy. Striking anticipations of Kong and, indeed, of specific scenes in the film, are to be found in eighteenth- and nineteenth-century illustrations to Part II Chapter V of *Gulliver's Travels* (in which Gulliver is kidnapped by a giant monkey)—especially in drawings by Pierre Bailly, Granville, Robida, and Job, some of which are reproduced in this volume. We must turn to Böcklin's picture "The Isle of the Dead" in order to see the artistic source of Skull Island, the home of Kong. The enterprising student of pre-Kong lore must further brace himself to locate and examine the many illustrations of nineteenth-century exhibitions of gorillas in zoos and circuses; he must prepare to trace, through countless pictures, the shift from fantasy to reality as Africa was explored and her teeming animal life became increasingly familiar to Western man.

From literature it would be possible to harvest an equally rich collection of references, anecdotes and stories about fantasy apes and gorillas. According to Bourne, "Greek literature refers to the 'licentiousness' of baboons and other monkeys. They were said to attack women and children with the idea of copulating with them." Bourne also mentions interesting ape stories in the *Arabian Nights* and in Voltaire's *Candide* (1759). In the former we find Scheherazade's tale of "The King's Daughter and the Ape," which concerns the nymphomaniac daughter of a sultan. This princess felt the urge to copulate almost incessantly. So, at her servant's suggestion, she obtained a baboon who had intercourse with her as often as she desired. Her activities with this accommodating ape were observed disapprovingly by a butcher who slaughtered the baboon and then offered himself as the lady's new lover. He soon discovered that it is not easy to ape an ape. The princess's needs proved too exhausting for him. But eventually, on the advice of an old witch, he gave the girl an emetic which forced two worms to emerge from her body. This cured her nymphomania permanently (though the baboons of the world were apparently left to wallow in their insatiable lust). In *Candide* there is an episode in which Cacambo and Candide, in the Amazon jungle, shoot a couple of monkeys whom they observe pursuing two nude girls. To their surprise, the girls are grief-stricken. They discover that far from saving the girls from a fate reputedly worse than death, they have killed their lovers. Perhaps the first celebrated ape character in literature was the well-bred Sir Oran Haut-Ton in Thomas Love Peacock's satirical novel, *Melincourt* (1817). Sir Oran is, of course, an orang-outang. Although he cannot speak, his master has taught him good manners and how to play the flute; he has also bought him a baronetcy and a seat in Parliament. The character was suggested to Peacock by the trained orang-outang of the Scots eccentric Lord Monboddo (1714–99).

The ruthless ape evidently emerges in literature in the pages of Edgar Allan Poe's tale, "The Murders in the Rue Morgue" (1841). Unlike the well-bred simian of *Melincourt*, Poe's orang-outang is a brutal creature that goes berserk with a razor and murders two helpless women. The police are, of course, baffled by the crime which is only solved through the investigations of C. Auguste Dupin, the first of the great detectives of fiction. Although the *lecherous* ape figures in many stories earlier than the mid-nineteenth century, it is noteworthy that except for Poe's tale, most literary accounts of *murderous* apes post-date the publication of Darwin's *The Origin of Species* (1859) and *The Descent of Man* (1871). This development may in part be explained as an expression of man's desire, at least in fantasy, to repudiate his newly-discovered and somewhat humiliating kinship to the lowly simian. Probably nothing shocked the Victorians (and knocked them off their self-appointed pedestal in nature—just below the angels) as much as Darwin's observation in *The Descent of Man*: "The Simiadae . . . branched off into two great stems, the New World and the Old World monkeys: and from the latter at a remote period, Man, the wonder and glory of the universe, proceeded." Man, Victorian thinking ran, might still recognize a reflection of his own behavior in the *lecherous* orang-outang, but his actual family relationship to the ape could be observed or even denied by so brutalizing the anmal in fiction that any identification with most human beings would be impossible to accept.

Like the *bête humaine* of Zola's novel, Mr. Hyde in Robert Louis Stevenson's novel, *The Strange Case of Dr. Jekyll and Mr. Hyde* (1886) is not, of course, an ape or even an ape-man, but his repulsive, bestial appearance prefigures many of the ape-monsters of later fiction and film. (Rouben Mamoulian's memorable 1932 film version, starring Fredric March, strongly emphasizes Hyde's ape-like features and supposedly ape-like behavior.) In addition, Stevenson's splitting of the main character into the virtuous hero and his bestial evil self anticipates the division we find in *King Kong* between Ann's hero (bashful Jack Driscoll) and the monster "hero" of the movie.

The late nineteenth and early twentieth centuries—before the making of *King Kong* in 1933—provide numerous examples of the ape or apeman as both hero and villain. Mention should be made of the subterranean, predatory white apes that H. G. Wells envisages to be among our future descendants in *The Time Machine* (1895), and the apeman, produced by surgically accelerated evolution in the same author's horrific *Island of Dr. Moreau* (1896). (The Morlocks, Wells' name for the white apes in *The Time Machine*, are perhaps the first simians in fiction to abduct a heroine.) Frank Norris presents an elaborate study of human brutishness (in the tradition of Zola's *La Bête Humaine*) in his Naturalistic novel, *McTeague* (1899), while Jack London vividly depicts man's prehistoric savagery in *Before Adam* (1906) and explores the bestiality underlying social order in *The Abysmal Brute* (1913). Related themes are treated dramatically in Eugene O'Neill's Expressionist play *The Hairy Ape* (1922).

Of special interest is Thomas Dixon Jr.'s *The Clansman* (1905) which provided D. W. Griffith with basic plot and character material for his epic film, *The Birth of a Nation* (1915). No gorillas appear in Dixon's notorious novel, but there is a relevant rape episode involving the renegade black, Gus, and a white girl named Marion:

> Gus stepped closer, with an ugly leer, his flat nose dilated, his sinster bead-eyes wide apart gleaming ape-like, as he laughed:
> "We ain't atter money!"
> The girl uttered a cry, long, tremulous, heart-rending, piteous.
> A single tiger-spring, and the black claws of the beast sank into the soft white throat and she was still.

The images by which Gus is described—"ape-like," "the black claws of the beast"—serve to remind us that the ape and the Negro have been all too often associated in the minds and literature of racists. This revolting subject is explored with much erudition by Winthrop D. Jordan in chapter VI Part 2 ("Negroes, Apes, and Beasts") of his masterly *White Over Black*

(1968). The association of ape and Negro relates to *King Kong* in so far as the film has sometimes been interpreted as a white man's sick fantasy of the Negro's lust to ravish white woman. According to this interpretation, Ann Darrow is abducted by a horde of blacks (who have previously offered to buy her from Denham) to be offered to their god, Kong, who is the super-black, super-rapist; but Kong is, like other blacks, enslaved by the whites and eventually destroyed by them after trying to wreck their society while he seeks to satisfy his mad lust.

Racist elements are present, but less overtly, in Edgar Rice Burroughs' *Tarzan of the Apes* (1912) and its many sequels. More to the point here is that in his novel Burroughs creates a proto-Kong in the form of the ferocious anthropoid ape, Kerchak, who murders Tarzan's father while the hero is still a baby and is later killed by Tarzan himself (who had been raised by a most maternal ape named Kala). Kerchak is, in effect, preparation for the mightiest of fictitious apes, and *Tarzan of the Apes* together with Conan Doyle's *The Lost World* (also published in 1912) brings us within sight of Skull Island and Carl Denham's Eighth Wonder of the World. Burne Hogarth's famous illustrations to the Tarzan stories (his earliest drawings date from 1937) show the influence of *King Kong* in the pictures of Kerchak; this is particularly evident in the recent pictorial edition of *Tarzan of the Apes* (1972) by Hogarth and Burroughs.

Prehistoric man and his ape-like rivals are central to such fiction as H. Rider Haggard's *Allan and the Ice Gods* (1920) and H. G. Wells's short story, "The Grisly Folk" (1921). One non-violent comedic treatment of the simian also deserves attention. This is John Collier's *His Monkey Wife, or, Married to a Chimp* (1931); it has so far failed to inspire the making of a "Queen Kong" but can nevertheless be recommended to thoughtful young men contemplating matrimony. C. G. D. Roberts' unjustly-neglected *In the Morning of Time* (1919) contains tales of dinosaurs—presented even earlier and with greater popular success in *The Lost World*—as well as primitive men and their conflicts with Neanderthalers. An equally neglected novel, John Taine's *The Iron Star* (1930), concerns a party of white men on safari in Central Africa where they are confronted by a horde of ape-like creatures led by a giant ape; in due course, this giant ape, like his grotesque army, is discovered to be human, the product of degeneration under the influence of rays emanating from a strange meteor. Reference must finally be made to *The Beast*, a story by Edgar Wallace which Bob Thomas (*Selznick*, 1970) rather dubiously claims as the original inspiration for the making of *King Kong*. As the reader will find, some articles in the present volume argue that Wallace had little if anything to do with inspiring or making the film—even though his name appears on the credits alongside Merian C. Cooper's. Others urge his direct and indirect influence on more compelling grounds than those offered by Thomas.

The first ape movie was perhaps Pathé's *An Apish Trick* (France, 1909), a ten-minute film in which a man begins to behave like an ape after his wife has given him an injection. Pathé followed this effort with another short film, *A Monkey Bite* (1911) in which some people who are bitten by a monkey begin to act like the monkey. *King Kong*'s specific movie antecedents probably begin, like so many film innovations, in the work of D. W. Griffith's many one and two-reel pictures for American Biograph included *Man's Genesis* (1912) and its sequel, *Brute Force* (also known as *In Prehistoric Days* and *Wars of the Primal Tribes*, 1913), two quasi-comedic melodramas of primitive man in which brutish ape-like men and one rather improbable dinosaur make appearances. In making these films, Griffith, usually responsive to public taste at this period, was perhaps inspired by the popular success of *Tarzan of the Apes* and *The Lost World* both of which had first appeared in print in the same year as *Man's Genesis*. Robert M. Henderson in *D. W. Griffith: His Life and Work* (1972) notes: "Griffith was strongly attracted to the story of primitive man and his struggles. Many years later, in the thirties, Griffith made a last attempt to start up his career with another remake of the same general story for Hal Roach, retitled *One Million B.C.*, starring Victor Mature and Carole Landis. Griffith was removed from the picture long before it was finished, but the basic story remained Griffith's. The film was re-made in 1967, long after Griffith's death." [4]

Monkeys, chimps and gorillas inevitably appear in many Tarzan movies, beginning with the first in 1918. An early documentary, *Bali the Unknown* (1921), a Prizma-color film by Harold H. Horton, was subtitled *Ape Man Island*. *The New York Times* reviewer dismissed this subtitle as "silly," explaining "There is nothing resembling a subhuman in the picture. An odd hermit, or some native dressed for the part, is shown briefly, but to use this unconvincing bit as the basis for a title of the picture as a whole smacks of ballyhooism . . ." Another silent documentary, Ben Burbridge's *Gorilla Hunt* (1926) showed the animals being killed but also revealed their essential amiability. On the lighter side, Douglas Fairbanks' *The Thief of*

---

4 *One Million B.C.* was co-directed by Hal Roach and Hal Roach Jr. The film, alternatively titled *Man and His Mate*, was released in 1940. The remake, was directed by Don Chaffey and titled *One Million Years B.C.*

Bagdad (1924) was parodied in 1925 by an all-star cast of performing chimps in a mini-fantasy titled *Grief in Bagdad*. Except for these pictures—and *The Monkey Talks* (1927) directed by Raoul Walsh for Fox pictures—during the 1920s, First National and Warner Bros. seem to have almost cornered the movie market on gorillas, ape-men, dinosaurs and monsters generally, beginning with *The Lost World* (1925), directed by Harry O. Hoyt for First National and utilizing Willis O'Brien (subsequently Chief Technician on *King Kong*) as technical director. This film and other immediate antecedents and inspirers of *King Kong*, including the unfinished *Creation*, are discussed at length in articles included in this volume. *While London Sleeps* (1926), directed by H. P. Bretherton for Warner Bros., was a Rin-Tin-Tin picture about the destruction of a man-beast under the influence of a master-criminal who used the creature to terrorize London and to kidnap the heroine (played by Helene Costello). *The Missing Link* (1927) directed by Charles F. Reisner for Warner Bros., from a story and scenario by Darryl F. Zanuck, dealt with an expedition to Africa in search of an animal midway between man and the anthropoid apes in the development of the human species. Essentially a love story despite its title, *The Missing Link* showed how the hero, Arthur (Syd Chaplin), won the heroine after subduing a real-live "Missing Link" with the aid of Akka, his pet chimp. *The Gorilla* (1927), directed by Alfred Santell for First National, and starring Walter Pidgeon in one of his earliest movie roles, was the first of at least three screen adaptations of Ralph Spence's comedy. This version was described by *The New York Times* reviewer as a picture "very much as if Mack Sennett in a restrained mood had turned to Edgar Allan Poe's 'The Murders in the Rue Morgue' and decided to adapt it to the screen in his inimitable manner, but without custard pies, or even mud. *The Gorilla* has the advantage over Poe . . . because they are able to show a man-made brute about eight feet tall with proportionate depth of chest and length of forelimbs, a 'gorilla' that is indeed impressive." *Stark Mad* (1929) directed by Lloyd Bacon for Warner Bros., concerned an expedition to Central America organized by James Rutherford (Claude Gillingwater) in search of his son Bob and Bob's guide, Simpson. One night when the party go ashore and camp in a Mayan temple, Irene (Jacqueline Logan), Bob's fiancée, mysteriously disappears. While they are trying to find her, Rutherford and his companions discover a gigantic ape chained to the ground. Later, Rhodes (Henry B. Walthall), captain of the ship that had brought them to Central America, is seized by a monster with hairy talons (the episode anticipates a sequence concerning a monster

spider, originally intended for *King Kong* but deleted from the completed picture). In the course of other events, of less relevance to *Kong*, Irene is rescued and it is learned that Rutherford's son was murdered—though not by the huge ape. *The Gorilla* (1931) was another screen adaptation of Ralph Spence's comedy—this time a talkie directed by Brian Foy and once again starring Walter Pidgeon.

Probably the most remarkable "gorilla" in a film prior to *Kong* was none other than Marlene Dietrich who donned a gorilla costume for the "Hot Voodoo" number in Josef von Sternberg's *Blonde Venus* (1932). In the same year, Johnny Weissmuller embarked on his most celebrated screen role in a film titled *Tarzan the Ape Man* (directed by W. S. Van Dyke). Mention should also be made of the murderous apes in *The Jungle Mystery* (a Universal serial directed by Ray Taylor, 1932) and in the first version of *Murders in the Rue Morgue* (directed by Robert Florey, 1932), as well as of the beast-men in *Island of Lost Souls* (directed by Erle C. Kenton, 1933), based on H. G. Wells' aforementioned novel, *The Island of Dr. Moreau*. Other significant atmospheric and narrative antecedents such as Frank Buck and Trader Horn are discussed at some length by various articles in this collection.

King Kong (1933) of course, fathered a vast brood of monkeys, ape-men and giant gorillas. The films in which they appear are too numerous to list fully. Among them we can merely notice the disappointing sequel, *Son of Kong* (directed by Ernest B. Schoedsack, 1933), and *Mighty Joe Young* (also directed by Schoedsack, 1949). Shortly after its original release, *King Kong* was parodied in *King Klunk* (1933), a "Pooch the Pup" cartoon. Later animated cartoon treatments of the ape or gorilla include the "Bugs Bunny" cartoons *Gorilla My Dreams* (1947) and *Apes of Wrath* (1959), both for Warner Bros.; *The Cultured Ape* (a Halas and Batchelor cartoon, 1960); the *Magilla Gorilla* series (Hanna and Barbera cartoons, 1964–66); *The King Kong Show* (Videocraft International cartoons, 1966–69); *The Jungle Book* (Disney cartoon feature, 1968), and, parenthetically, mention should be made of John Daborn's *Cupid and Psyche* cartoon (1968). Memorable gorilla episodes occur in such Universal serials as *Flash Gordon* (directed by Frederick Stephani, 1936) and *Tim Tyler's Luck* (directed by Ford Beebe, 1937), in such Republic serials as *Darkest Africa* (directed by B. Reeves Eason, 1936), *Perils of Nyoka* (directed by William Witney, 1942) and *Panther Girl of the Kongo* (directed by Franklyn Adreon, 1955, and subsequently re-edited and released as the feature, *The Claw Monsters*), and in such Columbia serials as *The Monster and the Ape* (directed by Howard Bretherton, 1945). Also noteworthy are the sequence of the gorilla on the bridge in *Swiss Miss* (a Laurel and Hardy picture directed by John G. Blystone, 1938) to which James Agee refers in his important essay, "Comedy's Greatest Era"; the third and most tepid adaptation of Spence's play, *The Gorilla* (directed by Allan Dwan, 1939, mainly as a vehicle for the Ritz Brothers); *The Ape* (directed by William Nigh, 1940); *The Monster and the Girl* (directed by Stuart Heisler, 1941); *Never Give a Sucker an Even Break* (directed by Edward Cline, 1941) in which W. C. Fields exchanges a bottle of whisky with an ape; *Dr. Renault's Secret* (directed by Henry Lachman, 1942) in which J. Carrol Naish appears as an apeman-butler; *Gorilla Man* (directed by Ross Lederman, 1942); *The Ape Man* (directed by William Beaudine, 1943); *Captive Wild Woman* (directed by Edward Dmytryk, 1943) concerning an ape-woman; *Nabonga* (also called *Gorilla*, directed by Sam Newfield, 1944); *Return of the Ape Man* (directed by Philip Rosen, 1944); *Gildersleeve's Ghost* (directed by Gordon Douglas, 1944) in which Harry Peary and "Nicodemus" are harassed by a most unghostly gorilla; *Africa Screams* (an Abbott and Costello picture directed by Charles Barton, 1949); *Mark of the Gorilla* (a "Jungle Jim" adventure starring Johnny Weissmuller and directed by William Berke, 1950); *Bedtime for Bonzo* (directed by Frederick de Cordova, 1951) in which Ronald Reagan becomes surrogate father to a chimp; *Bonzo goes to College* (also directed by de Cordova, 1952) a sequel to the last-mentioned picture which shows the chimp, now educated, leading his college football team to victory; *Gorilla Bill* (originally *Homme aux Gorille*, a Diamant Berger picture released in the U.S. through United Artists, 1952); *Neanderthal Man* (directed by veteran filmmaker E. A. Dupont, 1953) about a serum that transforms a scientist into a primitive man; *Gorilla at Large* (directed by Harmon Jones, 1954), a murder mystery starring Lee J. Cobb, Raymond Burr and Anne Bancroft; *Phantom of the Rue Morgue* (directed by veteran film-maker Roy Del Ruth, 1954); *Bowery Boys Meet the Monsters* (directed by Edward Bernds, 1954) in which Satch and Slip confront a gorilla and other wild animals in a mad doctor's menagerie; *Monster on Campus* (directed by Jack Arnold, 1958) concerning a serum that transforms a professor into a ferocious beast; *Konga* (directed by John Lemont, 1961); *King Kong vs. Godzilla*[5] (directed by Thomas Montgomery and Inoshiro Honda, 1963); *The Ape Woman* (directed by Marco Ferreri, 1964)—not a mini—"Queen Kong," but a rather distasteful comedy about a young woman whose body and face are covered with hair; *Sands of the Kalahari*

(directed by Cyril Endfield, 1965) in which the survivors of an airplane crash battle a horde of apes; *King Kong Escapes* (directed by Inoshiro Honda, 1968); *Planet of the Apes* (directed by Franklin J. Schaffner, 1968) and its sequels—all based originally on Pierre Boulle's novel; *The Gorilla of Soho* (directed by Alfred Vohrer, 1968), a German film about a murderer in a gorilla suit; *The Yellow Submarine* (directed by George Dunning, designed by Heinz Edelmann, 1968) which contains a brief cartoon appearance of Kong; *2001: A Space Odyssey* (directed by Stanley Kubrick, 1968) which contains the notable sequence of the dawning of intelligence among the apemen of the Pleistocene period; *Trog* (directed by Freddie Francis, 1970) which shows us anthropologist Joan Crawford coping with a "missing link"; and most recently, *The Ruling Class* (1972) which includes a monster gorilla in a fantasy sequence. Kongophiles will be able to extend this list indefinitely.

The most memorable image from *King Kong* is surely that of Kong himself atop the Empire State Building—a terrifying vision of defiant bestiality transcending man's technology. While Kong himself deserves most of our attention in this scene, the skyscraper also merits consideration. Its presence in the image testifies to public fascination with such architectural achievements in the twenties and thirties—and in particular with the Empire State Building which had been erected only just over a year prior to the making of *King Kong*. Just before construction began, Richmond Shreve, designer of the Empire State Building, noted: "one year from now it will have been completed . . . fifty millions of dollars . . . 20,000 tenants . . . two million square feet . . . fifty thousand tons of steel . . . rising nearly a quarter mile . . . stone from Maine and Indiana, steel from Pittsburgh and Elmira, cement from Pennsylvania and New York, timber from Oregon or the Carolinas, brick from the Hudson River Valley or from the clay pits of Connecticut, glass from Ohio, marble from Vermont or Georgia or Italy . . . [materials] from all the world must come together and fit together with accuracy of measurement and precision of time." (Quoted in John Burchard and Albert Bush-Brown, *The Architecture of America*, 1961, pp. 368–369). The "boast" is comparable to Denham presenting Kong, "The Eighth Wonder of the World" and perhaps to how Cheops might have talked about the building of the great Pyramid; it also indicates that the Building itself was, from the outset, conceived as a symbol for the whole of the U.S.A., for its wealth of natural resources and for its technological expertise. Burchard and Bush-Brown observe that from the 1890s onwards "American architecture . . . was anxious to excel, to have something that could be put before all the world

---

5 The name of Kong's rival is evidently a conflation of *God* and *gorilla*.

and announced with pride as American. We found it in the skyscraper. But for the moment there was a more direct connection with our imperialistic spirit as well. For the individual who commissioned it, the skyscraper, trying to go higher than any competitor, was the demonstration of a personal imperialism, even if it was that of a ten-cent-store owner. . . . The most distinctive American accomplishment . . . [during 1913–33] was the conquest of vertical space through brilliant engineering . . . in the United States . . . architects . . . evolved a type of building—the city skyscraper—so daring, so virile that. . . . It proclaims to all the triumph of industrial efficiency." (*op. cit.*, pp. 221–222, 304, 345). Winston Weisman states: "Ever since the early days of its history, the concept of a tower had been associated with the skyscraper . . . a reference to towers had an appeal that was aesthetic and expressive. How widespread was its use may be realized by its employment in religious, civic, domestic and exhibition architecture . . ." ("A New View of Skyscraper History," pp. 143–144 in *The Rise of an American Architecture*, 1970, by H-R. Hitchcock, Albert Fine, Winston Weisman, and Vincent Scully). Weisman might also have added The Tower of Babel (with which man challenged God), and more recently the launch-tower from which space projectiles leave the Earth to penetrate the universe, and the oil-engineer's tower through which man taps the wealth of his planet. Although it was not originally realized, the skyscraper is essentially an open-ended structure. "What matters," says John A. Kouwenhoven, "is the vertical thrust, the motion upwards . . . the point at which you cut it off is arbitrary and makes no difference." (Kouwenhoven, *The Beer Can by the Highway*, 1961). Patently, for these writers as for many other people, the skyscraper was the most potent symbol of America's apparently limitless strength and technology before the A-Bomb and the Apollo Program dwarfed the achievement represented by the Empire State Building. Hence the special significance of Kong atop the world's largest building (as it was in 1933). Symbolically, Kong challenges man's power in all dimensions —first on the horizontal plane he proves his mastery by smashing up an express train while it is thundering along the old New York El; then, on the vertical plane he scales the gigantic phallus of stone, steel and glass that at the beginning of the thirties was thrust as high as our architects could penetrate into the firmament. His bestiality is conquered, however, not only by Beauty but the technological skill that

had, since the Wright Brothers, made man master of the air.

The book that now lies open before you illuminates many aspects of the cinema's most enduring "classic" of fantasy and horror. The origin of the film, its making, its significances and influences are discussed and explained in the articles and essays that follow. In addition, a rich array of pictorial material is provided in order to demonstrate the continuing popular attraction of Kong—the Beast who has been "loved" by the public not only in the original film but also through innumerable drawings, sculpture, and stills as well as cartoons, comics, advertising materials, posters, "King Kong" shirts, ties, sweaters, buttons ("King Kong Died for Our Sins"), dolls, construction toys, jigsaw puzzles, ashtrays, keychains, greetings cards. . . .

In an article published in *The New York Times* (September 21, 1969) and reprinted in this book, Fay Wray, who played Ann Darrow in the film, mentions the sympathy Kong evokes when he is finally struck down. "There is no doubt about such sympathy," she says. "Even I, seeing the film a year or so ago, felt a great lump in my throat in behalf of Kong." She mentions Paul Johnson's appreciation of Kong as "more than a monster. He is a genuine character, a creature of intelligible rage, nobility of a kind and, above all, pathos. A prehistoric Lear, in a sense." As Fay Wray and Paul Johnson suggest, sympathy for this "creature of intelligible rage" emerges from a recognition that it is not Kong, but Carl Denham and the rest who are bestial. Sympathy for the Beast has not in any way weakened Kong's grip on the public imagination. Far from it. Along with Mickey Mouse and Chaplin's Tramp, Carl Denham's Eighth Wonder of the World remains one of filmdom's few permanent and universal contributions to popular mythology. The culmination of ages of myth, fantasy and fear, Kong endures as modern man's most potent self-image. It is a self-image of man divided within (or against) himself, opposing the rational to the irrational, the civilized to the natural, the mechanical to the physical, the technological to the magical-fantastic, and the European to the Afro-Asian. Kong is a reflection of the bestiality in us that dominates or controls our technological achievements—for Auschwitz, Hiroshima and Vietnam are no less expressive of man's true nature than the Empire State Building or rockets to the Moon. This celluloid tale of Beauty toppling the Beast affirms finally that our bestiality can be mastered (though perhaps, alas, only in fantasy) by the power of Love.

THE MAN WHO SAVED *KING KONG* *

Steve Vertlieb

There is a place, a vault of dreams where never realized plans and almost forgotten film projects sit, alone and lost, on a dusty and cluttered shelf accumulating endless, endless time. Some were movies that never came to be, and while many of these abandoned productions must be mourned over and lamented, there has been an occasional instance when the decision for change has been the right one, the proper one, a choice that forever shaped the history of motion pictures.

In 1940 the world was deprived of a film called *The War Eagle* that was to have been made by M.G.M. Had it been filmed the chances are great that the picture would have emerged a fantasy classic, for it was the project of General Merian C. Cooper, the man responsible for bringing to the screen the single most impressive fantasy film of all time.

The War Eagle was in its early planning stages when "Coop" returned to active military service, thereby terminating its production. A costly endeavor, the picture would have painted the fantastic portrait of a race of cavemen astride giant, prehistoric birds, who invade and attempt to conquer modern-day New York. Cooper probably based his story on H. G. Wells' fantastic novel, *The War in the Air*, in which barbaric Asiatic aviators invade New York in huge, wing-flapping airplanes. If the basic premise of this plot sounds familiar, it should. This would have been the third time that a film about a massive invasion from the past had been produced. The first feature-length film to have employed prehistoric creatures in a modern setting was First National's daring version of Sir Arthur Conan Doyle's *The Lost World* released in 1925 and starring Wallace Beery, Lewis Stone, and Bessie Love. However, it was the second attempt at filming this surface theme that truly captured the imagination of the public and which continues to inspire unparalleled excitement for audiences more than forty years after its original release.

The film, of course, was *King Kong* and it was largely the result of an idea formed years earlier in

* Originally published in *The Monster Times*, Volume One, Number One, January, 1972, and revised by Mr. Vertlieb especially for this volume.

the mind of Merian Coldwell Cooper, the creative genius behind some of the most exciting and visually impressive films of the past fifty years. Many men with considerable talent helped to form what would become the final version of *King Kong*, but throughout its innumerable growing pains there seemed to be only one man who remained faithfully behind the project from its modest beginnings. Merian Cooper was born in Jacksonville, Florida on October 24, 1894 and seemed almost ready even then to break loose from the confining bars of his crib and live in the most extraordinary fashion conceivable to his fertile imagination. He was appointed to Annapolis in 1911 by Florida Senator Duncan Fletcher, but he left school in his final year and signed onto the Transatlantic run as an able seaman, hoping to join the French or the British air service.

Passport difficulties prevented the realization of these goals, and he found a job in the States as a reporter for the *Minneapolis Daily News*. Newspaper work was promising and the later joined the *Des Moines Register-Leader*, and the *St. Louis Post-Dispatch*. Soon, however, he left the *Post-Dispatch* to join the Georgia National Guard which chased Pancho Villa in Mexico.

At the start of the First World War, Cooper enlisted into the Army Aviation Service and went to France as a first lieutenant. Promotions came quickly in battle and before long he was Captain Cooper, but fate stepped into the picture in September of 1918 when he was shot down behind German lines and taken prisoner. His lips and hands were badly burned, and he was confined to a hospital. German doctors performed plastic surgery. He was to remain there until the Armistice.

In 1919 he joined the Polish army and, with Major Cedric Fauntleroy, formed the Kosciusko Squadron to aid the Poles in resisting the Bolshevik invasion. While commanding the squadron he was again shot down behind enemy lines and taken prisoner. He was sent to a prison camp and held there, near Moscow, for ten months. With the help of a professional smuggler he escaped and reached the Latvian border in twenty-six days.

Cooper joined *The New York Times* in 1921 as a reporter and feature writer, and soon wrote an anonymous autobiography titled *Things Men Die For*.

He next arranged to represent *Asia* magazine on an around-the-world-exploratory cruise with Capt. Edward Salisbury. His articles resulted in a second book, written in collaboration with Salisbury, called *The Sea Gypsy*. During the cruise Salisbury's cameraman quit, which prompted Cooper to call in his old friend, Ernest B. Schoedsack, from Paris. Together they filmed the sights of Ethiopia, which they hoped to turn into a documentary. A fire destroyed the footage but not their desire to dramatize true-life adventure.

They purchased two cameras and 50,000 feet of film and together with Marguerite Harrison went to the Persian Gulf where they made a film detailing the annual migration of the Bakhtiari people. They processed the footage themselves back in Paris. The final print, now called *Grass*, was purchased for theatrical release by Jesse L. Lasky of Paramount. Critical reaction to the film was positive so Lasky dispatched the pair to Siam to make a jungle adventure film with a pre-arranged story line. The enormously exciting *Chang* was the result in 1927, and it no doubt served as the inspiration for countless *Bring 'Em Back Alive* type pictures for years to come.

The release of *Grass* in 1925 had started an irreversible chain of events and now the team of Cooper and Schoedsack was off to Africa to shoot "location" footage for the famous story of cowardice, *Four Feathers*. Released in 1929 as "The last of the big silent films," the film starred Richard Arlen and a young girl named Fay Wray. This was the sturdy background of the man who was to save *King Kong*.

Cooper, alone, persisted in his faith that *Kong* would one day become a reality, and were it not for his far-sighted efforts on behalf of the world's most celebrated gorilla, *King Kong* would have turned out a very different film, indeed. *King Kong* began to form in Cooper's mind as early as 1929. In 1930 he completed the first "treatment" of the story. From the beginning he had envisioned a modern re-telling of *Beauty And the Beast* in which a giant gorilla would be transported from his home in primitive jungle to the skyscraper forest of Manhattan. There he would meet his end atop the tower of the awesome Empire State Building, fighting for his right to existence against civilization's bullet-spewing pterodactyls.

Cooper's fascination with apes stemmed from his days in Africa shooting footage with Schoedsack for *Four Feathers*, but the force that triggered his inspiration for *Kong* would seem to have been the publication of *The Dragon Lizards of Komodo*, the true story of nine-foot carnivorous lizards on Komodo Island in the East Indies, published in 1927. The book was written by a friend of Cooper, W. Douglas Burden, a director of the Museum of Natural History in New York City, and set Cooper thinking of how easy it would be to utilize these lizards within the framework of the film that was taking shape in his mind. He would take a camera crew to Africa once again and shoot footage of a normal gorilla, and then transport that animal to the island of Komodo for a fight with an actual dragon. Later at the studio he could always enlarge both of the animals on film to make them appear abnormally big, and then shoot additional scenes of the gorilla atop a model of the Empire State Building.

Cooper consulted with Burden about a name for his huge protagonist. "Coop" had an affinity for names of one syllable, and the more unusual sounding they were the happier he would be. As all of the native dialogue used in the final film was to be authentic, he finally decided upon using the actual language of a small East Indies tribe. Their word for gorilla was "KONG." He added a title to his character to impress his power upon audiences and the simple result was King Gorilla or, in the preferred translation, "King Kong."

Now, the problem was to find studio backing—not an easy task in a depression. Producer David O. Selznick and his brother, Myron, were in New York trying to raise money in hopes of beginning a new independent production company that David would head. Cooper presented the idea to the Selznicks but they had their own problems at the time and *Kong* did not strike them as the way to solve them. The moment had not yet arrived. The year was 1931. In September David Selznick became executive vice president in charge of production at RKO. The studio had suffered through years of mismanagement and was on the verge of bankruptcy. Selznick took on the enormous task of saving the company. One of his first official decisions was to call in his old friend, Merian Cooper, to assist him in cleaning up the mess. One of Cooper's assignments was to evaluate projects either in, or planned for production that were held over from the previous regime. Decisions would be made then on whether they were worth continuing or if it would be financially wiser simply to scrap the projects and move ahead to newer, sounder ventures.

Fate stepped into the life of "Coop" and his pet project for, among the productions he was asked to look into and evaluate as David O. Selznick's executive assistant at RKO was a proposed feature-length picture to deal with prehistoric animals on the screen.

Creation introduced Cooper to an ambitious special effects technician named Willis O'Brien. O'Brien had almost single-handedly invented a marvelous photographic process called Stop Motion that he had used very successfully six years earlier in another film called *The Lost World*. However, the art had been still in its infancy when "Obie" made *The Lost World* for First National and he had been working hard on perfecting it while at Radio. Many of the bugs had been eliminated since 1925 and O'Brien was prepared to prove it.

As he explained to Cooper, Stop-Motion was the slow, tedious procedure of bringing inanimate objects to life on the screen. The process was nearly identical to the method of animating cartoons except that he worked with small rubber miniatures or models built to permit full, "natural" movement of the body. To give his animals the illusion of life he would move a limb a fraction of an inch and then proceed to shoot a frame of that position. Then he would set up the altered position and again shoot further frames. When all of the various body movements were recorded on film and projected, the animals seemed to move of their own accord and possess a very real life force of their own.

Cooper was deeply impressed with the possibilities of using this special technique on the screen. However, it wasn't the filming of Obie's *Creation* that excited him but the thought of using Stop-Motion procedures in his own, unrealized film of *King Kong*. By creating models of the animals he would not only be able to shoot the entire picture in the studio, thereby eliminating the need for extensive "location" filming halfway around the world, but he would be able to achieve undreamt of authenticity in the appearance and movements of his animals. Building and shooting sets on a small scale could capture the desired eeriness of Kong's primeval jungle far better than could a real jungle, over which the studio art directors would have no control.

This was the beginning of a dream coming true for Cooper. Destiny had brought these two men together to create the most astounding motion picture of the age. Now, all Cooper had to do was convince the board of directors at RKO.

The New York executives weren't as excited about the plan as Cooper and Willis O'Brien. Radio Pictures was on such insecure footing at this stage that the corporation directors would probably have balked at the bluest-chip investment. In Cooper and O'Brien's favor, however, was the complete and continued support of David Selznick. It was this support that prompted the worried executives in New York to authorize the filming of one reel which would be shown at a future sales meeting. Only after the accountants saw a sample of Cooper's product would they be able to estimate the picture's marketability.

Cooper was in a tight bind, and he had little choice. He could either make the test reel and hope for approval or start from the beginning again by seeking backing elsewhere. There was no choice. He had to go ahead. Choosing the sequence to put on film would not be easy. Whatever he presented to the overseers of the money would really have to stimulate their imaginations and loosen their wallets. He made his choice. The scene to be filmed would be of the giant ape violently shaking frightened men off a log and into a great ravine below. Additionally, some footage of Kong's battle with a menacing allosaurus in the primeval jungle would be shot.

The big day arrived at last in 1932 as Cooper arrived at the sales meeting with his baby tucked under his arm. The meeting was called to order, the men took their seats, and the projector was turned on. This was the ultimate moment. When the lights came on again, Cooper had his answer. There was overwhelming enthusiasm for the footage and he was granted immediate permission to begin work on *King Kong*. Cooper had won his victory, and *Kong* would at last be made.

That year Cooper was promoted to a higher post. He was now Selznick's executive assistant. He was producing two films simultaneously for the studio—*King Kong*, and an adaptation of Richard Connell's well-known 1924 short story, *The Most Dangerous Game*. Directorial supervision of *Kong* was divided between Cooper and Schoedsack, each working separately on his own chore. Cooper directed most of the jungle sequences, as well as those final exterior scenes set in New York.

Shooting of *The Most Dangerous Game*, begun some weeks earlier, ran into the production schedule of *King Kong*. Actor-Director, Irving Pichel co-directed the thriller with Schoedsack, while the latter raced to the adjoining set to oversee *Kong*. Some identical sets and identical players populated the sound-stages of both pictures. They were, indeed, sister productions, although *Game* was a much more modest effort.

An important set needed for the filming of *King Kong* was the great wall that separated the native population from Kong and his assortment of monstrous companions. It would have to be enormous and magnificent. Hollywood is a town cluttered with props from films gone by and films yet to be made. Cooper set about exploring the town he knew so well in search of a suitable wall. He didn't have much luck. Returning home he began to wander about the forty-acre back lot of RKO Pathé in Culver City. Staring him in the face was the skeleton of a huge gate Cecil B. DeMille had built in 1927 for his production of *King of Kings*. "Coop" "appropriated" the gate and quickly assigned a crew of studio workmen to re-model the structure for his purposes. He ordered two giant doors built for the center of the wall and fabricated a native village in miniature directly in front of the wall. (In some shots of the wall in the finished film one can spot certain Romanesque columns held over from the DeMille film.)

Meanwhile, Selznick had decided to go elsewhere for employment. In February, 1933, he departed RKO for Metro-Goldwyn-Mayer. In his place as production head of the studio was his former executive assistant. Cooper was now fully in charge.

Generally assumed to have been a part of the original test reel was a brief sequence that involved huge, carnivorous spider crabs. When the angered Kong shakes his unfortunate victims off the log and into the ravine below they are hungrily devoured by the waiting spiders. While the print was still in its "work" stages Cooper decided that the spiders slowed up the pacing of the film. He wanted to keep it tight at all times so he deleted the scene, and it was apparently never shown to anyone outside the immediate studio complex.

Famed mystery and adventure writer, Edgar Wallace, was under contract to RKO at this time and was assigned the task of writing a scenario based on Cooper's original story. Cooper agreed to share screen and book credit for authorship with Wallace, but Wallace died before he even had an opportunity to work on the screenplay so Coop was without a writer temporarily. Fortunately, there was Ruth Rose, a writer for whom he had great respect. She was, coincidentally, married to his friend and collaborator, Schoedsack. Cooper decided to keep the project in the family and so he assigned Miss Rose, along with fellow writer James Creelman to compose the final script.

The "Old Arabian Proverb" that precedes the story's unravelling stands as a profoundly beautiful warning to all who may fall under the spell of the goddess of love: "And The Prophet Said—And lo, the beast looked upon the face of beauty. And it stayed its hand from killing. And from that day, it was as one dead." The "Old Arabian Proverb" was written for the film by that old Arabian, Merian C. Cooper, as a part of his original treatment for the film in 1930; it has since become a genuine slice of American mythology.

For the official novelization of *Kong*, Cooper turned to an old newspaper friend, Delos W. Lovelace, who wrote a faithful adaption of the story. The novel was published by Grosset and Dunlap in 1933 and the author's credit at the top of the page read as follows: *King Kong* By Edgar Wallace and Merian C. Cooper; Novelized by Delos W. Lovelace. Cooper, a man of unflinching loyalties, had kept his promise.

As it turned out, ninety-five percent of *King Kong* was filmed directly on the studio lot just as Cooper had predicted. There was very little actual location footage done and costs were kept to a minimum. The exterior sequences taken aboard Captain Englehorn's embattled old steamer while it was still docked were really filmed on a tramp steamer in San Pedro Harbor. Kong's sole public appearance as "Carl Denham's Monster" in a New York City theater was filmed at the Shrine Auditorium in Los Angeles. All of the scenes surrounding that long-remembered appearance were filmed in one day. On the stage the fallen captive, bound tight to a steel cross, bore a significant resemblance to the crucifixion of Christ.

Rather than display Kong on a theatrical stage as was finally agreed upon, Cooper's first conception of that unveiling was to present Kong to New York in a huge, outdoor stadium in broad daylight. Choices being considered for the location were Madison Square Garden and Yankee Staudium. O'Brien went as far as sketching his version of the scene when the director decided in favor of the theater. Presumably, the Shrine Auditorium was intended to represent New York's Radio City Music Hall.

O'Brien drew a series of preliminary sketches of the animal at various stages of the film. In the film the cities and jungles were fashioned by Mario Larringa and Byron L. Crabbe. All of the animals in the picture were built by the skilled hands of Marcel Delgado, model-maker-supreme, and brought to life by the genius of Willis O'Brien with his chief assistant, E. B. Gibson.

Production of *King Kong* was completed after one year at a cost of $513,242.02. For the premiere on the West Coast a full-size bust of Kong was put on display in the forecourt of Sid Grauman's Chinese Theatre in Hollywood. It was the full-scale bust that had been used in the production of the movie for some of Kong's closeups. Of course, most of the ape's appearances on the screen had been filmed in Obie's "Stop Motion" process but several times in the film the full scale bust was used. For one of the final sequences, the long shot of Kong climbing up the side of the Empire State Building to do battle with the metallic serpents of the air, an actor was signed to don a gorilla suit and scale a miniature set of the building that had been erected on one of the sound stages. While many actors have laid claim to the job it is believed by some that animal-man, Charles Gemora, played the walk-on . . .

or climb-up.[1] (In later years, Gemora played a variety of strange parts, including the Martian in George Pal's *The War of the Worlds*, Paramount, 1953.)

In an adventure film like *King Kong* music plays a vastly important role in creating the proper atmosphere. In many instances film music can make a good film seem better than it really is. And as for the bad ones, this writer long ago lost count of the miserable pictures that were literally saved by an excellent music score. Similarly, a bad score can critically wound an otherwise decent film. *King Kong* was one film that appeared to have everything going for it. The head of RKO's music department until 1936 was Max Steiner, one of the screen's most prolific composers. In his unpublished autobiography, *On the Right Track*, Steiner recalls the growing skepticism on the part of the studio's executive officers regarding the box-office appeal of *Kong*. They repeatedly had to be persuaded out of their collective defeatism. They thought that the gorilla looked unreal and rather phony, and they were no longer impressed with the animated sequences. When it came time for scoring the film they advised Steiner merely to borrow tracks from previous studio films and dub them into the sound track of *Kong*. The word was out that no additional money was to be wasted on a film that might turn out to be the mortal blow to an already staggering studio. In other words—no new score and no costly orchestrations.

Fortunately, Cooper re-entered the scene and proved his complete faith in *Kong* once again. "Coop" urged Steiner to write a fresh score for the film and reassured him that he would pay extra costs from his own pocket. The result was Steiner's finest hour, the dynamic, heart pounding score for *King Kong*.

The composer set about creating a vast plain of emotional experience. From the moment the film begins with the ominous three bars that fans around the globe, universally recognised as Kong's theme, to the final, memorable fadeout, the listener is caught in a raging onslaught of sound. The slow, gradually building tension of the first hint of arrival on Skull Island is masterfully conveyed by Steiner's subtle integration of the deceptive sound of breakers near the shore with the warning drums of unseen natives from somewhere on the beach. As Denham and his crew cautiously leave the shelter of their ship and enter the apparently empty village, they hear a distant chanting somewhere near the great wall ahead. As they walk steadily nearer, the sounds gain strength and momentum until, at last,

the intruders come upon a dazzling sight: the ritualistic sacrifice of a young maiden to something the natives continually call "KONG! KONG!"

The momentary safety of the explorers on Skull Island is abruptly interrupted when the tribal chief catches sight of them and calls a halt to the ceremony. Steiner accents every movement of the chief's strut as he walks toward the intruders. His slow, deliberate steps are contrasted dramatically to the wild, gyrating advance of the menacing witch doctor. This is only a prelude to the unrestrained frenzy of the natives as they invite KONG to partake of their gift, the now-captive Ann Darrow. It is here that Steiner captures the fury and vengeful fanaticism of the island's populace in an intoxicated rage. The music begins as the natives are already swept up by the exhilaration of what they plan to do. It throbs, and builds to a fever pitch, communicating an excitement from the screen that cannot fail to touch anyone in the viewing audience, and concludes suddenly at its very peak leaving the helpless spectator literally gasping for breath.[2]

King Kong had its Hollywood premiere at Grauman's Chinese Theatre on Friday evening, March 24, 1933. The souvenir-program book contained the following publicity blurb: "Out of an uncharted, forgotten corner of the world, a monster . . . surviving seven million years of evolution . . . crashes into the haunts of civilization . . . onto the talking screen . . . to stagger the imagination of man."

Mystery magazine celebrated the event by beginning its own serialized version of the story in their February 1933 issue. Bruce Cabot and Fay Wray were pictured on the cover, and the blurb above the title billed the tale as "The last and the greatest creation of Edgar Wallace."

On opening night in Hollywood, premiere jitters were building and managed to leave practically no one untouched. However, this night was not the beginning of the suspense but its climax, for rumors about *King Kong* had been circulating for months.

Radio Pictures purchased one of the longest commercials in advertising history when, on February 10, 1933, the National Broadcasting Company aired a thirty-minute radio program to let America know of the impending birth of King Kong. It was a show within a show; a sort of coming attraction, complete with specially tailored script and realistic sound effects. Reaction to the broadcast was exactly as hoped for—it was tremendous.

Original publicity releases and newspaper ads gave

---

1 These facts remain speculative, however. There are indications that Cooper may have taken his dreams to the Disney studio where the controversial sequence was *Rotoscoped*, the process by which live action is drawn over an animated, utilized by Disney in many feature-length cartoons.

2 Sheet music for piano was published for the score, and Steiner recorded a fifteen-minute suite from the film with the RKO Studio Orchestra. Many recent re-recordings of this music are now available.

out verbal previews of what was to come: "Monsters of Creation's Dawn Break Loose in Our World Today" . . . "Never before had human eyes beheld an ape the size of a battleship" . . . "They saw the flying lizard, the fierce brontosaurus, big as twenty elephants . . . and all the living, fighting creatures of the infant world." . . . "The giant ape leaped at the throat of the dinosaur and the death fight was on. A frightened girl, in 1933, witnessed the most amazing combat since the world began."

Trailers (Coming Attractions) at the time, normally accustomed to previewing the most exciting scenes in a picture in order to entice a given audience, were deliberately secretive and noncommittal. Only a huge, frightening shadow was seen by theatergoers, accompanied by warnings like "This is only the shadow of King Kong. . . . See the greatest sight that your eyes have ever beheld at this theater—beginning Sunday."

Sid Grauman was a showman and had earned his reputation from years of inventive staging. On this night of all nights he wasn't going to be caught with his curtains down. Grauman arranged for a very special seventeen-act extravaganza to precede the first showing of *King Kong*. He hired dancers, singers and musicians for the gala evening. To be sure, it was a night that no one who was there would ever forget. Recreated in these pages is the original program produced for that memorable evening more than forty years ago.

Finally, the moment that the huge audience in Hollywood had waited for was at hand. The house lights dimmed, the projectionist started his machine and a hush fell over the crowd. On screen, the mammoth Radio Pictures tower beeped excitely atop a spinning globe. It faded out and into a *Radio Pictures Presents* plaque. Finally, the logo faded out, and onto the waiting screen came the title, in great block lettering, K I N G   K O N G. And it did come! From the background, the title suddenly zoomed up front in a dramatic 3-D effect to take its rightful place, prominently, in the foreground. It, and the film which followed have remained there ever since.

As big and exciting as the Hollywood premiere was, *King Kong* really gave its world premiere some three weeks earlier to the city that graciously destroyed itself for movie history. It was fitting and proper that New York City serve as host for the unveiling of Carl Denham's Monster, King Kong, the eighth wonder of the world. On March 2, 1933, *King Kong* created almost as much chaos for real as he did in the film. This was no ordinary premiere for, so great was the demand to see the new film that, in the midst of America's worst Depression, two enormous theaters were required to play the film simultaneously in order to fill the public's demand for seats. Both the Radio City Music Hall and

the Roxy Theatre, with a combined seating capacity of ten thousand, were filled for every performance of the film from the moment when the doors opened at ten-thirty A.M. on Thursday, March 2.

The theaters took out combined ads in *The New York Times* the day preceding the opening. Kong, himself, was pictured atop the Empire State Building holding Fay Wray in one paw, and crushing a biplane in the other. The caption next to the ape and atop the title read:

KONG
THE MONSTER

"Huge as a skyscraper . . . crashes into our city. See him wreck man's proudest works while millions flee in horror. . . . See him atop the Empire State Tower, battling planes for the woman in his ponderous paw. *King Kong* outleaps the maddest imagination."

As in Hollywood there were stage shows here also. "Stages Shows As Amazing As These Mighty Theatres," proclaimed the advertisement. 'Jungle Rhythms'—brilliant musical production. Entire singing and dancing ensemble of Music Hall and New Roxy. Spectacular dance rhythms by ballet corps and Roxyettes. Soloists, Chorus, Symphony Orchestras, Company of 500. Big enough for the Two Greatest Theatres at the same time.'

Kong played to standing crowds for ten complete performances daily. On the day of the opening a second ad appeared in New York's entertainment pages. The publicity blurbs read, in part, "Shuddering terror grips a city. . . . Shrieks of fleeing millions rise to the ears of a towering monster . . . Kong, king of an ancient world, comes to destroy our world—all but that soft, white female thing he holds like a fluttering bird. . . . The arch-wonder of modern times.'

Mordaunt Hall, critic for *The New York Times*, said in his review on March 3, 1933, "It essays to give the spectator a vivid conception of the terrifying experiences of a producer of jungle pictures and his colleagues, who capture a gigantic ape, something like fifty feet tall, and bring it to New York. The narrative is worked out in a decidedly compelling fashion, which is mindful of what was done in the old silent film, *The Lost World*. . . . Human beings seem so small that one is reminded of *Gulliver's Travels*. One step and this beast traverses half a block. If buildings hinder his progress he pushes them down, and below him the people look like Lilliputians."

Hall's obvious liking for the film was just as obviously shared by more than a few New Yorkers. When, in 1933, President Roosevelt declared a moratorium and closed the banks, the following ad appeared in New York's papers: "No money . . . yet New York dug up $89,-931.00 in four days (March 2, 3, 4, 5) to see *King Kong* at Radio City, setting a new all-time world's record for attendance of *any* indoor attraction." This is all the more startling considering that general admission prices were far less expensive than they are today.

It was rumored several years ago that a special fifteen-minute introductory film was made for the premiere showing of the feature in Hollywood that explained, basically, how the technical wizardry in *King Kong* was accomplished. Supposedly, the "prologue" was never again seen outside of the official premiere. Yet, according to the man behind the ape, Merian Cooper, no such film was ever made. He emphatically states that the film in question does not now, and never has existed—as the studio wanted to keep their new discoveries private. After all of the work, expense and risks involved in the making of this revolutionary film no one at RKO, least of all General Cooper, was about to advertise their secrets.

Similarly, it has been assumed that the recently rediscovered "censored" scenes from *Kong* were originally deleted by the censors in time for the film's big theatrical reissue in 1952, and that the censored scenes had been considered too brutal and . . . sexy. The scenes included shots of Kong playfully and naïvely inspecting the torn dress worn by Ann Darrow (Fay Wray), and then removing parts of it, lifting them to his nose and sniffing the strange scent; holding a villager between his teeth; violently smashing down a structure upon which natives were standing and hurling spears; grinding the head of a writhing native into the mud on the ground with his foot; climbing the outer wall of a New York hotel at which Ann Darrow was staying, in search of his captive at large, and finding the first woman he sees asleep in her bed, then drawing her to him out through the window, examining her in mid-air and, realizing that he has picked the wrong girl,[3] callously allowing her to slip through his fingers and fall to the ground below; and, lastly, chewing casually on a native New Yorker. The truth is that the much-publicized scenes were, in fact, deleted because of their strong content but this occurred first in 1938—not in 1952.

In 1933, as in all subsequent re-releases, the picture was box-office dynamite. Full-page ads in the trade journals were headed by the impressive lead-in, "The Answer To Every Showman's Prayer." And it was. This was no case of attempting to sell a loser, for *Kong* was truly a theatrical bonanza for all film exhibitors sharing in the feast.

It is interesting to note that, as compelling as the visual imagery in the picture was, its sound effects were

thought unique enough to permit re-use in later studio productions again and again. Some of the human misery inflicted by the great ape was shared by the similarly helpless men of *Kong*'s sister production, *The Most Dangerous Game*. For instance, the unforgettable screams of Denham's crew, hanging onto a precariously balanced log, as Kong shakes them one by one into the yawning pit below, served also as the blood-curdling cries of Joel McCrea's shipmates, being eaten alive by sharks after the wreck of their ship in the opening sequence of *Dangerous Game*.

Fay Wray's awesome scream is equalled in its popularity only by Johnny Weissmuller's well-known cry as Tarzan, The Ape Man. No one has ever attempted a guess at why Fay's screaming should have so completely overshadowed the shrieks of all other actresses throughout the four decades since *Kong*'s first release, but few would doubt her right to the title of the world's most celebrated screamer. Cooper had her work a full day in the recording studio—screaming. She screamed up and down the scale so that the correct note of terror would be injected into her performance. So, it was not surprising to learn that RKO used that contract scream in the voices of countless other actresses whose tonsils were not as healthily endowed. When Helen Mack opened her fragile lips to cry out in *Son of Kong* it was not her voice audiences heard but that of Fay Wray. As late as 1945 her scream could be heard for Audrey Long in Robert Wise's *Game of Death*, a remake of *The Most Dangerous Game*.

But, of all of the memorable sounds to come from *King Kong*, the immortal score by Max Steiner has been heard the most. Kong's thrilling and intricate themes have been played in such later films as *Son of Kong*, *The Last Days of Pompeii*, *Becky Sharp* (the first full Technicolor feature), *The Last of the Mohicans*, *The Soldier and the Lady* (from Jules Verne's *Michael Strogoff*), *Fang and Claw*, *Back to Bataan*, and *White Heat*.

Sets and props used in *Kong* also had ways of turning up before the cameras on other pictures. The huge log that Kong hurled furiously into the spider pit was seen in that very same jungle in *The Most Dangerous Game*, and spiders must have a very strong sense of survival, for one of the three original spider-crabs built for the test-reel survived long enough to put in an appearance in O'Brien's *The Black Scorpion* (Warner Bros., 1957). The doors that Cooper had built into the heart of De-Mille's Roman wall were transposed two years later from the tropical heat of Skull Island in the East Indies to the Arctic wastelands for duty in the second filmed version of H. Rider Haggard's classic fantasy, *She*. The wall perished spectacularly, finally, during the burning of Atlanta sequence for Selznick's *Gone With The Wind*

---

[3] The young actress who fell to her death was Sandra Shaw, a New York socialite who, under her real name of Veronica Balfe, married Gary Cooper on December 15, 1922.

(MGM, 1939). It may be mentioned, as an historical note for airplane aficionados, that although Army planes were called for by Denham at the film's conclusion it was actually a flight of Curtis F8C Navy Fighter planes that violated New York's "Be Kind to Animals Week" in 1933 and added injury to insult upon the proud relic of a bygone era.

Kong, unlike many other film favorites seems to grow in stature with the passing years and is more cherished today than when it was first released back in the depths of the Depression. A preview audience in San Bernardino, California couldn't have suspected that when they entered the theater on an evening late in February 1933, that they had been chosen by the warm hand of fate to see the first public performance of *King Kong*.

At the box office *King Kong* grew more financially rewarding with every new release and must rank close to *Gone With The Wind* in its number of new re-releases to first-run theaters in 1938, 1942, 1946, 1952, 1956 and most recently in 1970 for a limited engagement at "Art Theaters" across the country. Today's film fans and critics have begun to notice all manner of subtleties that escaped the more naïve filmgoer of the thirties. Its serious psychological, social, and cultural implications are now explicated in the vast commentary that has grown over the years.

In 1932 the cast and crew of *King Kong* sent a Christmas card to Merian Coldwell Cooper that portrayed him, in caricature, shouting "Make it bigger. Make it bigger." The wish became command and *King Kong* was born. Carl Denham, a thinly disguised replica of Cooper himself said, on the eve of his great adventure, "I'm going out and make the greatest picture in the world, something that nobody's ever seen or heard of. They'll have to think up a lot of new adjectives when I come back." Denham kept his word, and so did Cooper. He gave the world the finest, best loved, and most faithfully remembered fantasy in the history of motion pictures. And all of us have had the problem of inventing new adjectives to account for the experience of the film.

Were it not for Cooper and his deeply rooted faith in *Kong* the movie might never have been made . . . or, worse, it would have been made without its gifted creator continually at the helm. Without his belief in the possibilities of Stop Motion; without his insistence that Max Steiner create an original music score for the film when the money men were against the idea; and without his feeling for authentic, far-off adventure, *Kong* would have turned out a different film indeed and, quite probably, would be long forgotten by this time. However, Merian Cooper was faithful to his best aesthetic, technical, and commercial instincts and he, more than any other individual, shares the double responsibility for having first imagined and then saved the screen story that has so pervasively entered our cultural experience.

MISSING LINKS: THE JUNGLE ORIGINS OF *KING KONG* *

Gerald Peary

What strange, inexplicable beings inhabit the unexplored jungle regions of the earth? Carl Denham of *King Kong* was neither first nor alone in seeking pragmatic answers to this always provocative question. By the time Kong was brought back alive to rule the Hollywood bestiary in 1933, there had been established a long-standing tradition of similar sojourns into the depths in earlier "jungle quest" movies.

This very particularized genre usually has adhered to a rather formalized narrative pattern, regardless of whether the film was fictional in content, and wildly speculative, or documentary, a recording of factual events. A party of explorers from civilization travel into the dark, forbidden tropics on some kind of scientific mission, typically aimed at reversing a traditionally held biological theory about the area in surveillance. After the explorers have stood steadfast through a series of minor adventures and perils initiating them into the mysteries of the jungle, they are rewarded handsomely for their perseverance. Before them appears some tremendous aberration of nature which challenges, or even undermines, the so-called "normal" patterns of existence.

At its simplest symbolic level, the "jungle quest" demonstrates vividly that all the mysteries of the world can never be uncovered, for a dinosaur or strange variety of ape can suddenly storm out of the jungle bushes, turning standard scientific thought on its head. It is precisely this kind of inexplicable occurrence which endows the "jungle quest" movie with its inexhaustible vitality and appeal.

The lure of the jungle was felt early in the history of filmmaking, as turn-of-the-century documentarians sought out thrilling alternatives to the literalist, mundane world view typified in the Lumière Brothers "actualities," photographic duplications of the commonplaces of everyday life. Enterprising cameramen aimed to capture on film those events and locales which no one in civilization ever had witnessed, a goal leading inevitably into the jungle, understood broadly as the relatively unknown. Carl Denham in *King Kong* later echoed these early cameramen-adventurers in explaining his insatiable search for Kong: "I'll tell you, there's

something . . . that no white man has even seen. You bet I'll photograph it!"

The surprising financial and artistic success of Flaherty's *Nanook of the North* in 1922 made the full-length documentary suddenly a commercially viable product. It prompted a series of expeditions to the jungles and elsewhere with plans of producing ambitious, lengthy documentaries. Several of these projects are relevant to *King Kong*, not so much as direct influences as for their demonstration of *Kong's* kinship with the more imaginative, unorthodox topics of the documentary filmmakers.

Bali, the Unknown: or Ape Island, made even before *Nanook* in 1921, concerned itself with the possibilities of a prehistoric "ape man" civilization on Bali. *Gorilla Hunt*, a 1926 feature of FBO Studio (forerunner of *King Kong's* RKO), followed the adventures of a real-life Carl Denham type named Ben Burbridge, who traveled into Africa in search of gorillas to bring back alive in captivity. After a series of thrilling encounters with various jungle animals (elephants, pythons, crocodiles), Burbridge finally accomplished his task, catching six gorillas for return to civilization.

Closest of all to *King Kong* in its purposes was a film which was never made. In February 1925, a troupe of twenty-nine persons arrived in Singapore with ambitions to capture on film a legendary "ape man" periodically sighted in the area. Promised funding for the project from California never arrived. Faced with unpaid hotel bills, the movie company was forced to give up and return home to Missoula, Montana. The real "ape man" thus eluded filming.

Actually the commonality of *King Kong* with "jungle quest" documentaries is an easily explainable phenomenon, for Merian C. Cooper and Ernest B. Schoedsack, co-directors of the movie, broke into film as part of the post-*Nanook* documentary rush. They were employed as cameramen and artistic advisors for Captain Edward Salisbury on his travelogues called *The Lost Empire*

---

* This essay was prepared especially for this volume and is published by permission of the author.

(featuring his adventures in the South Seas, Ceylon, and Arabia) and *Gow, the Headhunter* (about the island of Fiji). Both of these works were made around 1924, though not placed in general release until approximately five years later.

More important for their subsequent careers was a decision by Cooper and Schoedsack to combine talents with famed newspaperwoman Marguerite Harrison on a film called *Grass*, which reverently pursued a tribe of obscure Iranian nomads on a forty-eight-day trek into the mountains. The object of this rugged journey, made annually by the tribe, was summer grassland for their flock, a considerably more sober aspiration than that featured in most "quest" pictures. *Grass* was released by Paramount in 1925, and widely praised for the seriousness of the filmmakers' intentions.

The critical success of *Grass* led Paramount to finance another faraway journey for Cooper-Schoedsack, this time to make *Chang* in 1927 in the Siamese jungles. The obvious parallels between the locales of *Chang* and *King Kong* signalled only one shift by the two filmmakers, now working alone, toward their future interests. Probably more important was the qualification of the documentary with strong fictional elements. The cast and environment were absolutely authentic. For the first time, however, the plot was pre-planned and fabricated, though still far from the uninhibted fantasy of *King Kong*.

Of further note was the initial utilization by Cooper-Schoedsack of a member of the simian family as an essential ingredient in telling their story. Providing the comic relief was a gibbon monkey named "Bimbo," who perhaps qualified as a distant cousin of King Kong himself.

Chang surpassed all expectations by Paramount for profits from an esoteric semi-documentary. Cooper and Schoedsack were rehired immediately for an expensive, ambitious project, two years of shooting on a film adaptation of A.E.W. Mason's *The Four Feathers*, a Kiplingesque novel of betrayal and redemption in the British Foreign Service. The co-directors journeyed to Africa for authentic location photography and bridging scenes in 1927, then came back to Hollywood to shoot the romantic story with Paramount stars against the documentary footage. This common filmic practice today was probably initiated on that picture.

Cooper later claimed to have thought first of the giant gorilla which would evolve as King Kong while shooting the African sequences of *The Four Feathers*. One scene of a jungle fire must have stuck particularly in mind. Flocks of adult baboons battled for safe spots high in the trees, protecting their roosts by mercilessly sacrificing their young to drown in the waters below. Such inspired Darwinian survival tactics would be worthy even of Kong.

In returning to film the Hollywood sections of *The Four Feathers*, Cooper-Schoedsack were granted the chance to make a second link in their minds crucial to the momentous success of *King Kong*. Acting in the gentle portions of the movie, thousands of miles from the baboons, was a very young actress named Fay Wray, signed to portray the proper Englishwoman fiancée to the film's hero, Richard Arlen. Was this budding startlet already envisioned by the filmmakers as the future object of King Kong's sexual passion? One can only guess.

Ernest Schoedsack, minus Cooper, made one more semi-documentary of the *Chang* variety at Paramount before moving permanently to RKO. This was a very late silent film, in 1931, called *Rango*. Shooting in the jungles of Sumatra, Schoedsack used a native cast to relate his fictional story.

As with both *Chang* and *Four Feathers* before, simian relations of King Kong figured prominently in the tale. Rango, the titular hero, was an ourang-outang slain by a tiger, leaving his father, Tua, to mourn him up in the trees, a touching contrast to the parental callousness of the baboons in *Four Feathers*. The poignant moment of grief prefigured, in a totally different context, the sad demise of King Kong himself only two years later.

There was, of course, a simpler and considerably less perilous way to make jungle movies than to travel into the tropical wilds. That was the way of Méliès, who demonstrated early the almost limitless means of simulating reality without ever leaving the studio. Despite Cooper-Schoedsack's years in the jungles by the time of *King Kong*, they followed Méliès' examples religiously, and shot almost all of the movie on indoor sets in California.

Méliès' pioneering influence on the then infant genre of jungle fantasies was incredible and complete, though almost all by inference. Except for a sixty-five-foot version of H. Rider Haggard's *She* and reconstruction of Devil's Island for a short on the Captain Dreyfus case, Méliès seemed distinctly disinterested in creating jungle settings. Nevertheless, it was his development of the essential ingredients of trick photography—rear projections, single frame shooting, elaborate miniature models —which would become the basic tools of future jungle fantasies, indeed of all fantastic adventure films. That King Kong moved at all, much less with animated grace and subtle facial expression, must be attributed ultimately to Méliès' technical wizardry.

Furthermore, the repeated choice by Méliès of Jules Verne-type stories as the subject matter of his most popular films (*Journey to the Center of the Earth, A Trip to the Moon*) surely was the source and structural inspiration of countless analogous "jungle voyage" fantasies in the cinematic future, in which scientists from civilization explored unmapped jungle regions of the earth and met with uncanny adventures.

Most important of all was Méliès' dramatic introduction of fiction and the realm of the fantastic as appropriate subject matters for film. He showed moviemakers that the pathway to the unique could be realized as capably through imaginary constructs as by shooting footage in untraveled parts of the world.

By the years before World War I, the ideas of Méliès in France had been disseminated to America, but with only moderate effect. The first "jungle cycle" of 1913 in the USA reflected an obvious acknowledgement of the technical possibilities offered by Mèliès, but more dominant was a reliance on naturalistic elements in the films to establish jungle versimilitude. *Beasts of the Jungle,* the three-reel Solax picture which success spurned the cycle, mixed with its actors and Fort Lee, N.J. studio setting, a minor menagerie consisting of two lions, a tiger, a monkey, and a parrot, all live and all imported to New Jersey for the occasion.

Alice Guy Blache, the remarkable woman who ran Solax, publicized the picture extensively, for she was understandably anxious to recoup the considerable 1913 investment of $18,000 in the production. *Beasts of the Jungle* was ". . . the first picture in which as many different animals have been used . . ." and ". . . in which the performers appear in the scenes with the wild beasts." This publicity paid off so profitably that other studios quickly made jungle films, a cycle capped at Famous Players by Adolph Zukor's extravaganza, *Captain Kearton's Wild Life and Big Game in the Jungles of India and Africa.*

In 1912, Edgar Rice Burroughs had contributed to *All-Story* magazine an elaborate and brilliant jungle adventure story entitled "Tarzan of the Apes," a literary work worthy in imagination to Méliès on film in its creative geography. Burroughs had, of course, never set foot in Africa, Tarzan's magnificently evoked homeland.

The switch for the popular Tarzan from books to the movies was an inevitable extension of the jungle fantasy picture, a movie form in search of its first hero. In 1918 the gargantuan D. W. Griffith muscleman, Elmo Lincoln, was called to the Louisiana location for *Tarzan of the Apes.* He replaced the former lead, who had abandoned the movie after spraining his ankle in a fall.

With hair at shoulder length and weirdly bobbed, Lincoln was a no-nonsense, completely physicalized Tarzan, the perfect primitive embodiment for the non-talking movies. He proved so adept at swinging through the firmament that he remained on the screen afterward in *The Romance of Tarzan* and *The Adventures of Tarzan.* Contemporary with Elmo Lincoln's emergence as the first star of the "jungle fantasy" movie was the public unveiling of the genre's primary artistic genius, special effects man, Willis O'Brien, whose designs for the Edison Company in 1917–1918 were startling prefigurements of his later unparalleled conceptions for *King Kong.* Experimenting then with clay models and stop-action photography, O'Brien masterminded a series of five-minute caveman shorts featuring mobile, animated prehistoric animals in deadly combat. The first of these was called *The Dinosaur and the Missing Link,* an amazing preview of the battle far ahead between King Kong and the fierce tyrannosaurus.

These tiny Edison films provided testing ground for Willis O'Brien's sophisticated laboratory experiments, allowing at last in America for a full exploration of Méliès innovations by a person who matched the Frenchman both technically and temperamentally. It was O'Brien who grasped the artistic possibilities opened up by Méliès, who carried the literally magical abilities of the filmmaker to create alternative worlds of the imagination, each with its own laws, its own unique essence.

It had been one thing to juxtapose human and jungle animals for dramatic effect in the manner of *Beasts of the Jungle* and its followers, including the Tarzan series. But it was extraordinarily different to transform the whole environment into a visionary reality in the way of Méliès and O'Brien. What Méliès had accomplished in animating the surface of the moon, the center of the earth, the polar regions, O'Brien managed for the jungle.

He took his prehistoric Stone Age setting from his Edison shorts and lifted it with little change into the twentieth century, the modern age, yet hid his locale in the midst of a lost jungle. Almost as a god, O'Brien set his anachronistic environment in motion, then waited, as Méliès before him, for explorers from civilization to stumble upon it.

Later in 1933, these journeyers would find King Kong, O'Brien's ultimate creation, awaiting them. But in 1925, the year of Willis O'Brien's first major designing assignment, the explorers ran smack against the ape men and dinosaurs of Sir Arthur Conan Doyle's *The Lost World.*

In February, 1925, First National Studio brought its most coveted film product, *The Lost World,* into Broadway's Astor Theatre for the premiere New York showing. The spectacularly publicized opening followed crisply on the tail of a cleverly executed Boston preview run—so monumentally successful that New York journalists shipped reporters ahead to Massachusetts for advanced "scoop" reviews.

Such reverential press coverage usually was restricted to theatrical productions during the silent era of the movies. But *The Lost World* was special, unique, the culminating moment of years of jungle fantasies, an immediate candidate to reign as the "king" of the "jungle voyage" genre. The film was an immense popular success; and contemporary critics appeared as convinced of the genuineness of the filmic achievement as the crowds.

A look at this heralded work half a century later, however, shows a movie quite embarrassingly over-praised in its initial run. *The Lost World* is far from qualifying as "the most marvellous film of all time," as one 1925 critic enthusiastically described it. There is simply no way to ignore the inept, plodding direction of Henry Hoyt, whose action sequences are so lifeless and crude that they seem at times a regression all the way to Edwin S. Porter's 1907 *Rescue from an Eagle's Nest*.

The sustained interest in *The Lost World* has only slightly to do with its intrinsic artistic values, much more with its forebearer role of conceptions which Willis O'Brien would transport and sharpen eight years later into the seemingly eternal appeals of *King Kong*. Skull Island, home of Kong, readily identifies as Doyle's Lost World in a new guise—moved out of the Amazon regions of South America and into the untracked waters of the South Seas.

Not only do the two locales share somewhat similar topography and extremely kindred inhabitants (primitive human tribes and dinosaurs live in proximity in both places), but the existences of these mutant environments make sense only in context of the same fascinating pseudoscientific theory postulated by Arthur Conan Doyle in his novel. Doyle argued the possibility on earth of a freakish land in which Darwinian processes had been jolted so that evolution moved forward and yet was suspended at the same time. There creatures of all genetic forms and from all periods of the earth's life coexisted, even the ostensibly extinct: dinosaurs, "ape-men," primitive Indians. And with the introduction of the Professor Challenger expedition in *The Lost World*, "contemporary man" would join in the fray.

This coexistence was hardly of the peaceful variety, however. In this overcrowded land, the Darwinian battle for the survival of the species was the central issue of existence, occurring in many variations every second of the day. The Lost World was a land in upheaval and tumult, a shrill, screaming, bloodbath parody of the romantic notion of a hidden, eternally tranquil sanctuary somewhere in nature. Likewise, Skull Island proved to be anything but a land representing a Golden Age.

O'Brien's animated jungle environment of "dinosaur eat dinosaur" in the movie of *The Lost World* wisely took its visual inspiration from the brilliantly detailed descriptions of Conan Doyle in the novel. But the final London sequences, in which the explorer party returns home, found O'Brien expanding on his own far beyond the brief paragraphs which abruptly halted the book.

Doyle had offered up a single tiny pterodactyl, which flew about London for a bit before heading back toward its South American homeland. But O'Brien added to the return to Britain his most phenomenal animated creation to this point, a 120-foot brontosaurus, which escaped into the streets, created havoc among the populace, caused London Bridge quite literally to fall under its weight, then finally swam up the Thames to disappear into the sea.

It was this finale which most amazed the contemporary critics of the film. "How was it done?" queried one reporter for *The Boston Herald* about O'Brien's climatic moments. "We have seen seas open and shut. . . . We have seen flying carpets and horses . . ; but how a naturally moving animal as big as a ship could chase real people down a real street and apparently break through a real bridge is too much for us. We'd better just believe it happened."

As noted earlier, Merian Cooper claimed conception of King Kong while making *Four Feathers* in 1927. Yet a more likely initial inspiration came via Willis O'Brien in 1925 with this lost, anachronistic dinosaur giant in *The Lost World*, stomping its way through the London streets, unleashing destruction like that which Kong would bring to New York. The brontosaurus even stopped to stick its head through a third-story apartment window, an action so novel as to be reiterated in *King Kong* when the giant gorilla snatched Ann Darrow out of her upper-story hotel room. Furthermore, the brontosaurus's fall through London Bridge, the city's most visible and representative public site, recurred in Kong's tumble from the Empire State Building.

An even more literal link to King Kong was through the "ape man" of *The Lost World*, who chased the Londoners about the Amazonian jungle. Although played unconvincingly by an actor in painted makeup and furpiece attire, this character still was interesting enough to O'Brien to figure in the conversion to *King Kong*. At least one "ape man" adventure was repeated so closely in the second movie that there could be no mistaking the original source.

When Driscoll and Ann fled Kong by climbing down a rope and dropping into the waters below, they echoed Edward Malone's escape from the ape man down the side of a steep plateau. The dramatic level of excitement in each case was the same, as the primate adversary fought back by pulling the rope, hand over hand, back up the ravine. Only at the last moment did the dangling heroes loosen their grasps and fall to safety, avoiding the unpleasantness of being mauled by the jungle beast lurking at the top.

There was an infinitely more obscure literary source than Doyle which also affected the future shape of *King Kong*, a 1927 pulpish, gothic mystery called *The Avenger*. This long-forgotten novel was one of 173 works of British author, Edgar Wallace, who later went to Hollywood in 1931 and cooperated with Merian Cooper on the "idea" of *King Kong*. Wallace also composed an early script version of the intended movie before dying suddenly in 1932, many months before the picture was released. (There is a current controversy between the Wallace forces and those of Cooper over what this means in terms of the signficance of Wallace's contribution. For example, see Behlmer's Foreword and Bezanson's essay in this volume.)

If *The Lost World* grandly inspired the symbolic geography and prehistoric concerns of *King Kong*, this novel, *The Avenger* still managed a modest influence on certain plot elements and also introduced early forms of several of *Kong's* characters. A movie company travels on location to the gloomy English provinces (Skull Island). Jack Knebworth, movie producer (Carl Denham), reaches among the anonymous extras on his movie and brings forward a new female star, beautiful Adele Leamington (Ann Darrow, Denham's soupline discovery). Adele finds herself plagued on the set by a mysterious ourang-outang named Bhag (King Kong), who chases her across the provincial terrain.

Different from both the "ape man" of *The Lost World* and Kong, Bhag does not run free in nature. He is pet and obedient servant to Edgar Wallace's villain, who orders him to strange and terrible deeds. And, as it is discovered, most primates in movies of the same period, the later silent era, were employed similarly, as faithful pet-assassin of the chief ogre of the picture.

Several examples of the "evil ape" traditions may be cited: *The Leopard Lady* (Pathé, 1928)—a Cossack employed by the circus owns an ape which assists in thefts and murders. *Where East Is East* (MGM, 1929) —"Tiger" Haynes, a wild-animal trapper played by Lon Chaney lets loose a killer gorilla to eliminate his evil-ex-wife. The gorilla murders the former spouse, then turns on "Tiger" himself. *Unknown Treasures* (Sterling Pictures, 1926)—Simmons, the villainous caretaker, unleashes his ape to strangle a man named Cheney. Later the ape revolts and kills Simmons; *The Wizard* (Fox, 1927)—Dr. Coriolus, whose son was given the electric chair, obtains an ape and trains it for revenge; *Circus Rookies* (MGM, 1928)—a comic version of the typical story above. Oscar Thrust, animal trainer, sends

"Bimbo, the Man-Eating Ape" after the woman who has rejected him. But Bimbo predictably turns on his master and administers a severe spanking.

Almost all of these apes and gorillas were thrown into the movies much more for easy melodramtic thrills than for any developed conceptual reasons. There were several other strange "ape films" in the same time period, however, which appear to have some affinity with the slightly more subtle concerns of *The Lost World* and *King Kong*. These films should be noted: *A Blind Bargain* (Goldwyn, 1922)—tells the story of a mad Dr. Lamb (Lon Chaney, of course) who attempts to reverse the Darwinian processes by changing men back into their simian ancestors. Luckily, his experiments are stopped short when one of the doctor's "ape man" patients crushes him to death.

Stark Mad (WB, 1929) was a "jungle quest" fantasy, totally lost today. This is unfortunate, for the film appears from descriptions possibly to have been a genuine influence on *King Kong*. One scene from the plot summaries sounds particularily striking and relevent: those on an expedition into the South American jungles enter a Mayan temple to find a gigantic ape chained to the floor. *Ourang* (Univ., 1930) was a film apparently never released. Yet if it had followed true to its advance advertisements, *Ourang* would have prefigured *King Kong's* bestial sexual theme in its story of a woman carried off by ourang-outangs through the jungles of Borneo. The preview publicity shot in the Universal ad in *Variety* even showed a woman struggling in the arms of the ourang-outang, an amazing foreshadowing of the trials and subjugations of Ann Darrow.

By 1930, then, the *King Kong* project was forming separately from at least three different directions: from Willis O'Brien's *Lost World* experiments, from Cooper-Schoedsack's documentary work and filming of *The Four Feathers*, from Edgar Wallace's novel of *The Avenger*. Furthermore, jungle movies were undergoing a new cycle of popularity, revived by the fantastically successful *Trader Horn* at MGM, shot in super-spectacular fashion by W. S. Van Dyke on African location with ninety-two tons of technical equipment. *Variety* commented in January, 1930, "So many people are going into woolly Africa with cameras that the natives are not only losing their lens shyness but are rapidly nearing the stage where they will qualify for export to Hollywood."

The time was ripe for *King Kong*, though what was still needed was an interested studio. Thanks to the infamous *Ingagi* incident of early 1930, RKO clearly would be amenable to such a project.

In April, 1930, the representatives of "Congo Pictures, Ltd." walked up and down Market Street in San

Francisco offering the theaters a chance to purchase rights to this picture, *Ingagi*, "based on an exploration into the Belgian Congo by Sir Hubert Winstead of London." Every theater except one turned down the movie as an obvious "raw fake." But the Orpheum decided not only to exhibit *Ingagi* but to promote it vigorously.

A tabloid newspaper filled with sensational pictures from *Igagi* was distributed door to door in the area. A jungle exhibition was set up in the lobby. And the Orpheum drummed up $4,000 worth of business the opening day, $23,000 for the first week. RKO Studio, owner of the Orpheum, picked up national rights, and soon *Ingagi* was showing everywhere. It doubled existing house records in Seattle, was termed "the talk of the town" in Chicago, and soon was among the box-office champions of the whole country.

"Photography is poor," noted *Variety*. "Accompanying lectures, synchronized on the film, are supposed to have been done by Winstead, but the speaker uses a plain American accent." None of this mattered to the public, nor the fact that three-fourths of the picture was devoted to the tired, standard shots of elephant herds, hippopotami, and various animals running about the jungle.

All attention was directed to the last ten minutes of *Ingagi* which showed a tribe of completely naked "ape women" (though modestly obstructed from full view by thickets) sacrificing a black woman to a gorilla. *Ingagi* publicity turned also to this final scene, blatantly emphasizing the sexual aspects of the sacrifice, the perverse union of woman and jungle animal. The crowds kept coming.

Many groups, including Better Business Bureaus on the Coast, were offended by the flagrant sexual selling of *Ingagi* to the public. But rather than demanding its censorship on these grounds, they chose another stratagem of attack: an investigation of the suspicious-looking "documentary footage," especially of the sacrifice. They turned their fascinating conclusions over to the Hays office.

In the middle of May, 1930, the Hays organization officially announced the findings. "Congo Pictures, Ltd." had never stepped a foot out of the West Coast. *Ingagi* was a conglomeration of stock footage from old prints. Three thousand feet of the movie were duped from an anicent documentary of the Lady McKenzie expedition called *The Heart of Africa*. The "gorilla woman" finish was shot with actresses in blackface at the Selig Zoo in California.

Following a conference at the Hays office, Hiram Brown ordered *Ingagi* out of all his houses in the RKO circuit, ending forever its brief but happy run. In its month-and-a-half showing, April–May, 1930, *Ingagi* had been such an astounding sensation that promoters everywhere had scurried for old jungle documentaries to be dubbed with sound and re-released. *Variety* explained their colorful plans: ". . . all they have to do is get someone with an English accent to dub the lecture, call him Sir-Something-or-Other, the great hunter, and their fortune is made."

But the cancellation of *Ingagi* ended the speculation, and promoters looked elsewhere, to the 1930–31 gangster cycle for example. Only RKO kept indelibly in mind the incredible gold mine at hand in combining gorillas, beautiful and sensual women, and the extra ingredient of jungle sacrifice. By 1931, Willis O'Brien, Ernest Schoedsack, Merian Cooper, and Edgar Wallace were all busily at work for RKO. Fay Wray would join them in 1932. And *King Kong*, at long, long last, was just around the corner.

H. RIDER HAGGARD: CREATOR OF *KING KONG?** *

Elden K. Everett

Despite being one of the most famous films ever made, there are still some mysteries surrounding the 1933 RKO production of *King Kong*. Younger film heads, raised on a diet of Godzilla and other city-rampaging monsters, don't realize what an astonishing film this was in its day.

Who created the giant ape? Press releases have kept alive the tradition that mystery writer Edgar Wallace wrote a novel called *The Beast*, which was the basis of the film. But although Wallace was brought to Hollywood to work on the script, his posthumous book —*My Hollywood Diary*—a collection of his letters to his wife during the Kong period (he died while working on it) shows that he had little to do with the film, and apparently little interest in the project.** **

The fact seems to be that, even though Ruth Rose wrote most of the script, the idea was that of that quiet genius of animation, Willis O'Brien. O'Brien had been discovered in San Francisco in 1914 by industrial film maker Watterson Rothacher. O'Brien had made a couple of short films animating clay dinosaurs, and was able to come to New York and make several such films for Edison. Legal problems were attached to his 1919 short film *The Ghost of Slumber Mountain*, and he spent several years making industrial films before becoming animator in 1925 for the classic: *The Lost World*.

The next few years found O'Brien, backed by Rothacher, working on another prehistoric film called *Creation*. What O'Brien's original idea for the giant ape consisted of, no one now knows. It's interesting to note, however, that a few months after the spectacular release of *Kong*, that RKO rushed out a follow-up called *Son of Kong*. This second adventure was a low-budget thriller made in part of O'Brien's original footage not used in the first film. It ends with a truly spectacular climax. On Skull Island, where Robert Armstrong and Helen Mack are cast away, the volcano erupts and the

island begins to sink into the seas. Kong Jr. holds them in his hand as the waters rush in, and the final scene is of the hand sticking up out of the water, as the ape gives his life to save the two lovers.

Was this O'Brien's original story concept—the way the original film was to end? Was the second ending—Kong fighting the biplanes atop the Empire State Building—decided on late by RKO? A surprising discovery I made recently indicates that this may be the case.

H. Rider Haggard is world-renowned for his adventure stories. During the 1960s, three of his books were filmed: *She* (with Ursula Andress), *The Return of She*, and *Watusi* (based on his *King Solomon's Mines*). I can't provide a complete list of Haggard films, although there have been five or six versions of *She* (including the 1916 *Hidden Valley*). This classic story of an immortal high priestess in a ruined city in the heart of Africa is probably best-known of his works, although *Mines* has also been filmed before. The 1937 English production of it featured Roland Young and Paul Robeson, and the 1950 version, filmed in Africa featured Stewart Granger and Deborah Kerr.

Other Haggard stories filmed include two versions of his Boer War story "Jess" (the 1916 version starred Theda Bara), a 1920 Austrian film of *Moon of Israel*, and the 1916 Universal version of *Mr. Meeson's Will* (with Lon Chaney as a grizzled old sailor).

Haggard, in the 1880s had spent many years in colonial Africa, and his adventure stories portray the Dark Continent more convincingly than anyone who has come along since. His understanding and respect for the blacks of Africa is reflected on almost every page, a fact that did not endear him to some of the chauvinistic white colonials of the Empire.

Haggard's favorite character was Allan Quartermain the old white hunter introduced in *King Solomon's Mines*. Allan, aided by his friends (which included a silly-ass Englishman named Good, an all-around good fellow whose only fault was a penchant for shooting every animal they encountered, as a God-given right

---

* Reprinted by permission of the author.
** But see Bezanson's article in this volume. *Eds.*

bestowed on an English gentleman); Hans, the Hottentot tracker, and the giant warrior, Umsopogaas, a sort of black Conan: appeared in literally dozens of Haggard's books including: *Allan's Wife, Allan and the Holy Flower, Allan and the Ice Gods, The Ancient Allan, A Tale of 3 Lions,* and even a rare "teamup," *She and Allan.*

One of these books: *Heu-Heu; or; The Monster,* is the one that interests us here. My copy is a Grossett and Dunlap reprint, copyrighted 1923–1924. The story is being told years later to Haggard and Good, as a tale that had happened many years before, while Allan was just a young man.

It seems that Allan and Hans were doing some trading, driving a team of ox-carts into the African bush to swap trade goods for ivory. After a hot day pregnant with thunderstorms, they are caught in a maelstrom of sheet lightning, which kills a number of the oxen. Allan and Hans take refuge in a mysterious cave. While the storm spends itself outside, they find some wall-paintings in the cave, done by primitive bushmen, and one of them astonishes Allan. He describes it: "Imagine a monstor double life size—that is to say, eleven or twelve feet high. . . . Imagine this thing as a huge ape to which the biggest gorilla would be but a child, and yet not an ape but a man, and yet not a man, but a friend!"

He disbelieves Hans' story that this is a living creature worshipped by the local natives. After the storm, they have lost most of the oxen from the lightning, and they trek into a familiar place, the Black Kloof, a valley housing the witchdoctor, Zikali, who in this, as well as other books, sets Allan a strange task he must complete before he will give them the oxen they need.

Rather against their will, Allan and Hans follow an Arab-speaking native into a long journey to a lost land surrounded by huge swamplands. In the center of this marsh, surrounded by prehistoric men and animals, Allan finds that the picture he had seen of the ape is indeed the living deity worshipped by these natives.

There are here several subplots going on, a jealous high-priest who wants to marry the chief's daughter, a native woman who falls for Allan etc., but the chief (although fearful of the ape-god Heu-Heu) is afraid that he will have to sacrifice his daughter to placate the monster. He describes the scene almost word-for-word for the same sequence in *King Kong:* "The third night from this is that of the full moon, the full moon that marks the beginning of harvest. On that night we must carry my daughter, on whom the lot has fallen, to the island in the lake where stands the smoking mountain and bind her to the pillar upon the Rock of Offering that is set between two undying fires. There we must leave her, and at the dawn so it is said, Heu-Heu himself seizes her and carries her off into his cavern, where she vanishes forever!"

From here on, there is a lot of running around and intriguing, of a logic comparable to Doc Savage, when Allan and Hans rescue the girl from the pillar, substituting the dead body of another woman. When dawn comes up, sure enough, here comes the giant ape to claim his sacrifice!

Allan and Hans have decided to put an end to this whole sacrificial business, and they blow up some sluice-gates with a couple of drums of gunpowder. This diverts the river so that it floods into the underground chambers of the volcano, and predictably enough, the whole island blows up.

Haggard, however, cops out here—it turns out that the fifteen-foot-high ape is actually the high-priest on stilts inside an ape-costume. But as this is revealed, the island is sinking, and the man in the ape-suit climbs higher and higher on the mountain trying to save himself, finally disappearing from view as the waters wash over him—pictorially very similar to the *Son of Kong* footage originally created by Willis O'Brien.

So. . . . The question is whether or not O'Brien had read the Haggard novel and being intrigued by some of the scenes in it, transferred them into his own fantasy-conception. We may never know, but it's interesting to speculate.

EDGAR WALLACE AND KONG*

Mark Bezanson

Edgar Wallace's role in the writing of the screenplay for *King Kong* was cut short by his death from pneumonia on 10 February 1932, two months into the film's production. However, an original copy of the scenario he prepared for the film has survived. Kept in a vault in England by his daughter Penelope, the script depicts many of the film's key scenes as well as several graphic episodes that were never used. The 110-page work appears to be Wallace's personal draft, containing corrections and interpolations in his own handwriting. Apart from its intrinsic interest, it suggests that Wallace imagined and articulated on paper much of the narrative structure, many of the details of action and considerable amounts of the tone of this enduring film classic.

Wallace recalls in his *Hollywood Diary* the excitement of his new task.

> Merian Cooper called and we talked over the big animal play we are going to write, or, rather, I am going to write and he is directing. He has just had an approval from New York, and I am going to turn him out a scenario.**

Wallace started the screenplay on New Year's Day and finished it five days later. On January 5th he wrote, "Cooper is very pleased and today I am finishing the scenario and letting him have it."* Wallace, who had never previously shared the writing process with others, was extremely deferential to his collaborators. He, Willis O'Brien, and "Coop" would go over the script page by page. Wallace's later remarks show that he understood the collaborative nature of Hollywood screenplay development:

> I had to rewrite certain lines of *Kong*, but of course this sort of thing will go on all the time; one expects it.**

Cooper at the time seemed pleased with Wallace's work, at least as Wallace saw it:

> Cooper called me up last night and told me that everybody who had read *Kong* was enthusiastic. They say it is the best adventure story that has ever been written for the screen.**

Wallace's primary task was to provide an integrating narrative framework for several key scenes already worked on by Cooper and O'Brien.

Although Wallace was hired to arrange a suitable format for the studio material, his original script proved to be a brilliant prefiguring of some of the more important underlying themes and moods of the final film. In certain respects, in fact, the original script is better than the finished film.

The Wallace screenplay, for example, avoids the ponderous talky opening sequences of the completed film. Denham in New York and the sea voyage to the island are absent from this script. Almost immediately the action gets underway with a telegram from a shipwreck off Vapour Island (so-called because of its steaming volcanoes). Denham, instead of being a filmmaker, is a big-time circus man and former friend of Phineas Barnum. Like Frank ("Bring-em-back-alive") Buck, he is an explorer searching for wild animals to fulfill his dream of presenting the greatest show on earth. The aggressive and cynical aspects of his entrepreneurial character are revealed in the first brilliant scene in the scenario in which an ape is tearing the petals off a rose.

Capt. Englehorn
You see? It is der dawn of human intelligence, is it not? The admiration of the thing.

Denham
Yeah! And he's pulling it to pieces—that's human.

---

* This essay was prepared especially for this volume and is published by permission of the author.
** All quotations from Edgar Wallace, *My Hollywood Diary*, (London: Hutchinson and Company, 1932). All references to and quotations from the KONG scenario are from Penelope Wallace's personal unpublished copy of Edgar Wallace's *Kong*.

Stevens
I suppose you'll exhibit him, Mr. Denham?

Denham (contemptuously)
Him? No! You can buy that kind of bimbo for two bits.

And a few lines further

Stevens
What did you expect to get?

Denham
Something colossal, something you could show in the polo ground [sic] or Madison Square Gardens and pack the place at a dollar a head.

Then the menacing hint that sets the tone for the rest of the scenario is introduced:

Something that's never been seen before.

The action moves swiftly with some cross-cuts from Denham's tramp steamer to a lifeboat that has survived from a shipwreck and is headed for the island. As Denham scoffs at the captain's mention of sea serpents off the island, the scenario cuts to the lifeboat holding a crew of ex-cons, the heroine Shirley (Ann), and her heroic rescuer, John (Jack). Suddenly a brontosaurus attacks the boat; the viewer abruptly crosses the threshold into a strange world. Wallace delineates the camera's role to present the action from the viewpoint of the monster. Next, the survivors' frantic escape from the brontosaurus leads the party into the forest to a campsite that has evidently been the scene of some recent mayhem. Dialogue is minimal and terse; the images are graphic: a gun barrel twisted out of shape; a human skeleton in the trees drops its skull to the ground. Soon two beasts devour one another; a man is swallowed by a weird snake with little hands; a pterodactyl swoops in from the horizon, unknown carnivorous monsters lurk just beyond the site. With doom impending, a tough ex-con, demands that John hand Shirley over to him and the ex-cons for their own sexual disportment. Just as Louis is about to rape Shirley, a horrible loud sound erupts from the jungle. It's Kong! Wallace's imagery brings the scene to life:

64   EXT. CLEARING-DAY
Animals' terror sequence at the sound of Kong. A succession of shots. The drumming continues throughout these shots. A number of

crocodiles slide into the water, a brontosaurus escapes into the bushes. A stegosaurus makes a rapid exit. Some other animals fly past. The pterodactyl on his nest also hears Kong and gathers his young around.

Kong lifts up the tent and sees Shirley. So begins the "strangest love story ever known."

Kong carries the girl through the primeval forest, destroys the pursuing sailors, beats an allosaurus to death, then makes for his cave in the mountains. Protecting the girl from the intrusion of hungry, cold-blooded reptiles, Kong commences peeling off Shirley's dress (a comparison is made to the monkey pulling off the rose petals.) He caresses her and then sleeps by her side across the threshold of his cave. Kong is a beast, the terror of his domain, but, then he becomes a lover. Wallace writes:

153   EXT. LEDGE-DAY
Close shot of Kong's face. He is making strange sounds.

154   EXT. LEDGE-DAY
Close shot of Zena (interchangeable name for Shirley), still fearful, but with just a little more confidence than she had. The upper hand of Kong comes away and the tips of his fingers go over her face and down the side of her cheek. She has an expression of disgust and revulsion, but, as though he were human and understood, she tries to control that expression.

Then the girl bathes her face with water from a pool and dries her face on her tattered dress. A close shot of Kong looking at her. He goes to the pool and imitates her actions. Then he brings her a pterodactyl egg as a gift. As he fixes her a nest, John appears on the scene to rescue her.

Subsequently, the scenes are the same as in the completed film till New York, where Wallace imagines Kong doped and held captive in a circus cage at Madison Square Garden. While Denham is boasting to the audience about his colossal captive, Shirley is lured into a tiger cage by a jealous circus woman. When a tiger attacks Shirley, Kong breaks out of his cage and kills the cats while the crowd disperses in panic. The remaining scenes in Wallace's script parallel those in the final version of the film except for the train wreck. Kong climbs the Empire State Building as thunder and lightning storm over the city.[1] He is machine-

---

[1] This storm is represented in early posters for the film. *Eds.*

gunned by the police in planes, but not before he snatches one of the circling biplanes out of the sky. Then, holding his hand over his broken heart, he caresses the girl for the last time. A lightning bolt strikes the flagpole he is holding and destroys him. His fall is not shown.

Throughout the script Wallace's imagery is powerfully visual, his dialogue laconic, the action steadily precipitous, the drama engrossing. Though the tone established by Wallace's scenario is more sinister and macabre than the final version's, the sense of terror and awe, the feeling of revulsion and pity anticipate those we experience in the film.

Wallace was gifted with a cinematic vision, and, if he had lived, might have become a great screenwriter. In England alone more than forty-one of his books were made into films. He had plans to direct Constance Bennett in a film of his own, and Cooper, who was amazed at the speed and dexterity with which Wallace worked, had already promised to let him adapt *The Most Dangerous Game* after completing the screenplay of *Kong*. (RKO executives didn't like the title *Kong* because it sounded too much like Cooper's *Chang* as well as too oriental. Wallace suggested *King Ape;* later the two were combined.)[2] Wallace, who started off as a journalist and an amateur documentary film maker, was a kind of British Simenon; he was known to write a novel in a weekend, and is credited with some 170 novels, seventeen plays, and hundreds of short stories. In 1938, one-fourth of the books printed in Britain were either originals or reprints of his fiction.

---

[2] Early posters for the film advertise *Kong. Eds.*

There is no question that the final draft of the screenplay was the work of Ruth Rose (Mrs. Ernest Schoedsack). Several other writers, including James Creelman (who adapted *The Most Dangerous Game*), had been tried out and eventually replaced by Rose, who had never seen Wallace's script, and who prepared a fresh script after conferences with Cooper. In addition to supplying the opening sequences and the business of the sacrificial ceremony, she relocated Wallace's circus scene to Carnegie Hall, introduced more destruction into Kong's escape, and depicted Kong being machine-gunned by the airplanes and falling to his doom on the streets below. Cooper directed the major sequences: the jungle scenes with the actors, Kong's rampage in Manhattan, the final climax atop the Empire State Building. Schoedsack worked on the opening scenes of the film and directed the actors on the steamer and the landing on the island.

Although Merian Cooper has taken the main credit for conceiving and realizing the picture of the mighty ape, *King Kong* could never have been born without the tireless genius of Willis O'Brien, whose character was inscribed in every movement, glance and gesture that Kong made. And Wallace, who was working on several other projects and had just been notified of his renewed contract with RKO, certainly contributed the initial narrative pattern for the evolving structure of the film with its moods and tones of gothic romance. *King Kong* seems to have become part of everyone who worked closely on the film. It took the collective energy and genius of people like Cooper, O'Brien, Rose, Schoedsack and Wallace to resurrect the mighty ape from that remote and awesome landscape that prefigures the darkest shapes of our own souls.

80   EXT. CAMP - DAY

MEDIUM SHOT - The convicts and John struggling.
Sound close by of Kong. The struggle ceases.
All the men look up in the same direction.

81   EXT. CAMP - DAY

FULL SHOT - Noise of Kong. The screen of trees
is drawn aside and Kong appears, stands for a second,
then comes forward.

[Kong is a huge ape about
30 feet high] EW

82   INT. TENT - DAY

MEDIUM SHOT - Shirley and Louis struggling.

83   EXT. TENT - DAY

MEDIUM SHOT - A big hand picking up the tent.

84   EXT. CAMP - DAY

MEDIUM FULL SHOT - The men look on in horror,
paralysed.

85   INT. TENT - DAY

CLOSE SHOT of Louis in the tent, also looking up
in terror, and a big hand coming down and grabbing
him.

21   EXT. SPEEDBOAT - DAY

A picture taken under the water as through the
animal's eyes. You can see the keel and the lower
part of the hull of the boat moving slowly across.
The eyes come right up out of the water and view
the whole of the boat.

Pan up till you are clear of the water. Shake
the camera as the animal shakes his head and drops
of water pour up and come down before the camera.

22   EXT. SPEEDBOAT - DAY

MEDIUM FULL SHOT of the boat and the people staring.

23   EXT. SPEEDBOAT - DAY

TRUCKING SHOT - the camera approaches the keel and
hull of the boat. Boat suddenly rises and heels
over as the head comes beneath it.

24   EXT. SPEEDBOAT - DAY

FULL SHOT of the boat overturning. The men are
swimming ashore for their lives. John is
supporting Shirley.

25   EXT. DINOSAUR - DAY

MEDIUM SHOT of the head of a dinosaur coming up
and darting down on a man. Beast and man
disappear.

From time to time during this dialogue Shirley has
been looking up with a startled expression. Suddenly
she grasps John's arm.

                    SHIRLEY
                 (excitedly)
          Johnny, Johnny, did you see that
          Bird? (120)

                    JOHN
                 (looks up)
          I've seen several queer-looking birds.(121)

                    SHIRLEY

          This was terribly big. It came down
          and went straight up in the air again -
          a horrible-looking thing - like the
          things you see in a nightmare. (122)

                    JOHN

          It's gone now. (123)

                    SHIRLEY
                 (tremulously) tries to smile)
          I'm not feeling quite as brave as I
          did! (124)

                    JOHN
                 (pats her arm)
          I haven't felt brave since this trip
          started. (125)

45   EXT. CLEARING - DAY

     FULL SHOT towards tree. He is in a clearing.

46   EXT. CLEARING - DAY

     MEDIUM SHOT - Henri looks round apprehensively, then
     looks up.

47   EXT. SKY - DAY

     FULL SHOT in the sky. A little speck grows rapidly
     larger, dropping like a plummet. It is a huge
     pterodactyl.

48   EXT. CLEARING - DAY

     MEDIUM SHOT of Shirley, John and Tricks looking
     towards tree. Sudden consternation in every face.
     Horror in Shirley's.

                      SHIRLEY

         Oh, Johnny! (126)

49   EXT. CLEARING - DAY

     MEDIUM CLOSE SHOT of Henri. He sees the bird. He
     takes a knife from his belt and strikes at it. The
     bird comes into view. There is a terrific struggle.
     Suddenly the bird lifts the man. He is still
     struggling.

In a special *King Kong* issue of *Midi-Minuit Fantastique* (October-November, 1962), Jean Boullet first proposed that Jonathan Swift be seriously considered as the "veritable auteur" of (or at least inspiration for) *King Kong*. Calling attention to the narrative parallel between the capture of Gulliver in the land of the Brobdingnags by a monkey in Book II of *Gulliver's Travels* (1726), and the final sequence of the movie, Boullet supports his provocative thesis by reproducing drawings from illustrated editions of *Gulliver's Travels*, all of which were published long before the motion picture was conceived. Some of these are also reproduced in the present volume.

The crucial portion of the *Gulliver's Travels* text reads:

From GULLIVER'S TRAVELS, Book II

But, the greatest Danger I ever underwent in that Kingdom, was from a Monkey, who belonged to one of the Clerks of the Kitchen. *Glumdalclitch* had locked me up in her Closet, while she went somewhere upon Business, or a Visit. The Weather being very warm, the Closet Window was left open, as well as the Windows and the Door of my bigger Box, in which I usually lived, because of its Largeness and Conveniency. As I sat quietly meditating at my Table, I heard something bounce in at the Closet Window, and skip about from one Side to the other; whereat, although I were much alarmed, yet I ventured to look out, but not stirring from my Seat; and then I saw this frolicksome Animal, frisking and leaping up and down, till at last he came to my Box, which he seemed to view with great Pleasure and Curiosity, peeping in at the Door and every Window. I retreated to the farther Corner of my Room, or Box; but the Monkey looking in at every Side, put me into such a Fright, that I wanted Presence of Mind to conceal my self under the Bed, as I might easily have done. After some time spent in peeping, grinning, and chattering, he at last espyed me; and reaching one of his Paws in at the Door, as a Cat does when she plays with a Mouse, although I often shifted Place to avoid him; he at length seized the Lappet of my Coat (which being made of that Country Silk, was very thick and strong) and dragged me out. He took me up in his right Fore-foot, and held me as a Nurse doth a Child she is going to suckle; just as I have seen the same Sort of Creature do with a Kitten in *Europe*: And when I offered to struggle, he squeezed me so hard, that I thought it more prudent to submit. I have good Reason to believe that he took me for a young one of his own Species, by his often stroking my Face very gently with his other Paw. In these Diversions he was interrupted by a Noise at the Closet Door, as if some Body were opening it; whereupon he suddenly leaped up to the Window at which he had come in, and thence upon the Leads and Gutters, walking upon three Legs, and holding me in the fourth, till he clambered up to a Roof that was next to ours. I heard *Glumdalclitch* give a Shriek at the Moment he was carrying me out. The poor Girl was almost distracted: That Quarter of the Palace was all in an Uproar; the Servants ran for Ladders; the Monkey was seen by Hundreds in the Court, sitting upon the Ridge of a Building, holding me like a Baby in one of his Fore-Paws, and feeding me with the other, by cramming into my Mouth some Victuals he had squeezed out of the Bag on one Side of his Chaps, and patting me when I would not eat; whereat many of the Rabble below could not forbear laughing; neither do I think they justly ought to be blamed; for without Question, the Sight was ridiculous enough to every Body but myself. Some of the People threw up Stones, hoping to drive the Monkey down; but this was strictly forbidden, or else very probably my Brains had been dashed out.

The Ladders were now applied, and mounted by several Men; which the Monkey observing, and finding himself almost encompassed; not being able to make Speed enough with his three Legs, let me drop on a Ridge-Tyle, and made his Escape. Here I sat for some time five Hundred Yards from the Ground, expecting every Moment to be blown down by the Wind, or to fall by my own Giddiness, and come tumbling over and over from the Ridge to the Eves. But an honest Lad, one of my Nurse's Footmen, climbed up, and putting me into his Breeches Pocket, brought me down safe.

I was almost choaked with the filthy Stuff the Monkey had crammed down my Throat; but, my dear little Nurse picked it out of my Mouth with a small Needle; and then I fell a vomiting, which gave me great Relief. Yet I was so weak and bruised in the Sides with the Squeezes given me by this odious Animal, that I was forced to keep my Bed a Fortnight. The King, Queen, and all the Court, sent every Day to enquire after my Health; and her Majesty made me several Visits during my Sickness. The Monkey was killed, and an Order made that no such Animal should be kept about the Palace.

Drawing by Granville: From an English Edition of
Gulliver's Travels

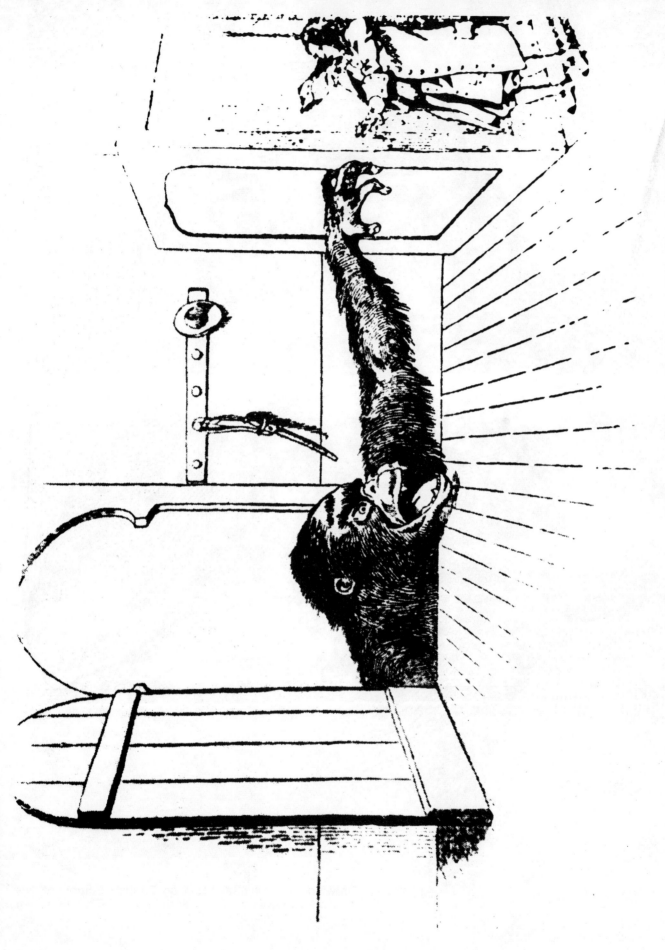

Drawing by JOB: From an Illustrated Edition of *Gulliver's Travels*

Artist Unknown: From an Italian Edition of *Gulliver's Travels*

Artist Unknown: From an Italian Edition of *Gulliver's Travels*

Artist Unknown: Possibly from a modern interpretation of *Gulliver's Travels.*

PIERRE BAILLY

Drawing from the Press-book for *King Kong*
Courtesy of Elliott Stein

Drawing by Willis O'Brien *Courtesy of Mrs. Darlyne O'Brien*

Drawing by Willis O'Brien
Courtesy of Mrs. Darlyne O'Brien

Drawing by Willis O'Brien *Courtesy of Mrs. Darlyne O'Brien*

Drawing by
Willis O'Brien

Courtesy of
Mrs. Darlyne
O'Brien

Drawing by
Willis O'Brien

*Courtesy of
Mrs. Darlyne
O'Brien*

Drawing by Willis O'Brien *Courtesy of Mrs. Darlyne O'Brien*

PART II

HAIL TO THE KING

KING KONG: A REVIEW

Mordaunt Hall, *The New York Times*

At both the Radio City Music Hall and the RKO Roxy, which have a combined seating capacity of 10,000, the main attraction now is a fantastic film known as "King Kong." The story of this feature was begun by the late Edgar Wallace and finished by Merian C. Cooper, who with his old associate, Ernest B. Schoedsack, is responsible for the production. It essays to give the spectator a vivid conception of the terrifying experiences of a producer of jungle pictures and his colleagues, who capture a gigantic ape, something like fifty feet tall, and bring it to New York. The narrative is worked out in a decidedly compelling fashion, which is mindful of what was done in the old silent film *The Lost World*.

Through multiple exposures, processed "shots" and a variety of angles of camera wizardry the producers set forth an adequate story and furnish enough thrills for any devotee of such tales.

Although there are vivid battles between prehistoric monsters on the island which Denham, the picture maker, insists on visting, it is when the enormous ape, called Kong, is brought to this city that the excitement reaches its highest pitch. Imagine a 50-foot beast with a girl in one paw climbing up the outside of the Empire State Building, and after putting the girl on a ledge, clutching at airplanes, the pilots of which are pouring bullets from machine guns into the monster's body.

It often seems as though Ann Redman [*sic*] who goes through more terror than any of the other characters in the film, would faint, but she always appears to be able to scream. Her body is like a doll in the claw of the gigantic beast, who in the course of his wanderings through Manhattan tears down a section of the elevated railroad and tosses a car filled with passengers to the street. Automobiles are mere missiles for this Kong, who occasionally reveals that he relishes his invincibility by patting his chest.

Denham is an intrepid person, but it is presumed that when the ape is killed he has had quite enough of searching for places with strange monsters. In the opening episode he is about to leave on the freighter for the island supposed to have been discovered by some sailor, when he goes ashore to find a girl whom he wants to act in his picture. In course of time he espies Ann, played by the attractive Fay Wray, and there ensues a happy voyage. Finally through the fog the island is sighted and Denham, the ship's officers and sailors, all armed, go ashore. It soon develops that the savages, who offer up sacrifices in the form of human beings to Kong, their super-king, keep him in an area surrounded by a great wall. Kong has miles in which to roam and fight with brontosauri and dinosauri and other huge creatures.

There is a door to the wall. After Denham and the others from the ship have had quite enough of the island, Kong succeeds in bursting open the door, but he is captured through gas bombs hurled at him by the white men. How they ever get him on the vessel is not explained, for the next thing you know is that Kong is on exhibition in Gotham, presumably in Madison Square Garden.

During certain episodes in this film Kong, with Ann in his paw, goes about his battles, sometimes putting her on a fifty-foot-high tree branch while he polishes off an adversary. When he is perceived on exhibition in New York he is a frightening spectacle, but Denham thinks that he has the beast safely hackled. The newspaper photographers irritate even him with their flashlights, and after several efforts he breaks the steel bands and eventually gets away. He looks for Ann on the highways and byways of New York. He climbs up hotel façades and his head fills a whole window, his white teeth and red mouth adding to the terror of the spectacle.

Everywhere he moves he crushes out lives. He finally discovers Ann, and being a perspicacious ape, he decides that the safest place for himself and Ann is the tower of the Empire State structure.

Needless to say that this picture was received by many a giggle to cover up fright. Constant exclamations issued from the Radio City Music Hall yesterday. "What a man!" observed one youth when the ape forced down the great oaken door on the island. Human beings seem so small that one is reminded of Defoe's [*sic*] "Gulliver's Travels." One step and this beast traverses half a block. If buildings hinder his progress, he pushes them down, and below him the people look like Lilliputians.

Miss Wray goes through her ordeal with great courage. Robert Armstrong gives a vigorous and compelling impersonation of Denham. Bruce Cabot, Frank Reicher, Sam Hardy, Noble Johnson and James Flavin add to the interest of this weird tale.

BEAUTY AND THE BEAST*

William Troy, *The Nation*

At least one of our national characteristics is illustrated in the RKO-Radio production of *King Kong* which loomed over the audiences of both Radio City movie-houses last week. It is a characteristic hard to define except that it is related to that sometimes childish, sometimes magnificent passion for scale that foreigners have remarked on our building of hundred-story sky-scrapers, our fondness for hyperbole in myth and popular speech, and our habit of applying superlatives to all our accomplishments. Efforts to explain it have not been very satisfactory; the result is usually a contradiction in which we are represented as a race that is at once too civilized and not civilized enough. If Herr Spengler interprets the extreme gigantism of the American mind and imagination as the sign of an inflated decadence resembling that of Alexandria and the later Roman Empire, others discover in it the simpler expression of a race still unawakened from childhood. At Radio City last week one was able to see the contradiction pretty dramatically borne out; an audience enjoying all the sensations of primitive terror and fascination within the scientifically air-cooled temple of baroque modernism that is Mr. Rockefeller's contribution to contemporary culture.

What is to be seen at work in *King Kong* is the American imagination faithfully adhering to its characteristic process of multiplication. We have had plays and pictures about monsters before, but never one in which the desired effect depended so completely on the increased dimensions of the monster. Kong is a veritable skyscraper among the apes. In his own jungle haunts he rules like a king over the rest of the animal world; and when he is taken to New York to be exhibited before a light-minded human audience he breaks through his chromium-steel handcuffs, hurls down two or three elevated trains that get in his way, and scales the topmost heights of the Empire State Building with the fragile Miss Fay Wray squirming in his hairy paw. The photographic ingenuity that was necessary to make all this seem plausible was considerable, and in places so remarkable as to advance the possibility of a filming of certain other stories depending largely on effects of scale—*Gulliver's Travels*, for example, and possibly even *The Odyssey*. But, unfortunately, it was thought necessary to mitigate some of the predominant horror by introducing a human, all-too-human, theme. "It was not the guns that got him," says one of the characters at the end, after Kong has been brought to ground by a whole squadron of battle planes. "It was Beauty killed the Beast." By having Beauty, in the person of Miss Wray, lure the great monster to his destruction, the scenario writers sought to unite two rather widely separated traditions of the popular cinema—that of the "thriller" and that of the sentimental romance. The only difficulty was that they failed to realize that such a union was possible only by straining our powers of credulity and perhaps also one or two fundamental laws of nature. For if the love that Kong felt for the heroine was sacred, it suggests a weakness that hardly fits in with his other actions; and if it was, after all, merely profane, it proposes problems to the imagination that are not the less real for being crude.

* *From* The Nation 136, *no.* 3533 (1933): 326. *Copyright* © 1933 *by* The Nation.

Having risked a great deal on the success of *King Kong*, RKO mounted a major promotional effort. The illustrations that follow sample some of the posters, lobby cards, and other advertising for *King Kong*.

Early poster using drawing by Willis O'Brien. Note that film is known as *KONG* and that Edgar Wallace gets top billing. (See article by Mark Bezanson in this volume.) [*From Dennis Gifford, A Pictorial History of Horror Movies, 1973, Hamlyn Publishers, London & New York.*]

Courtesy of Steve Vertlieb

NO MONEY

yet

NEW YORK DUG UP

$89,931

IN 4 DAYS
(MARCH-2-3-4-5)

to see

"KING KONG"

AT RADIO CITY

SETTING A NEW ALL-TIME WORLD'S RECORD FOR ATTENDANCE OF ANY INDOOR ATTRACTION

COOPER-SCHOEDSACK PRODUCTION..RKO RADIO PICTURE

This opened the day President Roosevelt declared a moratorium and closed the banks in 1933 - as I recall it.

Remember these grosses were when admission prices were much lower than they are at the present time.

Merian C. Cooper

Early Lobby Card

KING KONG
with
FAY WRAY....
ROBERT ARMSTRONG
BRUCE CABOT
A COOPER-SCHOEDSACK PRODUCTION
28
FROM A STORY BY
EDGAR WALLACE
AND MERIAN C. COOPER
RKO Radio PICTURES
DAVID O. SELZNICK
Executive Producer

KING KONG

with
FAY WRAY....
ROBERT ARMSTRONG
BRUCE CABOT
A COOPER-SCHOEDSACK
PRODUCTION

RKO
Radio
PICTURES

Reg. U. S. Pat. Off.

DAVID O. SELZNICK
Executive Producer

FROM AN IDEA CONCEIVED BY
EDGAR WALLACE
AND MERIAN C. COOPER

NEVER TOPPED! NEVER EQUALED!
the one and only

KING
KONG

with
FAY WRAY
ROB'T. ARMSTRONG
BRUCE CABOT

Re-released by
R K O
RADIO
PICTURES

Copyright 1956, RKO Radio Pictures   Country of Origin U.S.A.

1930s Poster

Poster Prepared in 1942

KI
KO
Heaven Help Us All!
King Kong, the ape
as big as a battleship,
is loose!
FAY WI
R K O
RADIO
MERIAN
COOPE
From the story b
MERIAN C. COOPE
and EDGAR WALLAC

Lobby Card

Poster for 1943 Re-release

Poster Design

Poster Design

Poster Design

Publicity Still

Publicity Still

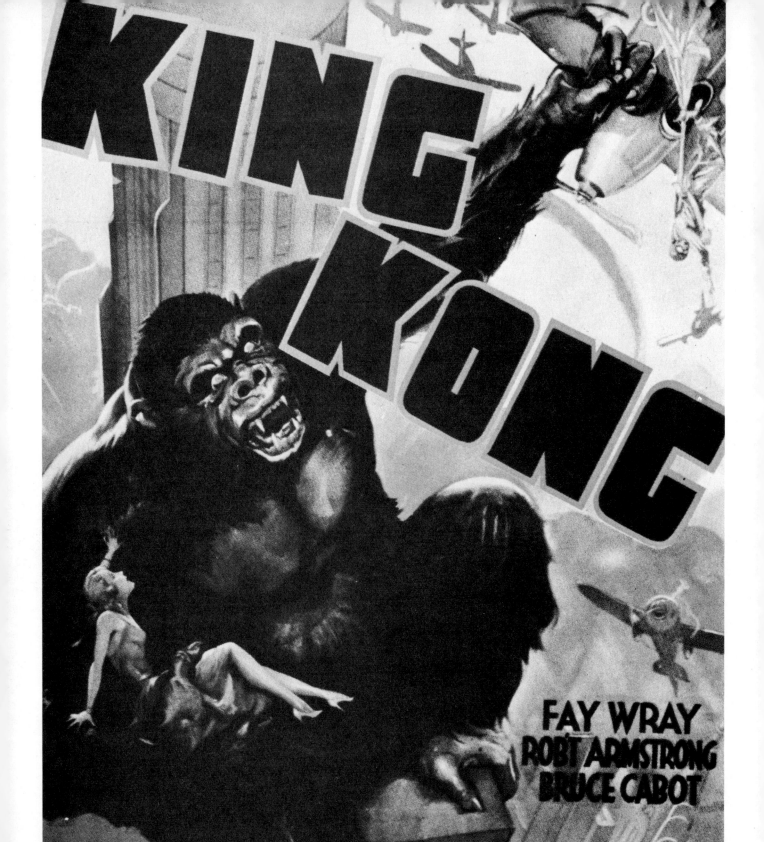

KING KONG

FAY WRAY
ROB'T ARMSTRONG
BRUCE CABOT

A PERSONALLY DIRECTED
MERIAN C·
COOPER
ERNEST B·
SCHOEDSACK
PRODUCTION
FROM THE STORY BY MERIAN C·COOPER and EDGAR

Janus Films presents

KING KONG

starring Fay Wray, Bruce Cabot, Robert Armstrong

the original uncut version

Unseen for 35 years

Fay Wray and Merian C. Cooper

MYSTERY

ONE OF THE
TOWER MAGAZINES

February, 1933
10¢

Beginning **KING KONG**—*the Last and
the Greatest Creation of* **EDGAR WALLACE**

The MAN with the RUBBER FACE
by H. Bedford-Jones

Warner Fabian's *New Murder Mystery on a Florida Houseboat*—BELLS IN THE NIGHT

PART III

THE BEAST
IN THE CRITICAL JUNGLE

WILLIS O'BRIEN, OR THE BIRTH OF A FILM FROM DESIGN TO STILL*

Jean Boullet

Like Méliès, like the great Eisenstein (who frequently used the same technique), and before Ray Harryhausen (who was to adopt it for *Mysterious Island* and *Jason and the Argonauts*), Willis O'Brien meticulously designed, sequence by sequence, almost shot by shot, a personal dream which later came to life as the sublime, the colossal, the fabulous *King Kong*.

As early as 1934, Jean Ferry published in *Le Minotaure* an article on *King Kong* [1] which has since become a classic, and in which he stressed the sculptural quality of certain scenes (such as "King Kong's battle in the cave against the monstrous serpent"). On this topic, Jean Ferry, who at that time was probably unaware of Willis O'Brien's designs (even today, everybody in Europe is still unaware of them), started drawing parallels between some sequences of *King Kong* and the creative work of certain great names associated with fantastic art. Jean Ferry, commenting on the "strictly Maldororian" [2] feeling of the stage scenery, considered the mock-ups of the prehistoric monsters worthy of claiming Max Ernst as their spiritual father. As for me, I would rather favor a comparison with the talented illustrators of Jules Verne, Rioux, and Beunett, with Arnold Böcklin also, if still another name did not force itself upon my mind—that of Gustave Doré.

I have never seen any Doré design more beautiful than Willis O'Brien's admirable composition depicting for *King Kong* the sequence of the tree trunk over the abyss—or rather, dreaming it up, since the script had not even been written yet. [3] This magnificent drawing, masterpiece of symbolism in chiaroscuro, ideally demonstrates these words of a patient to Freud: "I could draw you a picture of my dream, but I couldn't tell it to you."

For this fabulous dream, Willis O'Brien was to compose the most fantastic scenes one drawing at a time, several years before the screen adaptation of *King Kong*. [4] It is the dream of an obsession or, as Eisenstein put it, "the scenes are so hallucinatory at times that they could almost be drawn with one's eye closed."

The case of Willis O'Brien is probably unique: no creator had ever seen his dream come to life so thoroughly nor so perfectly, in its most minute detail and with so much attention paid to the designer's most rigorous layouts.

The comparison between Willis O'Brien's sketched mock-ups and the stills from *King Kong* is impressive. The tree trunk thrown like a bridge over the abyss, Kong's fight against the prehistoric monsters, the scene during which he snatches Fay Wray from the pterodactyl's claws (never was any scenery more "maldororian" than the one we have here), Fay Wray's clothes ripped off by King Kong shred by shred, the panic scenes in New York City, etc., are like so many detailed drawings set to motion. All at once the design palpitates and breathes; the dream comes alive. King Kong is a flesh-and-blood reality.

The design of the pterodactyl episode, compared to the still from the same scene, matches the mock-up so well that one hesitates to choose between the artist's initial art work and the still from the motion picture filmed two or three years later.

An oversize pterodactyl, looking like a nightmarish flying gargoyle and afflicted by the gigantism peculiar to King Kong himself, kidnaps Fay Wray and carries her into an apocalyptic sky.

All those who criticized *King Kong* for its paleontological improbabilities—such as the survival of large prehistoric reptiles side by side with a giant gorilla

---

* This article was translated by Madeleine F. Wright. It was originally published in French in Midi-Minuit Fantastique, No. 3 (Oct.-Nov., 1962).

1 Ferry's essay was reprinted in *Midi-Minuit Fantastique*, No. 3 (Oct.-Nov. 1962), pp. 25-30.

2 Translator's note: "Maldororian," an adjective coined by the author of this article, is used here to represent the visionary and surrealistic atmosprere of French poet Isidore Ducasse, Comte de Lautréamont's major work, *Les Chants de Maldoror*.

3 This sequence of the felled tree trunk bridging two cliffs over an abyss already had appeared in Harry Hoyt's *The Lost World* (1925)—a coincidence easily explained by the fact that both *The Lost World* and *King Kong* were "created" by Willis O'Brien. Another sequence common to both is that of the pterodactyl.

4 Editor's note: to the best of our knowledge and also according to Merian Cooper, Willis O'Brien designed only one sequence (the last one) of *King Kong* in 1931. The others were designed during the shooting of the film.

(the very highest form of mammal) usually forget that *King Kong* is first of all a fantasy, and definitely not an introduction to paleontology for grade or high school students. The colossal size of the pterodactyl created by the illustrator O'Brien supports this statement well enough. Willis O'Brien—himself a consultant in scientific reconstitutions for major museums of natural history—knew better than most that real live pterodactyls never exceeded the size of a jay or of a pigeon. Willis O'Brien never aimed at realism; he only sought the impact of the fantastic. By immortalizing the pterodactyl he had created as early as 1924 for *The Lost World*, O'Brien, expert in prehistoric monsters, let us understand that the "maldororian" cave in *King Kong*, its landscapes from another planet (the same dreamlike landscapes already appeared in *The Lost World*) and the analogy with "The Lost Valley" in the film spoke for themselves. The kind of atmosphere in which the monsters perform—straight out of a Jules Verne story; the unreal jungle with its treelike ferns; the lake shrouded in mist from which rises a nightmarish sea-monster (Willis O'Brien knew well that such creatures were herbivorous and did not devour explorers like so much mincemeat)—all these elements, intentionally absurd through their obvious inconsistencies, ideally recreate the dreamlike climate intended by O'Brien for *King Kong*.

Who could imagine for one second Fay Wray surviving the episode with the giant pterodactyl, especially since the latter is holding her by the middle, all claws bared!

This scene and that of the fight with the plesiosaurus in the cave, King Kong's climb to the platform balcony, the involuntary striptease of Fay Wray, peeled like a banana, her slip torn to shreds (a lace slip the color of champagne—I cannot see it in any other shade. Why?), the powerful rustle of the pterodactyl's leathery wings and their swishing noise when he swoops down to land; his claws digging into Ann Darrow's body like those of a vulture; King Kong snatching the pterosaurus in full flight and tearing him to pieces, with wing bones crunching between his teeth; Ann and Jack Driscoll crawling to safety among the rocks; the symbol of the endless liana hanging from King Kong's "balcony," like Romeo and Juliet's rope ladder, over a vertiginous abyss (the abyss of our dreams); the couple's being severed from the life-saving rope while King Kong slowly pulls up the twining tropical plant, their double fall into the void (a stunt frequently used thereafter)—that interminable, stumbling fall, like a slow-motion jump through the fathomless depth of nightmares into the blessed, life-saving waters below . . .

Who will dare challenge the intentionally and deliberately visionary character of this sequence after having reviewed—albeit briefly—such fantastic episodes?

The dreamlike atmosphere which serves as background for real adventures can also be found in Jules Verne's *Voyage to the Center of the Earth*, for instance. Verne, like O'Brien, had a rigorous scientific training, and the conscious poetic improbabilities which cram *Voyage to the Center of the Earth* and *King Kong* are deliberate. They belong to the area of the art device (how could anyone imagine Jules Verne believing for one moment in the raft supported by the melting lava and carried, like an elevator, to the top of the volcano's crater by the erupting Stromboli?).

I have recapitulated these consecutive episodes of the pterodactyl sequence in order to suggest to the reader the extent to which those who appreciate *King Kong* love it for its exceptionally poetic dream climate and agree with Jean Ferry, who called it admirable (Paul Eluard, approached for the chairmanship of a film club, answered one day: "I accept—but will you give *King Kong* again?"). The poetic impact of *King Kong* comes from its unique visionary atmosphere; and what unfolds under our eyes is a long dream, a dream which lasts an hour and a half (the film is always abridged) and reproduced on the screen in its most accurate detail. This we know, since we can compare O'Brien's original drawings to the stills from the film adaptation of this fantastic dream.

King Kong is—and this is probably unique in the history of the cinema—a dream filmed in its entirety.

This profoundly dreamlike aspect is further accented by the use of Arnold Böcklin's famous painting, *The Isle of the Dead*, reconstituted by Willis O'Brien to serve as the setting for the first part of *King Kong* under the name "Skull Island." The narrow bonds which unite Böcklin's strange painting (the picture is dated 1880 and is presently at the Kunstmuseum in Basel) and Skull Island (the kingdom of *King Kong* and later of *Son of Kong*) prove beyond any doubt that those who collaborated on the birth of *King Kong*—and Willis O'Brien first of all—did not draw at random, as some would have us believe. To the contrary, the use of Böcklin's *Isle of the Dead* demonstrates the sound art background of Willis O'Brien in the area of the bizarre and the deliberately contrived aspect of his choices and influences.

Isle of the Dead, which literally poisoned four generations of black-clad aesthetes with a taste for morbidity (it was Bela Lagosi's and Bram Stoker's favorite painting) was suddenly reborn, fifty-three years after its original creation to become, through O'Briens genius, King Kong's domain and the site of his exploits, thus proving the permanence and the continuity of works which owe nothing to chance, but partake through their common traits of a macabre, fantastic and supernatural world.

I do not know whether this parallel between the Skull Island of Schoedsack's two productions (*King Kong* and *Son of Kong*) and *The Isle of the Dead* of Arnold Böcklin has ever been established since 1933, but it seemed fairly important to disclose here the strange likeness between the two works: the cinema has actually revived a literary and artistic theme which is never credited—as far as we know—to *King Kong* and, still less (quite obviously) to the inspired and unrecognized works of this great artist, Willis O'Brien.

But let's return, after this digression, to the collective dreamlike quality of *King Kong* and to the real reasons why it influences so deeply those who remain forever affected by it.

If *King Kong* is a visionary film of such high quality, if it has been called a "masterpiece" so repeatedly, it is because it represents a very rare example of an "animated dream." Willis O'Brien has translated his dream into images, thanks to the magic of his art. The miracle of the cinema is to have given life to these mental projections, thus illustrating one of Otto Rank's thoughts: "In many ways, the cinema is like a certain kind of dream in which some facts, instead of remaining abstract, take on shapes preceptible to our senses." (*Don Juan* and *The Double*).

The poetic qualities of *King Kong*, "the visionary, strange and horrible power of its content," as Jean Ferry points out, proceed from a dream—Willis O'Brien's dream, a perfect, total, complete dream. And it is this dream, animated thanks to the technology of movie making, which gives *King Kong* its poetic impact.

King Kong may be the most remarkable—perhaps even the only—example of a man's entire dream (O'Brien's) turned into a masterpiece, thanks to technology, and thus made available to the world.

Which unconscious memories (from childhood books, maybe?) induced O'Brien to design the sequence of the gorilla appearing at the window? Is it the same forgotten reminiscence which dictated to Jean Ferry: "For a long time, the terror of seeing a gorilla peering through my window haunted my childhood insomnia."

And after all, why couldn't O'Brien, Jean Ferry, Ernest Beaumont, Schoedsack, Merian Cooper and the director of *The Amazing Colossal Man* have read and forgotten this passage from Swift in which Gulliver sees the head of a giant gorilla at his window?

What child has not read or owned an illustrated edition of *Gulliver's Travels*? What teen-ager has not

daydreamed in front of Job's, Granville's or Robida's illustrations?

One of Jean Ferry's sentences is particularly meaningful in this respect: "I am not trying to conjure up very complex recollections when I ask that the innumerable dreams built around this theme will be remembered." With the excerpt from Swift in evidence at the beginning of this issue of *Midi-Minuit*, we are not trying to relate this sentence to plagiarism but rather to the world of correspondence. Whether the authors of *King Kong* knew this passage from *Gulliver's Travels* or not is irrelevant and immaterial. But on the other hand it would be most interesting to find out whether, after having read it during their teen-age years, they might not have forgotten it; the head of King Kong at Fay Wray's window in the heart of New York City became—several years later—the artist's conscious translation of an unconscious remembrance.

Did Willis O'Brien ever possess, in his childhood library, a copy of Swift's *Gulliver* with an illustration precisely representing the gorilla kidnapping the hero "like a Baby in one of his Fore-Paws" and taking refuge at the top of the palace overlooking the city of Brobdingnag? We shall probably never know. Willis O'Brien and Jean Ferry need not be concerned—to dream the same dream as Jonathan Swift could hardly be detrimental to a good man!

King Kong, a poet's filmed vision from beginning to end (much in the same vein as Peter Ibbetson for the novel), does not exclude the possibility of a vast collective dream, and this is especially true of certain landscapes—that of the Theater, for instance, as Jean Ferry points out: "In the episode of the Theater, I literally recognized a striking scene from one of my most frequent nightmares—anguish and uneasiness included. A spectator, somewhat frightened, would like to leave, but the rest of the audience boos him for his cowardice and he stays. *I* am that spectator. A hundred times, in my dream, just before the disaster . . ."

Who has never experienced this in a dream? It is this "collective" quality of *King Kong's* vision which enables the film, dreamed and illustrated by Willis O'Brien, to move us so deeply. If Schoedsack and Cooper made such a success out of it; if Schoedsack felt the vital need to continue it with *Son of Kong*, then to revive it with *Mighty Joe Young*; if both Willis O'Brien and Ray Harryhausen had the same dream; if Job drew it so precisely; if the episode of the giant head at the bathroom window recurred in *The Amazing Colossal Man*: if so many dreamers recognize in *King Kong* the scattered fragments of a vast collective nightmare—all of this is due to the fact that Willis O'Brien's dream goes back to something very basic, a sort of incredibly intense and horrible fright.

Willis O'Brien's "illustrating," with plates worthy of Gustave Doré or of Max Ernst, a masterpiece neither written nor even conceived yet; the obvious coincidence of his inspiration with Swift's; the close similarity of "climate" between some of his designs and Jules Verne's illustrations for *Voyage to the Center of the Earth,* expressly and definitely prove that he, O'Brien, gave the very best pictorial interpretation of this "collective" dream, with he himself providing a living demonstration of the case quoted by Freud. By animating still drawings, he gave them life forever.

The undeniable genius of Willis O'Brien lies in the fact that he translated his vision onto paper so well; and if Freud's patient offered to draw his dream rather than to tell it ("I could not tell it to you."), Jonathan Swift chose to narrate his, and thus fired up the inspiration of numberless illustrators (Granville, Robida, Job, Pierre Bailly, etc.).

Only Méliès' *Selenites* and Ray Harryhausen's fastidious and carefully composed art work (drawn—of all things!—for *Gulliver's Travels,* which is absolutely bewildering, in view of the point we are trying to make; drawn also for the *The Mysterious Island* and *Jason and the Argonauts*) succeed almost as well in bridging the gap between the illustrator's inner dream and its actual screen adaptation. Eisenstein, who resorted so frequently to the method of the preliminary sketch, has admitted: "Sometimes, the scene which is being filmed loses all points of resemblance with the original drawing." But he immediately adds the following words, so illuminating in Willis O'Brien's case: 'Sometimes also, it's the design itself which comes alive on the screen, two years later." This remark from a great director throws a good deal of light on the work method of another great—and too often unrecognized creator:

"And suddenly the dream comes alive and becomes reality . . ."

Willis O'Brien's dream came alive under his pen; it became reality among the confusion of studios jammed with technological devices, and thanks to the technique of shot-by-shot filming; from Edgar Wallace's vague outline (strongly influenced—and this may be an understatement—by Conan Doyle's literary plot for *The Lost World*), the talented O'Brien drew a version of reality which was to consecrate two directors (Ernest Beaumont Schoedsack and Merian Cooper); a reality twice reborn like a phoenix, in *Son of Kong* and in *Mighty Joe Young* (the latter with the collaboration of Ray Harryhausen). This indestructible, colossal, fabulous *King Kong* was to thrill such different temperaments as those of (I name at random) Jean Ferry, Ado Kyrou, Brunius, Michel Laclos, André Falk, Jacques Doniol-Valcroze, Elliott Stein, etc.

If all the individuals mentioned above became so enthusiastic over the giant gorilla's exploits, it is because a man, Willis O'Brien, was able to change a fantastic dream, the collective memory of a childhood book, of a forgotten illustration, into a concrete, tangible reality; because he learned how to animate the dream which he drew tirelessly for the fabulous scenery, worthy of Dante's *Inferno,* on which Swift, Conan Doyle, Jules Verne, Gustave Doré and Max Ernst had hung fragments of their dreams, like white clouds of mist caught on the brambles in the graveyards of *The Sign of the Vampire.*

Willis O'Brien's dream, drawn first, then animated by him shot by shot to become at long last the most fabulous movie in motion-picture history—this very dream is *King Kong,* the eighth wonder of the world, the masterpiece of cinematographic dreamland, the true *Voyage to the Center of the Head,* which no one had dared undertake before him.

A KING IN NEW YORK*

Claude Ollier

In 1925, the captive brontosaurus hauled back from the jungle of *The Lost World* to London to be exhibited as a circus attraction breaks his chains, plays havoc with a number of objects around Piccadilly, then is engaged in combat on the famous bridge, until he stumbles and, sliding down the whole length of the structure, causes it to collapse under his weight. Six years later, Willis O'Brien, creator of the designs and models which were the basis of these special effects, was engaged by Merian Cooper (the coproducer with Ernest Beaumont Schoedsack of such adventure films as *Grass, Chang, The Four Feathers, Rango* and the future producer of the most notable films of John Ford) to contrive a series of tableaux illustrating the possibilities of a film project the action of which was to be built around a giant gorilla. Assisted by Mario Larrinaga and Byron L. Crabbe, O'Brien executed a dozen designs which served to crystallize the ideas of the promoter.

The entire first design represented King Kong on top of the Empire State Building: he holds the woman in his hand as the planes rake him with machine gun fire. The second design shows King Kong in the jungle shaking a tree in order to tumble some sailors out of its branches. And in the third, Kong is seen facing the sun and beating his breast as the woman this time lies at his feet. There were twelve designs in all, eleven of which were actually reproduced during the shooting and faithfully brought to life . . .[Interview with Merian C. Cooper in *Midi-Minuit Fantastique*, No. 6 (June, 1963), p. 40].

It would be most instructive to know in what order scenarists James Creelman and Ruth Rose (in private life Mrs. Schoedsack), having in mind the film's ultimate point of action, developed its other episodes.

Did they invent the last sequences entirely in reverse order so that the outcome, at least for them, would not be a surprise? It is precisely in this way that the most solid fictions are sometimes achieved; for the author who begins with the end of his story, developing his plot line as it were in reverse, is obliged under penalty of death to discover absolutely ineluctable lines of causality.

It may be, however, that Creelman and Ruth Rose proceeded in the way it is ordinarily supposed that scriptwriters work, which is to say in a forward movement like that of the hands of a watch rather than as retracers of a course of time as yet unrecorded. In either case, all the leading motifs of the film are to be found in O'Brien's initial inspiration, which provides indeed a veritable blueprint for the plot: Beauty, a privileged value, protected from a social milieu that is itself in distress, becomes witness to a mortal combat between the forces of mechanized civilization and the Gorilla-God of primitive nature. (Nor is it accidental that she should appear to be less terrified in these harrowing climactic moments than she is at her story's "beginning," a matter not to be explained simply on the basis that fear tends to work itself out through its physiological expression.) As to the Beast —it is shown to be more concerned, in its pathetic fury, with defending Beauty against the flying machines than itself: as it drops its guard for a moment to assure itself of its protégée's safety, it is machine-gunned in the back by the Spads of the rash U.S.A.F.

Thematically, the film stresses the conjunction between the stupefying power of theatrical spectacle and the stock market activity bound up with it, and the way this in turn inexorably leads to a catastrophic depletion and disorder—disasters of a kind which seem nonetheless to have been unconsciously wished for by the populace. Thus a main influence contributing to the chaos is the extravagant role played by a public entranced by the star system: the "prehistoric" lead promoted to the role of star is revealed to be a god of love and, for that reason, of destruction. Finally, and most importantly, the presence of the monster atop

* From Cahiers du Cinéma, nos. 166-67 (May-June 1965): 65-72. Copyright © 1965 by Les Editions de l'Etoile. English translation by Roy Huss and T.J. Ross copyright © 1972 by Roy Huss and T. J. Ross. Used by permission of Grove Press, Inc.

the skyscraper drives home the parallel between the worlds of the jungle island and the modern metropolis.

The scenario of *King Kong*, which culminates in so grandiose an image, is made up of ingredients out of three well-tried plots: *The Sorcerer's Apprentice, Beauty and the Beast,* and *The Lost World*. These ingredients are combined in a single work which possesses an uncommon richness of implication. It is shocking therefore to find the most favorably disposed among its earliest reviewers applying to this masterpiece of symmetry the epithet "infantile" (even granted that the first reel of the film—since fortunately restored—was missing when the film was first shown in France, toward the end of 1933). For the appeal of *King Kong* after all depends on the plastic beauty unequaled in its genre; on the remarkable quality of its dreamlike configurations; and on a power of erotic suggestion compelling enough to make generations of high school kids amorous of the big monkey—a creature at once scarifying and cosily protective.

It will be worth pausing, then, for a closer look at the action of this fable. How does it work? Consider first the prime mover of the action: a producer-author (who is in the bargain a capitalist, a director of production, a scenarist, a cameraman, and a set designer!) sets sail for the umpteenth time for an unexplored region where he hopes to film another in the string of exotic spectaculars for which he is renowned. And the initial steps of his project are shrouded in secrecy, including all specific details concerning the voyage; it is all very much indeed "a staging in the abyss." Not only are we faced with the unpredictable—only partly foreseeable—events which lie ahead when the shooting of the film actually takes place, but also with a most parsimonious yielding of information in the scenario of the film *we* are seeing. There is, to be sure, one clear motive for these early precautions: if the crew members had the slightest hint of what awaited them at journey's end, nothing would induce them to board ship. The guarded disclosures, offered piecemeal, also serve to reinforce the tone in general of an adventure movie; at the same time the slow, teasing unraveling of points of information allows for the dramatic underscoring of certain main themes and the suggestion by delicious foreshadowings of the real import of the drama to come. If, for example, the film's daredevil hero, Carl Denham (played by Robert Armstrong), is concerned for the first time in his career with engaging a leading woman for one of his productions, it is because both the critics and the public have joined in insisting that he now mix sex with his usual brand of exoticism. His present enterprise then is in large measure a response to a collective wish. Nor is it merely a matter of chance that brings Denham ashore to pick out his future star from among the anonymous crowd on the streets; in the course of his seemingly aimless stroll, his attention is drawn by the outcry of a woman being shoved about (as she is held in the grip of a fruit vendor who had caught her trying to snitch an apple from his stand). Her cry of anguish echoes with the mystery of an ambiguous expectation, a mystery whose force will not be dissipated until the arrival of the film company at their island destination. Although Denham has a scenario in mind for his island project, his method of working is one we would now find thoroughly up-to-date as he seeks to bring within the—of necessity—tentative framework of his scenario three uncertain and "unstable" elements: an unexplored terrain inhabited by a primitive populace, a young American woman, and a legendary creature which is neither man nor beast and in its essence quasi-divine. Inevitably, improvisation will be the rule. In preparation for the monstrous psychodrama he envisages in the forthcoming encounter between prehistory and the industrial age, Denham devotes the leisure hours of their ocean voyage to rehearsing his Beauty: decking her out in costumes specially designed for her role, coaching her in the arts of mime and devising exercises for her voice in the upper register to get it attuned for the most reverberative expressions of terror. In the case of the Beast, Denham will direct him as best he can, blithely backed up, when necessary, by gas grenades. Everything to do with the island conforms to a classically mythic pattern: thus, the Norwegian sailor who had turned the map over to Denham had himself never seen the fabled spot; it was from the native survivor of a shipwreck that he had heard about it. So too the Victorian style in narrating adventure stories—with its earnest tone, its leisurely pace, and its native and archaic flavor—is scrupulously adhered to. The voyage is menaced by an incoming monsoon gathering speed; by a deviation off-course from the standard maritime route; by a captain increasingly ill-at-ease with a restive crew—all topped off with the dangers of heat, fog, submerged reefs. But the isle awaits—it exists—as does Kong, whose name, once uttered, strikes upon the ears of the hardened seamen like some submerged memory risen from the stormy deeps of time.

His first day's shooting on the isle surpasses all of Denham's hopes. Then, in a stunning reversal of fortune, Denham is himself overwhelmed by scenes more visually breathtaking than anything he had dared to imagine—in consequence of the natives taking his star prisoner and in effect stealing his thunder as directors of the ensuing action! Denham regains the initiative by sheer dint of force, substituting for the film record of an exotic spectacle, which he had planned to make, the raw spectacle itself. He traps the monster and gets it on board his ship, with the plan of exhibiting it "in person" in New York, together with the heroic men who had taken it captive. Here is one of those rare instances when the real actors in an event promise to be more impressive and memorable than their pattern as traced on celluloid.

But there is another way, no less faithful to it, of looking at this fable and apprehending its meaning: we have in Denham a redoubtable businessman who—disturbed and stimulated by an economic depression of unprecedented magnitude, one which has shaken his country to its foundations—decides to mount a show which will be so enormous in scale as to exorcise, or at least overshadow by its own spectacle, widespread social anxieties. In face of the grave and unforeseen peril of the financial crisis, the authorities remain without either a coherent plan of action or the imagination to conceive any fundamental revision of the system. Leaving his country, where an anguished populace trembles before the specter of its doom, Denham journeys to an unknown and virgin terrain, where he finds a primitive people who are also exposed to a frightening menace, this one of a permanent, indeed quasi-eternal, nature. The natives, however, are capable of dealing with the threat in a manner which seems more or less to have worked, at least up to the moment of Denham's arrival in their midst. Drunk with his prospects for profit, and failing completely to recognize the local wisdom, which he treats with all the contempt of an honest white racist, Denham succeeds in record time, like the "imprudent merchant" of the fairy tale who makes too little of Beauty, not only in causing the death of several of his crew in grisly circumstances, but also in destroying the fragile equilibrium between God-Beast and man established on the island by the native witch doctors. Enraged by Denham's mindless and exploitative intervention, the majestic Beast shatters the ancient ramparts of the village and lays it waste. Nor is this enough to satisfy the marauder: obsessed with his contemptible objective, Denham mobilizes every technological resource at his disposal in order to transplant the gigantic hellbent creature to his own country, where he remains heedless of what this will cost his compatriots in life and property. Only by means of the most advanced weaponry is he able to check and—finally—destroy the monster. It is precisely in consequence of the heedless and destructive shenanigans of one of its leading citizens that the menace on the human scale which hovers over the New World is multiplied by a far more terrible menace of superhuman proportions. An enigmatic power beyond rational comprehension is now unleashed on the metropolis with a clearly punitive force: in confrontation with a mean, unjust, and degrading culture, a vengeful aspect of nature, in all its "horror" and violence, looms over the general chaos of civilization to rescue the one noble human it has encountered and to destroy whatever it sees as threatening to engulf her.

Having noted, then, some of the moral and social overtones developed through the interplay of the film's characters and its star monster, we may turn now for a closer view of the two main locales which are so deftly placed in parallel by the scenario—a scenario the "puerility" of which keeps proving most complex indeed. First, there is the domain of Kong—Skull Island—so named since it is shaped like a skull or an inverted cup: a tiny peninsula spread out at the foot of an immense mountain, Skull Island corresponds exactly to that other island, Manhattan, the tip of which juts out from the foot of giant skyscrapers. On Skull Island, a resourceful people subsist as best they can on the lowlands in proximity to the ominous cliffs, just as the denizens of the city swarm round the buildings within which all-powerful beings impassively toy with and juggle the fate of the crowd. In either sphere, we behold the bulwarks of prosperity and security giving way: on Skull Island, the shattering of the bolt on the gate of the village wall corresponds to the floodgates of the city burst open by the financial tidal wave of "the crash.' The equilibrium maintained by both spheres is smashed, with the difference that the dwellers on Manhattan will find themselves facing both perils—of nature and finance—together.

We may note too that it is the white man who sounds the gong to call to the rescue those same black men whom he had just before accused of cowardice and whom he then betrays to a massacre through his own folly. Thus a maddened Kong, at loose for the first time in the village, indiscriminately attacks first one group, then another. It is true that the whites clear the isle of the dread presence of Kong, but then it is also true that Kong had served on occasion to rid this land of other giant beasts roaming its surface. After the forays of the whites, little is left the islanders in any case but to bury their dead and to seek to rebuild their gate against those truly remorseless monsters who will be returning once more to breach the gate and with whom no pact is conceivable.

Thus we behold two jungle worlds in parallel. The remarkable meshing of special effects by which the jungle of Skull Island is created—models, transparencies, articulated scaffolds, "stop action"—becomes so powerfully suggestive that the dreamlike aura of Skull Island is transposed onto the landscape of that other, modern jungle, which is made up in great part of very real views of the American metropolis. This expansion of the fantasy through seeing one universe in terms of the other evidently constitutes the film's basic line of force. There is another law ruling each of these worlds, however, which merits note (the close study of which would provide a field day especially for stock market analysts).

Regarded purely as a marketable commodity in a capitalist society, the heroine, Ann Darrow, is virtually of no worth when we see her in the beginning as a penniless waif; as soon as Denham engages her, she takes on, in contrast, great potential value. Then when the natives of the isle offer her up to Kong, her value is further raised to the category of an object for barter. Once in the possession of Kong, she becomes an amorous cult object: another promotion. Recovered by Denham, she falls back a couple of notches in the scale of values, but her rate of exchange in consequence climbs dizzily. In repossessing her and elevating her out of reach of his mercenary counterparts, King Kong saves his lady fair from one kind of degrading "fetishism": the anger of Kong is explained as much by the larceny of which he has been the victim as by the frivolous disrespect shown him and his costar by the theater audience. The uneven destiny of Ann is perforce closely bound with the conditions of life prevailing in her social group: it is as exemplary in its glory as in its panic; and this is precisely the meaning carried from start to finish by the piercing modulations of her scream. "Your only chance is to scream," says Denham to her on the ship. From the beginning this cry predestines her for violence; indeed the misadventures of Ann in *King Kong* prefigure those of another American heroine, one equally predestined: Melanie of Hitchcock's *The Birds*. The link between the individual and the collective fate by progressive amplification and final generalization is continuously established in the two films. Melanie brings about the unleashed fury of the birds as Ann does that of the gorilla. After her, the neighborhood group, then society in the aggregate, then the nation as a whole, successively become prey to devastation. The famous "too lengthy" first part of *The Birds* matches exactly the first half of *King Kong*, during which nothing supernatural occurs, when the action includes no more than subterranean flickers of apprehension concerning the "favored" individual, these hints and intimations later communicating themselves rapidly to larger and larger social units. And one matter which in *The Birds* is treated extensively (Melanie's past efforts at social advancement) is in *King Kong* elided and condensed in Ann's shimmering outcry: it is her single faculty for projecting to perfection various facets of her terror by her voice alone which leads Denham to "discover" her, even as Melanie

Daniels is singled out by Mitch as he notices her little "innocent" machinations.

In any case, New York is saved from destruction, and it is Denham who has the last word as he delivers a funeral oration over the body of the vanquished beast. In contrast, the concluding scene of Hitchcock's film is still dominated by the presence of thousands of threatening winged creatures, seemingly in a state of truce before possible resumption of their attack. Only in prosperous times, like the America of 1963 (when *The Birds* was first shown), would such an ending heavy with uncertainty and menace be tolerated; the America of 1931, however, when *King Kong* began taking shape, was bound to insist on a standard "happy ending." (It is precisely in an era of the fatted calf such as the sixties that a "no limits" freedom of artistic expression is most readily allowed: 1963, for example, is also the year of *Dr. Strangelove*, a film in which New York is wiped out at the stroke of a presidential pen.)

But to return to Ann's nightmare experience (Fay Wray, who plays Ann, will also be especially remembered for her portrayal of Mitzi, the enticing and beleaguered beauty of Erich von Stroheim's *The Wedding March*). Nearly all the episodes during which our heroine changes masters take place at night. With a glance that increasingly mingles hints of lasciviousness with astonishment and terror, Ann endures in succession being virtually shanghaied by Denham, kidnapped by the natives, taken possession by a Kong on the sacrificial altar, and later repossessed by the creature in the high chamber of the palace (in a sequence which anticipates the inevitable finale when Kong climbs the skyscraper). A main exception: when the first mate Driscoll (Bruce Cabot) takes Ann and races off with her while Kong is occupied in his fight with the pterodactyl (or is it pteranodon?). At this point in the action there occur two vertically steep drops into the abyss—the sort of thing the cinema has found to be its most apt means for registering that kind of abrupt and incomplete resolution of tensions—and consequent swooning sensation—which marks the culmination of a nightmare. Thus we see Ann and Driscoll make their descent down a providential vine and take a dizzying fall into the waters incredibly far below. Dissolutions and recrystallizations of terror are by this exciting means woven together in a series of actions which conclude as Ann races along a sinuous path of escape, her hair flying free and her body at last somewhat relaxed after the convulsive tremors caused by her ordeal.

In another of the jungle sequences there is communicated one of the most hallucinatory and surreal sensations that the screen has ever given us: when she falls from on top the tree where Kong had placed her for safety, Ann witnessed a duel to the death between her guardian ape and an attacking tyrannosaurus. In this sequence the distinction maintained between the foreground where Ann is seen, helpless and appalled, and the middle distance where the monsters go through their paces, is as thin as a hairline—so that we are made to doubt our sense of a spatial demarcation between the two locations: the beasts are obviously quite near, since they keep bumping against the trunk of the overturned tree; and yet their confrontation (in medium-long shot) is enacted in a disorientingly close and "imponderable" perspective. Ann's terror stems both from the immediate proximity of the combatants (and the immense danger this puts her in) and from the weird sensation of unreality evoked by the spectacle. But if there were some basic "daylight" logic to the business, it would be shattered soon enough by the frightful glancing blows exchanged by the monsters. It is at this moment that the split between dream and reality is most flagrant: in large measure, what Ann is here witnessing is her own nightmare. Displacements of a similar kind, although less immediately evident, prevail almost continually during the scenes of combat; for example, the "too rapid" progression of the brontosaurus which, surging up out of the marsh, pursues a band of sailors across the jungle. In this instance, several effects of different origin are brought into play and combined: the breaks more or less visible in the succession of medium shots; the transition from medium-long to medium shots of Kong, with that extraordinary full face dolly-in on Kong's incensed features; and especially the jumps achieved by shooting "frame by frame." We may note, then, how even the minor flaws in the continuity of perspective or movement, far from destroying or enfeebling the credulity of the spectacle, are in accord rather with the presentation of a totally dreamlike state, a dream created by means of spatial illusion, optical displacements, and disruptions between individual shots and the overall continuity. The "doubtful" space created by the depth montages of O'Brien and the necessity of filming in fragmented time results in a visual pattern altogether of a kind with the sort of "collage" manifest in all visions of nightmare worlds —pointillistic effects of space and time, gaps, fringes, overflowings, and scenic incompatibilities, zones of vacant expenses where any suspicion of unreality is overcome in the all-engulfing eeriness. Moreover, the few "errors" in scale evident on occasion between the proportions of King Kong and those of the environment add to the compartmentalizations characteristic of dreams, in which agreements of size between objects are in constant evolution. (It is a pity that shots of Denham's companions being devoured by giant spiders at the bottom of the precipice from which the men had toppled have not been preserved in the extant version—at the wish, it would seem, of the producers themselves.)

From the purely plastic point of view, the creations of O'Brien, as fully limned on paper as created on film are of a beauty which is strange, sumptuous and overflowing: this jungle rich in its geographically inauthentic vegetation, inhabited by animals more legendary than scientifically prehistoric, derives directly from engravings that several centuries of tales of adventure have inspired. For example, one rediscovers in the scene of the subterranean lake the same chiaroscuro found in many a composition illustrating Jules Verne or Paul d'Ivoi. In certain compositions of rocky plateaus, the kinship with Gustave Doré is clearly evident. We know too that the tableau of Skull Island directly reproduces the celebrated "Isle of the Dead" of Arnold Böcklin. The director Fritz Lang had himself borrowed from three of Böcklin's works for the composition of two of the sequences of his epic film *Die Nibelungen*. Concerning the animation of the King of the Jungle, secrecy continues to shroud the different techniques that either successively or concomitantly went into the work. Because of the gorilla's superb posture and movement, it is hard to disabuse the spectator of the idea—which is false—that the "role" of Kong was played by a human being, so much does the character impose itself by its *élan vital*—one is tempted to say by its "humanity." Finally, on the matter of the film's cruelty, its horror runs the gamut of suffocation, devouring strangulation, quartering. There are also bonus bits unequaled in monster films: witness the enormous paw with the claws meticulously curved crushing the body of a hapless native in the spongy mire.

King Kong, masterpiece of the fantastic film and assuredly one of the most disturbing, was made in the most audacious period in film history. No doubt its impressiveness is due in large part to the skills of an exceptional team. Yet the answer to its success does not lie there, but rather in the sources from which the team was inspired to draw. O'Brien and his collaborators, renew, across the span of literature, painting, and engraving, a kinship with an abounding tradition of legends and illustrated myths. It is certainly more agreeable to explore among these materials than among the junk heaps of pseudoatomic science fiction, of which the dismal and ugly *Goldfinger* marks the nadir. A single regret perhaps: that the authors of the scenario had not faithfully pursued to the end the story that

Denham had promised to shoot. Another possible happy ending would have removed the major uncertainty overshadowing the second appearance of the bestial creature, a mystery still unsolved: what expression would King Kong have assumed if, in those last shots, Ann had loved him?

NARRATIVE, FABLE, AND DREAM
IN *KING KONG* *

R C Dale

The story of beauty and the beast is timeless. In antiquity it appears in many different forms, probably the most famous of which is the confrontation of Odysseus and Circe. Odysseus was wiser than his men: he resisted Circe's charms because he shared the common contemporary knowledge that witches had the power to enervate and destroy their lovers by secretly drawing off their blood in little bladders (according to Robert Graves, almost everybody knew that). But many other heroes fared less well, if we may trust the parabolic annals of antiquity, the Middle Ages and the Renaissance. One of the definitive victories of beauty, and the definitive version of the story, came from the eighteenth century: Mme. de Beaumont's fairy tale called *La Belle et la Bête*. Eighteenth-century fairy tales were closely allied to the popular form known as philosophical and moral (i.e., having to do with mores, manners) stories, thinly disguised fables with extremely clear messages. This whole tradition indulged itself in exoticism, eroticism, satire and social commentary. It eventually contributed a great deal to the later genre of the Gothic novel, which emphasized the first two of those characteristics and played down the others completely. *King Kong*, like its progenitors, the eighteenth-century fairy tale and the Gothic novel, and like its sister, the horror film, is rich in implication and imagination.

Somehow, despite the fantastic goings-on in which the film abounds, it succeeds in casting a rare spell over most of its viewers, a spell somewhat similar to that created by the best of the Gothic novels, such as Lewis's *The Monk*. The film manages to bypass the critical, censorious level of the viewer's consciousness and to secure his suspension of disbelief with what appears to be great ease. A number of French critics have attributed this phenomenon to what they call the film's oneiric qualities, its pervasive dreamlike control of some subconscious, uncritical part of the mind.

Indeed, it does succeed in dreaming for us, and we are swept along with the dream as helpless spectators, as if the dream were our own. Every viewer's reaction is obviously his own, but few can resist completely the involvement that the picture offers. Most film estheticians agree that this oneiric involvement is inherent to cinema, but rarely so well established as in the case of *Kong*. It may seem odd that a film based on patently fantastic happenings should succeed so well where many films based in conventional reality fail. There are a number of factors to explain this odd circumstance. First of all, *Kong* has a basic cinematic subject, an almost completely visual appeal as far as the action is concerned. Almost half of the film has no dialogue; instead, it builds suspense and involvement with emotion-reinforcing music. The special effects are extraordinarily well-handled. We recognize the animals are miniature models animated by means of stop-motion photography, but we allow ourselves to be deceived by them almost immediately. The fact that a brontosaurus, as a vegetarian, shouldn't really be chasing after meat, may flicker across our minds as we watch the action, but that logical objection is soon quelled by the struggle on the screen: the action never fails to fascinate. But probably the most important reasons for the film's success at capturing us as spectators are that it carefully establishes a reality of its own; it employs extensive use of archetypal myth imagery that appeals directly to our subconscious, and it uses an extremely effective narrative approach to its subject.

To facilitate leading us into its fantastic reality, the picture presents us with a classically simple narrative structure. It has a brief prologue, an introductory part set in New York and on the high seas; a second, crucial, part set on Skull Island, home of Kong; and a conclusion that returns us to the original locale. The narrator secures our good will by setting the beginning of his tale in familar surroundings—the docks of a great city. He then specifies the time—the present, 1933, the height of the Depression. As he sets the scene, he also economically presents the principal

* From *Persistence of Vision*, Joseph McBride, ed., Wisconsin Film Society Press, Madison, 1968.

characters. They are introduced to us without any editorial qualification expressed through angular viewing, exceptional cutting, or music.

We recognize Carl Denham as the central character in this section (and presumably in the film, although that is not to be the case) through the simple narrative principle of concentration, of following. Denham reveals himself as a strong, independent, masculine character who knows what he wants and who is used to getting it.

What does he want this time? asks the reporter with whom we have sympathetically boarded the ship for an interview. The narrator knows that we won't resist an interrogative identification with the reporter in a situation like this. Thus Denham isn't just talking to people, he's answering our question; and we are pulled into the interview.

He wants to find a woman to go off somewhere (he's not saying where) with that odd, oversized crew on a vessel with enough explosives aboard to blow up the harbor. But why does he want her? Not because he likes women. "Do you think I wanna haul a girl around?" But he needs her. "I'm going out and find a girl for my picture, even if I hafta marry one."

The narrator cuts to women standing in a breadline, then to a girl standing, hesitating, before a fruit stand. She reaches to steal an apple, but the owner rushes out and grabs her. Denham intercedes, takes her to a restaurant, restores her with food, and offers her the part in his picture. He tells her that he isn't bothering about her out of kindness or sexual interest in her, but can offer her ". . . money, fame, the thrill of a lifetime, and a long sea voyage that starts at six in the morning."

The narrator has succeeded in provoking our curiosity and our interest by making Denham into a man of mystery and intrigue, but nonetheless a perfectly believable one. Like all the great creators of fantastic narrations—Mérimée, Lewis, Hoffman—Cooper and Schoedsack lead us slowly and credibly away from reality. So far, they have centered our interest on Denham and his mysterious quest almost entirely through his own verbalization.

In the following section of the introductory part, the camera joins the microphone to intensify the mystery and to suggest without overt statement that we are slowly leaving behind civilization and the known. The photography becomes more muted and less obviously studio-shot, values of grey begin to appear, the lighting loses the uniformity of the sound-stage. The ship enters a fogbank as barrier after barrier closes between the crew and civilization. They pass through a reef that forms another gate into the unknown, and finally reach the point of primitive isolation that is their goal.

Before we get into the great battle that forms the central part of the film, let us turn from narration to subject—to what is being narrated. The narrator, we remember, has been very careful to lead us slyly into his own world. He is equally sly when it comes to confiding in us what he really intends to discuss in this film. He tells us straight off, in the title card that precedes the first part, that we're going to see a story involving beauty and the beast. The card bears a putative Old Arabian Proverb that proclaims: "And lo, the beast looked upon the face of beauty. And it stayed its hand from killing. And from that day, it was as one dead."

Denham reiterates this apparent subject on numerous occasions during the first part of the picture. As they are sailing off into the unknown, he sees Ann with a little monkey, in a sort of prefigurative situation, and remarks: "Beauty and the beast, eh? If beauty gets you . . . that's the idea of my picture. The beast was a tough guy, too. He could lick the world. But when he saw beauty, she got him; he went soft, he forgot his wisdom . . . and the little guys got him."

Shortly after he utters those words, we get a glimpse of him directing Ann in a screen test aboard ship. She appears in an extremely diaphanous gown, the picture of fragility and femininity, submitting unquestioningly to his orders. He tells her to look up, higher, higher, until she sees something horrible, so horrible that it petrifies her. "You're helpless, Ann, helpless. If you could scream—but you can't." At this point, certain peculiarities about Denham become pretty pronounced.

Denham, the apparent protagonist in the film, is very eager to obtain a girl—any girl—for his picture. He would marry one if he had to, and the marriage would presumably have no other purpose whatever. He picks a girl almost at random from the streets, a girl whose weakened condition and circumstances attract his attention. He photographs her entirely as an object and, in great eagerness to get right down to business, shoots her as she is about to be abducted by something monstrous, dangerous and undefined. Denham, as a master voyeur, is conducting an experiment in which he will be a recording observer—not an active participant. He has obtained a random example of femininity and now he intends to expose it to a vague, mysterious example of brute masculinity.

So much for Denham, the voyeur not interested in participating directly in courting and sex, who prefers to get his kicks vicariously and immaculately. But what of the narrator? Does he have any particular feelings about all this? Does he particpate in this objectification and degradation of woman? The answer, of course, is an unqualified yes. To begin with, he implicitly states his distrust of woman in the opening title (for which Denham can in no way be held responsible). Then he chooses to depict a breadline peopled exclusively by woman suggesting their debilitated position in the effete American culture. Only by getting away from it, he further suggests, can masculinity have its day. In the last part of the film, back in New York, it is women who drag their reluctant husbands off to see the captive, figuratively castrated Kong. The narrator continually informs the picture with his own particular brand of misogyny. Between him and Denham, the film holds the almost total and certainly pervasive conviction that woman, like Circe, incapacitates man.

The complicity in outlook between the two runs the course of the picture, but there is a greater separation between the narrator and Denham in the first than in the subsequent parts, especially the central part. In the first part, the narrator observes Denham making his voyeuristic preparations and draws our attention as fellow witnesses. He also notes such details as the three crew members lined up vertically and rather phallically on a ship's ladder grinning expectantly at Ann as she does her stuff for the screen test. (By the way, that shot forms a very rare—perhaps even unique—example in this part of the phallic imagery that completely dominates the remaining parts of the film; it appears, significantly enough, exactly when overt voyeurism occurs on screen.) In the first part, we consciously observe Denham laying his plans. Indeed, the narrator leads us deftly into the fantastic world of Skull Island by postponing visualization of it even after we have arrived there. As we peer over Denham's shoulder at the map of the island, we slowly become aware of the faint throbbing of drums in the distance. Then we rush to the deck to peer at indistinct forms in the far-off native village as Max Steiner's music sneaks in to increase our wonder and excitement.

The next day, we scan the beach and find it empty. Again, there is nothing tangible for us to reject, so we go along with the narrator. The music gets spookier as a landing party reaches shore. Amidst the sounds of drums and chanting, Denham suddenly stops, a look of excitement and wonder on his face. Only at this point does the narrator let us have a look at what is going on: the natives' ritual Kong dance. Although the dance itself is a bit on the silly side, the narrator doesn't allow us much time to think about it. Instead, he cuts back to Denham, who pushes aside some fronds and peeks through them at the dance. "Holy mackerel, what a show! If only I could get pictures before they see us." Thus the narrator again insists on Denham's voyeurism by forcing us to observe him

rather than the action he is watching. The narrator is waiting for the right moment, the moment when he can get rid of Denham and make us take his place as direct witnesses of the action. The sequence also serves structurally as yet another prefiguration of things to come by showing us the natives practicing ritual sacrifice of a young maiden to the dangerous threatening force that they must keep locked out of their small society: the monster gorilla that inhabits Skull Mountain. The narrator thus implies without direct statement a sort of analogical extension of Denham's personal voyeuristic inhibitions: society, no matter how primitive, must wall out the bestial impulse that Kong represents or be destroyed by it. Libido, the passionate and uncontrolled inhabitant of a mountain in the form of a giant skull, must be contained or society will perish.

The native chief reinforces Denham's recognition of Ann's sexuality. He offers to trade him six of his women for Ann, the "golden woman." Such a woman, he implicitly reckons, would keep Kong satisfied and out of the village for a good time. Denham, of course, won't accept the offer. After all, he is a gentleman. Or is that indeed the reason? It is interesting to note that the plot takes an important but almost imperceptible turn at this juncture. If we remember that the chief is proposing in effect to set up Denham's projected situation for him, we might wonder why Denham displays no interest at all in making some sort of deal with him about Ann. The reasons have to do more with narrative effectiveness than with demonstrating Denham's consideration for Ann.

But let us return with the narrator to the ship. On board after their visit to the island, Jack declares his love to Ann, and they kiss. Love-making scenes quite naturally bring out the voyeur in all of us, and this is the first moment in the film when we have actually been cast in that role. Up until now, Denham—in his mind, at least—has been doing that for us and we have been watching him do it for us. But now we are doing the observing without any intermediary other than the narrator, who keeps us at it for the next hour of non-stop involvement.

In order to do this, he must remove Ann from Denham's control, the control that a cautious man or a cautious society feels must exist over beauty or woman or the object of the libido. So the natives slip aboard ship, steal her off and take her ashore, up to the great gate leading into the land of unsuppressed desire. They chain her in an erotic crucifixion to two sinewy phallic stakes, and beat the gong that summons Kong to claim his sacrifice. The huge gate ponderously swings shut behind Ann, left alone and helpless in the land of the giant skull. The transition from reality to dream, from judgment to belief, from casual observer to vicarious participator on the part of the viewer has just been effected with consummate skill by the narrator. From here on, we are in the land of the libidinous dream, where everything is erotic in shape and in meaning. The great gate, for example, underwent one obvious and important modification for this film: when it was first built, for the Babylon sequences in *Intolerance*, it was closed by means of a huge gear system. In *Kong*, the gears are gone, replaced by a gigantic beam that slides across its front, slowly penetrating hoop after hoop in the gate and retaining wall.

The music begins to race, we hear a few tremendous growls, and Kong makes his appearance. The narrator cuts almost directly into an ECU of his eyes, as he leers laciviously at Ann. Kong's intentions are obvious. He beats his breast and picks up Ann. Jack runs up, sees what's happening, and immediately takes over the situation. He leads the men into the jungle, admonishing them. "C'mon, fellas, and keep those guns cocked."

But what has become of Denham since the role of antagonist clearly has shifted to Kong? Despite his precautions for staying clear of the action, he is swept up into it. He loses the desired control of the situation, becoming involved in the necessity for rescuing Ann, which he soon gives up as hopeless without outside help. Kong is the realization of his wildest dreams, but Kong is too much for Denham, who loses control and flees, abandoning the viewer to his own fate. The audience replaces Denham as the voyeur in a situation that has got out of control, in a situation involving no more control than a dream. Denham dematerializes because of his very superfluity.

Thus the narrator has effectively involved the viewer, who is immersed in his erotic dream. Every form assumes a strongly suggestive shape; a brontosaurus pricks his long, slithery neck above the surface of a swampy lake; Kong does battle with a cocky tyrannosaurus rex, a huge snake, and finally a pterodactyl. He also battles members of the crew, who find themselves caught stradding a colossal log spanning a chasm. They hold onto the log for dear life, but Kong shakes them loose, one by one, and they hurtle screaming to the floor of the chasm and their destruction. To detail all the sexual imagery in this part of the film would amount to talking about something in practically every shot. The narrator has absolutely plunged us into his completely consistent and convincing dream. We are carried along by it without protest, no matter how extravagant it becomes, no matter how obvious the animation and rear-screening, no matter how show-offish the cross-cutting between various actions and locales; we are carried along because the narrator

insists so pervasively on its inner reality that we simply cannot extricate ourselves from it.

During this part of the film, there is an absolute coincidence of dream symbolism and surface-level plot: each action builds suspense by delaying gratification of the beast's desires. As we advance deeper and deeper into the weird, wild landscape, over and beyond chasms, lakes, rivers, swamps, through thick banks of fog, farther and farther from the familiarity and security of civilization and exterior reality, we see that Kong is indomitable in his own territory. After each progressively briefer and more intense encounter, he beats his breast and bellows his defiance to the world. When finally he leads Ann up through his cave at the top of Skull Mountain and out an opening that forms the skull's eyesocket, we know that the moment has come when the natural king of the natural world is about to take his natural prize—and we don't care how impractical that may be. He picks up Ann in his immense paw, leers most lasciviously indeed, and then slowly undresses her (the last part of this scene did not survive the censors' shears for long).

But a moment later it's all over for Kong. A pterodactyl distracts him as Jack and Ann escape by jumping into the lake far below. The narrator goes underwater to show them swimming together toward the surace. Kong's days as a would-be rapist are over; Jack and Ann have just been through ritual fertilization by water together.

Kong pursues them, eventually shattering the huge phallic bolt that is meant to keep him in his own element. With that symbolic act of castration, he bursts into civilization and his downfall.

Denham fells him with gas, an unnatural and thereby unfair weapon devised by civilization, then he brings him back to civilization itself, to be gawked at by the feckless crowd. The narrator returns us to our former roles as observers of observers, resuming the misogynic attitude he displayed in the first part. Kong, out of his element, is clearly intended to be the pathetic object of our sympathy. At no earlier point in the film has the narrator asked such indulgence for one of his characters. He certainly did not ask us to sympathize with Ann when she was at bay in Kong's world, but when the situation is exactly reversed and it is Kong's turn to be crucified, we see by comparison exactly how misogynic the picture actually is. In order to demonstrate the hopelessness of Kong's plight when he is in an unnatural realm, the narrator reenacts the high points of the chase on the island. Now Kong derails an elevated train that resembles the snake he conquered on the island; again he carries Ann up to an eyrie at the top of the world. But this mountain is not the skull bursting with libido; it is the symbol of restraint and control, the tallest man-made structure in the world, a tremendous lifeless monument whose very shape mocks its function. This time he does not bellow his victory, and he cannot overwhelm the airplanes as he did the pterodactyl in his own realm. He manages to knock off a few of them, but eventually their unnatural bullets penetrate his chest and he knows he will die. He picks Ann up one final time, contemplates her, gently sets her down, and falls about as far to his death as any symbolic sex dream has ever had its dreamer fall.

The narrative in this last part has interspersed the technique of each of the first two parts—conscious observation and dream. The narrator has felt no constraint to limit himself to either of the modes, since he has prepared us by now to accept both of them. But we cannot help noticing which mode he uses to end the picture: the crowd, panic-stricken shortly before, now mills about curiously to have a good look at civilization's victim. Denham, again master of the situation, becomes his brash, exploitive self. "Oh, no," he explains to the onlookers, "It wasn't the airplanes. It was beauty killed the beast. And the last shot in the film shows us Denham standing before Kong's lifeless body. He looks at him with contemplation written on his face—and his hands in his pockets.

Civilization has had its show, but not quite the one that Denham had set out to give them. He—and they—thought that it would be passive amusement, movieland, harmless voyeurism. But it turned out to be more than that for them: it turned out to be a participating, enthralling, engaging experience that threatened to destroy their protected, circumscribed, civilized existences. Nonetheless, civilization has managed to triumph once again over the impulses of the unrestrained libido.

And we, thanks to an unparalleled brilliance of narrative technique, have been through it all. Furthermore, thanks to the intricate interplay of narrative, we understand at the end of the film—while society does not—that civilization and its obvious representative, Denham, are the real culprits in this tale: they who would meddle with natural forces, who would entice them, deny them, remove them from their rightful contexts, and then destroy them in the name of preserving civilization.

No other fantastic film has ever even approached *King Kong* in overall effectiveness. Many have borrowed principles and have copied ideas, but no director has ever managed again to combine symmetry of plot, imagery, drama and narration so well as the men—the unrecognized and uncelebrated Cooper and Schoedsack—who put together this archetypal masterpiece of fantasy.

WHO KILLED KING KONG?*

X. J. Kennedy

The ordeal and spectacular death of King Kong, the giant ape, undoubtedly have been witnessed by more Americans than have ever seen a performance of *Hamlet, Iphigenia at Aulis,* or even *Tobacco Road.* Since RKO-Radio Pictures first released *King Kong,* a quarter-century has gone by; yet year after year, from prints that grow more rain-beaten, from sound tracks that grow more tinny, ticket-buyers by thousands still pursue Kong's luckless fight again the forces of technology, tabloid journalism, and the DAR. They see him chloroformed to sleep, see him whisked from his jungle isle to New York and placed on show, see him burst his chains to roam the city (lugging a frightened blonde), at last to plunge from the spire of the Empire State Building, machine-gunned by model airplanes.

Though Kong may die, one begins to think his legend unkillable. No clearer proof of his hold upon the popular imagination may be seen than what emerged one catastrophic week in March 1955, when New York WOR-TV programmed *Kong* for seven evenings in a row (a total of sixteen showings). Many a rival network vice-president must have scowled when surveys showed that *Kong*—the 1933 B-picture—had lured away fat segments of the viewing populace from such powerful competitors as Ed Sullivan, Groucho Marx and Bishop Sheen.

But even television has failed to run *King Kong* into oblivion. Coffee-in-the-lobby cinemas still show the old hunk of hokum, with the apology that in its use of composite shots and animated models the film remains technically interesting. And no other monster in movie history has won so devoted a popular audience. None of the plodding mummies, the stultified draculas, the white-coated Lugosis with their shiny pinball-machine laboratories, none of the invisible stranglers, berserk robots, or menaces from Mars has ever enjoyed so many resurrections.

Why does the American public refuse to let King Kong rest in peace? It is true, I'll admit, that *Kong*

* *From* Dissent, *Spring 1960. Copyright* © *1960 by* Dissent. *Reprinted by permission of the author and* Dissent.

outdid every monster movie before or since in sheer carnage. Producers Cooper and Schoedsack crammed into it dinosaurs, headhunters, riots, aerial battles, bullets, bombs, bloodletting. Heroine Fay Wray, whose function is mainly to scream, shuts her mouth for hardly one uninterrupted minute from first reel to last. It is also true that *Kong* is larded with good healthy sadism, for those whose joy it is to see the frantic girl dangled from cliffs and harried by pterodactyls. But it seems to me that the abiding appeal of the giant ape rests on other foundations.

Kong has, first of all, the attraction of being man-like. His simian nature gives him one huge advantage over giant ants and walking vegetables in that an audience may conceivably identify with him. Kong's appeal has the quality that established the Tarzan series as American myth—for what man doesn't secretly image himself a huge hairy howler against whom no other monster has a chance? If Tarzan recalls the ape in us, then Kong may well appeal to that great-grand-daddy primordial brute from whose tribe we have all deteriorated.

Intentionally or not, the producers of *King Kong* encourage this identification by etching the character of Kong with keen sympathy. For the ape is a figure in a tradition familiar to moviegoers: the tradition of the pitiable monster. We think of Lon Chaney in the role of Quasimodo, of Karloff in the Original Frankenstein. As we watch the Frankenstein monster's fumbling and disastrous attempts to befriend a flower-picking child, our sympathies are enlisted with the monster in his impenetrable loneliness. And so with Kong. As he roars in his chains, while barkers sell tickets to boobs who gape at him, we perhaps feel something more deep than pathos. We begin to sense something of the problem that engaged Eugene O'Neill in *The Hairy Ape;* the dilemma of a displaced animal spirit forced to live in a jungle built by machines.

King Kong, it is true, had special relevance in 1933. Landscapes of the depression are glimpsed early in the film when an impresario, seeking some desperate pretty girl to play the lead in a jungle movie, visits souplines and a Woman's Home Mission. In Fay Wray

—who's been caught snitching an apple from a fruit-stand—his search is ended. When he gives her a big feed and a movie contract, the girl is magic-carpeted out of the world of the National Recovery Act. And when, in the film's climax, Kong smashes the very Third Avenue landscape in which Fay had wandered hungry, audiences of 1933 may well have felt a personal satisfaction.

What is curious is that audiences of 1960 remain hooked. For in the heart of urban man, one suspects, lurks the impulse to fling a bomb. Though machines speed him to the scene of his daily grind, though IBM comptometers ("freeing the human mind from drudgery") enable him to drudge more efficiently once he arrives, there comes a moment when he wishes to turn upon his machines and kick hell out of them. He wants to hurl his combination radioalarmclock out the bedroom window and listen to its smash. What subway commuter wouldn't love—just for once—to see the downtown express smack head-on into the uptown local? Such a wish is gratified in that memorable scene in *Kong* that opens with a wide-angle shot: interior of a railway car on the Third Avenue El. Strap-hangers are nodding, the literate refold their newspapers. Unknown to them, Kong has torn away a section of trestle toward which the train now speeds. The motorman spies Kong up ahead, jams on the brakes. Passengers hurtle together like so many peas in a pail. In a window of the car appear Kong's bloodshot eyes. Women shriek. Kong picks up the railway car as if it were a rat, flips it to the street and ties knots in it, or something. To any commuter the scene must appear one of the most satisfactory pieces of celluloid ever exposed.

Yet however violent his acts, Kong remains a gentleman. Remarkable is his sense of chivalry. Whenever a fresh boa constrictor threatens Fay, Kong first sees that the lady is safely parked, then manfully thrashes her attacker. (And she, the ingrate, runs away every time his back is turned.) Atop the Empire State Building, ignoring his pursuers, Kong places Fay on a ledge as tenderly as if she were a dozen eggs. He fondles her, then turns to face the Army Air Force. And Kong is perhaps the most disinterested lover since Cyrano: his attentions to the lady are utterly without hope of reward. After all, between a five-foot blonde and a fifty-foot ape, love can hardly be more than an intellectual flirtation. In his simian way King Kong is the hopelessly yearning lover of Petrarchan convention. His forced exit from his jungle, in chains, results directly from his single-minded pursuit of Fay. He smashes a Broadway theater when the notion enters his dull brain that the flashbulbs of photographers somehow endanger the lady. His perilous shinnying up a skyscraper to pluck Fay from her boudoir is an act of the kindliest of hearts. He's impossible to discourage even though the love of his life can't lay eyes on him without shrieking murder.

The tragedy of King Kong, then, is to be the beast who at the end of the fable fails to turn into the handsome prince. This is the conviction that the scriptwriters would leave with us in the film's closing line. As Kong's corpse lies blocking traffic in the street, the entrepreneur who brought Kong to New York turns to the assembled reporters and proclaims, "That's your story, boys—it was Beauty killed the Beast!" But greater forces than those of the screaming Lady have combined to lay Kong low, if you ask me. Kong lives for a time as one of those persecuted near-animal souls bewildered in the middle of an industrial order, whose simple desires are thwarted at every turn. He climbs the Empire State Building because in all New York it's the closest thing he can find to the clifftop of his jungle isle. He dies, a pitiful dolt, and the army brass and publicity-men cackle over him. His death is the only possible outcome to as neat a tragic dilemma as you can ask for. The machine-guns do him in while the manicured human hero (a nice clean Dartmouth boy) carries away Kong's sweetheart to the altar. O, the misery of it all. There's far more truth about upper-class American life in *King Kong* than in the last seven dozen novels of John P. Marquand.

A Negro friend from Atlanta tells me that in movie houses in colored neighborhoods throughout the South, *Kong* does a constant business. They show the thing in Atlanta at least every year, presumably to the same audiences. Perhaps this popularity may simply be due to the fact that *Kong* is one of the most watchable movies ever constructed, but I wonder whether Negro audiences may not find some archetypical appeal in this serio-comic tale of a huge black powerful free spirit whom all the hardworking white policemen are out to kill.

Every day in the week on a screen somewhere in the world, King Kong relives his agony. Again and again he expires on the Empire State Building, as audiences of the devout assist his sacrifice. We watch him die, and by extension kill the ape within our bones, but these little deaths of ours occur in prosaic surroundings. We do not die on a tower, New York before our feet, nor do we give our lives to smash a few flying machines. It is not for us to bring to a momentary standstill the civilization in which we move. King Kong does this for us. And so we kill him again and again, in much-spliced celluloid, while the ape in us expires from day to day, obscure, in desperation.

KING KONG: A MEDITATION

Kenneth Bernard

TARZAN AND KONG

It is logical that having written at some length on King Kong I should turn to Tarzan of the Apes, There are many striking parallels. For example, their native habitat is jungle. Further, Tarzan, like Kong, seems unable to find his generative organ, or, if he has found it, seems equally unable to divine its function. Hence in both cases a good deal of sublimated sexuality in the form of encounters with wild beasts. (A good question here is, how would Tarzan and Kong have gotten along? Perhaps they would have established what one critic has described as an innocent homosexual relationship. Can you imagine, for example, Kong and Tarzan floating down the Mississippi on a raft, sharing a perfect trust and understanding as well as naked moonlit swims under the stars?) But all this is really by the way, though not without a certain interest. What makes Tarzan of the Apes peculiarly interesting to me at the moment is his faculty of speech. Kong, for all his expressiveness, for all his frustrated flooding at the gates of articulation, is a dumb brute, whereas Tarzan has given utterance to several of our civilization's notable word and vowel configurations.

Take "HUNGAWA!" for example. (One is reminded, perhaps, of Eliot's "Hakagawa.") This is almost invariably the directive Tarzan gives to an elephant when a situation is critical. Miles off (down or up river), a young, frightened woman is about to be ripped into four pieces by bent saplings as lascivious sweating savages leer at her. (It is really very stupid of them, since all they can do afterwards is eat her.) But crashing through the bush on the tide of "HUNGAWA!" come Tarzan and his elephant (or sometimes elephants). She will be saved (though not won); the savages will scatter in jabbering fear as their meager huts are crushed by an elephant's foot. It would be a mistake, of course, to think that "HUNGAWA!" meant only "Hurry!" Sometimes it means "Push." And sometimes "Gather ye (elephants, beasts of the jungle, et cetera) round." On at least one occasion it was addressed to a lion and meant, roughly, "Cut it out! Behave yourself!" Upon (repeated) which,

the lion slunk off. In other words, context and tone (even repetition) are everything. One constant, though, is the imperative, the exclamatory. Urgency and command are always there. It is man's Ur-*cri* for crisis—in which man still feels the power to control. There would be something laughable in the businessman rushing by taxi to catch his train shouting "HUNGAWA!" (The cab driver would fix his wagon promptly.) But how appropriate for the astronaut at blast-off to scream "HUNGAWA!" to the TV audience. What a thrilling link of old and new.

Another notable expression of Tarzan's is the discovery, "Me Tarzan, you Jane." This is the quintessential boy meets girl. With the reservation that Tarzan does not know the generative function of his penis. It is quite likely that Jane does not either; otherwise she would learn to use "HUNGAWA!" for her own end. A horrendous scene would be Jane screaming "HUNGAWA!" like a fishwife at Tarzan and Tarzan scratching his head in befuddlement, as did Kong when he held the screaming blonde maiden in his fist for the first time. (Why is she screaming? What does she think I will do to her?) But Jane does not know about his penis. That is why she spends so much time swimming. But her relationship to elephants is significantly different from his. She obviously gets a different feeling from riding them than does Tarzan. It is not blatantly sexual, but quite clearly we would see nothing wrong with grape juice dripping down her chin while astride an elephant. Tarzan, on the other hand, never masturbates. He simply does not know it. Yet, contradictorily, we feel he disapproves of it (whatever it is), and speaks harshly to his household chimps when he catches them at it. Jane is probable more permissive* This slight difference in their natures would undoubtedly have pushed them to some

---

* We must also bear in mind, I think, that Jane is a barbarian American and Tarzan an Englishman, Lord Greystoke, to be precise. In whatever he does, there is a "natural outcropping of many generations of fine breeding, an hereditary instinct of graciousness which a lifetime of uncouth and savage training and environment could not eradicate" (*Tarzan of the Apes*, Chapter XX). Thus, though he may eat the raw meat of a lion he has just killed, his erections must in no way intrude, that is, rattle the teacups. There also, perhaps, just a *schmeck* of Anglophobia in having Jane, whose breeding is, after all, only acquired, civilize the apelike English lord.

domestic crisis in which Tarzan could not have shouted "HUNGAWA!" There would ultimately have to be a limit to the amount of swimming Jane could take, or flowers in her hair (what a clever game, that), or pineapple stuffed in her mouth, or tandem swinging through the trees. They are saved from this crisis by the discovery of Boy in the jungle. They have fulfilled the Biblical injunction and multiplied. Yet one senses some artificiality in all this. For example, "Me Tarzan, you Jane, him Boy" clearly does not have the epic rightness of the shorter phrase. Equally clearly, some accommodation has been made. And in this accommodation we have one of those mirror instances in which we see ourselves naked, so to speak. Because it is all right with us. We are content to have them find Boy in an overgrown cabbage patch. We *want* Jane to go on swimming and Tarzan to go on fighting crocodiles and renegade lions. Just as we do not want Kong to violate that blonde maiden, so too we do not want Tarzan to share carnal knowledge with Jane. Yet at the same time these are precisely what we do want. We want Kong to grow big and approach the blonde maiden with bloodshot, lustful eyes. Similarly, one day when Jane has arisen dripping from her swim and is awaiting her flower in the hair, we want Tarzan to rip off her garment and shout "HUNGAWA!" The elephants would undoubtedly come running but would not necessarily be a problem. Boy, in this event, would become the jungle's first juvenile delinquent; his reversion to abandonment would be too much after reigning as Tarzan's heir apparent. Perhaps he would seek his real father. Perhaps he would destroy Tarzan and Jane's first genital child. In sum, civilization would ensue. But this is not what happens. The balance is kept. Paradise is not lost. We have our cake and eat it, too, for in fantasy we penetrate the blonde maiden and Jane, are ravished by the vision of innocence outrageously, stupendously lost. Tarzan or Kong with erections are unthinkable, but somewhere in the furry depth, beneath that loincloth, they *lurk*, waiting to spring to life at our call. And at that moment, civilization will destroy itself, for we could not, in our finitude, in our infantilism, stand that much joy. We would go mad with it and run raging in the streets. Kong, because in effect he *wants* his erection, must be destroyed. Tarzan, the docile one, we allow to live. "HUNGAWA!" is no fit comparison for Kong's shrieks of rage on the Empire State Building as bullets pour into him. It is the pain and anger of all men in their betrayal. Deep within us we all cry out for the blonde maiden to violate, to plunge the very Empire State into her and achieve orgasm with the cosmos. But we do not, we cannot. We must content ourselves with a "HUNGAWA!" to the elephants and the lions, while Jane, sleek and wet (but ever clothed) with the lily-studded water, swims ever away, even as we join her and swim down, down into misty depths.

HOW BIG IS KONG'S PENIS?

In a recent meditation on King Kong and Tarzan of the Apes, I wrote the following: "We want Kong to grow big and approach the blonde maiden with bloodshot, lustful eyes." There are several interesting problems here. For example, Fay Wray, the blonde maiden, who is to say she is a maiden? (Actually, she is not even blonde.) When found by the impresario Carl Denham and taken to a waterfront café (read *dive*), she is alone and starving. She is down on her luck. She has come upon *bad times*. Denham clearly wants someone with nothing more to lose, and when he sees her there is a flash, or burst, of recognition. The cards, we can say, are pretty heavily stacked against maidenhood. Yet, surprisingly, Fay Wray *is* a maiden, which gives this adventure much of its fairy-tale quality. We know this from a scene that is not (and could not be) in the movie but which obviously had to take place. For years the island savages have been giving maidens to Kong. They are not going to break with tradition simply because Fay Wray is white. The whiteness is merely an added spice, or sauce. She must be maiden *and* white. The scene not included in the movie is that wherein the chief, the elders, and the midwives of the tribe examine a naked Fay Wray gynecologically. As all those black fingers probe and poke Fay Wray, she must be thinking that nothing can be worse than this, just as in the waterfront café she had thought she could sink no lower. How wrong she was and is. This limit to her imagination makes Kong's initial appearance all the more devastating. Kong is literally *beyond her wildest imaginings*. It is worth noting that Fay's first vision of Kong is an (arch) typical bride's first night fantasy of her husband. When Kong appears, Fay Wray is severed forever from the civilization that bred her. The unspeakable has become life. If her mind has not already been sprung by the savages' examination of her virgin body, it surely is now. She will never be the same. In any event, it is clear that the savages would not have offered her to Kong had they not been assured of her maidenhood. We could also adduce as proof the evidence of the first mate's love for her: his instinct would not have failed him: no *used* woman (and he surely knew them) could have aroused him to a pure love. But this is superfluous; the anthropological inference is conclusive enough.

A second interesting point in the quotation is the oblique reference to Kong's penis in the phrase "to grow big." Exactly how big *is* Kong's penis? It is a matter of monumental cultural and psychological interest. And a great mystery: for *Kong's penis is never shown; he is no common monkey in the zoo.* (Its abscence, of course, is the reason why it is dreamed about so much.) It is quite possible that Denham, before he leaves the island with Kong, emasculates him (in another unfilmed episode)* to assure his docility later on. (An interesting question here is, if this is so, what did the savages do with it or them? There is quite possibly an interesting totemic myth buried here.) That might well explain Kong's interest in the Empire State Building later on. Realizing that he is without his penis or its generative power (in fact or in his mind—for his defeat and humiliation at Denham's hands may well have resulted in a psychological emasculation, a temporary impotence), and that there is something he cannot do with Fay Wray without it, he seeks to attach another penis to himself. Here his ape brain reveals itself. (Question: Does Fay Wray have any inkling of what Kong intends? Probably, though only an inkling. Kong constantly shatters the limits of her nightmares. He plunges her from one insanity into another—but who is to say that heaven itself is not awaiting her within that final, absolute, insanity?) If this is so, we might well accuse Kong of certain immodesty. A penis (even erect) the size of the Empire State Building? But we cannot be sure, for we have never seen it. There is, however, some slight indirect evidence of size. When Kong storms the walls that separate him from the savages, seeking his stolen maiden, with what does he batter them? It is definitely a possibility. But still, not Empire State dimension, not even the upper dome. We can only put *that* gesture down to a rage beyond all reason.

Which still leaves us with the problem of Kong's penis. There is, of course, the peculiar behavior of Kong from the beginning. He obviously does not ravish Fay Wray immediately. He is not even sexually curious about her. How are we to explain his early *playfulness* with her and his later *libidinous determination?* (He has not chosen the Empire State idly.) The answer, I think, is to be found in his age. Kong, up through his island adventures with Fay, is a child. He sees her merely as a new and unusual plaything. (What has happened to his earlier playthings is problematical. As I have indicated elsewhere, I lean toward the idea that he ate them.) But, during his voyage to America (possibly even just before the voyage, if we bear the wall-battering in mind), he arrives at puberty,

and in America he is a young adult—hence his altered interest in Fay. But now there is no penis or penis power with which to effect his end. Part of his problem (assuming Denham's butchery, which we need not) is that he very likely has little recollection of his penis and what its varying aspects were. (Question: *Did Kong ever masturbate?*) He is also unsettled from the sea voyage, the gas, and the total change in environment. Hence his berserk casting about for a substitute.

But *we* need not be equally at sea. A simple scientific approach will give us at least a reasonable working hypothesis. One of Kong's first destructive acts in the New World is the wrecking of an elevated train and its track. The track is about twenty feet off the ground and reaches Kong's shoulders. Kong therefore must be about twenty-four feet tall. Further, we can usually count on a six-foot man having a three-inch inert and six-inch erect penis. Assuming the validity of comparative anatomy, we can say therefore that Kong's penis would be twelve inches inert and twenty-four inches, or two feet, erect. And this is a startling fact. Because it really doesn't seem so very big. Even its fatness would not increase its shock impact, for the fatter it is, the *shorter* it would seem. Possibly it is some horrendous blue or purple, or pointed, or wickedly curved—but even these would have limited shock value. A more experienced woman than Fay might even, *momentarily and in spite of herself,* entertain the thought of what it would be like. So we are left with this fact: that the penis Kong ought to have is insufficient to cause the terror and anxiety he inspires. Therefore the penis Kong has is the one he *ought not* to have. Of course one can suggest that the horror of Kong is in his size *in general,* that is, a twenty-four-foot ape—but only to reject it. For the entire drama of Kong is not built around his general size or destructiveness but around his relationship with Fay Wray. And the entire point of this relationship is that it is male and female, and that it aspires to the condition of consummation! The only question—and it harbors an anxiety that reaches into the very depth of our civilization—is *When?* When will Kong's twenty-four-inch erect penis penetrate the white and virgin (and quivering) body of Fay Wray? And there, of course, we have the solution. It is easily conceivable that in these circumstances some people, perhaps many, would say, "Who cares?" Precisely. Twenty-four inches is not *that* awe-inspiring. But people say no such thing. *It is obvious that Kong must exceed the estimates of comparative anatomy to inspire the universal dread that he does.*

Kong's penis, therefore, is at least six feet inert and twelve feet erect (or seventy-two and one hundred and forty-four inches respectively). In a state of sexual

---

* Dare I suggest how admirable this scene, as well as the earlier one between Fay Wray and the savages, would be, today, in Technicolor or Vista-Vision?

excitement it very likely rises over his head. *That* would certainly explain the battering at the savages' wall, and it certainly explains the terror in New York City's streets: a twenty-four-foot ape with a twelve-foot erection stalking the streets for this woman. The blasé mode is simply not possible in the face of such a Kong. No experience is equal to it. There is no room for wonder, only fear. And so, in the end, when Kong, half-crazed by the bullets and frustrations he has experienced, identifies sexually with the Empire State Building, he is not, after all, being immodest. He has sought only what all true lovers seek, in the only way that he could. He has brought his love to the threshold of his love and valiantly persevered to his last desperate breath. Dazed beyond recall, so near and yet so far, he loosens his grip, his fingers slip. No longer can he guide his newfound power into her. Kong cannot live erect in the New World. And uttering a last terrifying cry from within his battered heart (who will ever forget it?), he falls, falls ever so far, perhaps momentarily remembering the lushness of his island paradise, wet from dew in the silent and foggy primeval morning, falls to his cold and concrete death. In truth, as Carl Denham mutters, Fay Wray hath killed the beast.

THE MIND AND THE HEART OF FAY WRAY

It is clear to me that far too little attention has been paid to Fay Wray, the love of King Kong. Not only is her experience terrifying and transcendental (*sublime*, as Burke would have it), but it is also not lost on her. When Kong dies, Fay Wray knows that no other lover in her life will be equal to him. She may not be able to articulate the changes that have placed her beyond merely human experiences, but she has absorbed them, she is alive and (psychologically) whole: she has confronted King Kong and received his blessing among an alien breed. She will henceforth dwell among them but not be *of* them. Had she experienced sexual union with Kong, she would (also) have been omnipotent and omniscient. In this essay I should like to discuss several aspects of her psychopsychical journey.

THE DISAPPEARING BOTTOM

When we first encounter Fay Wray, she is the most ordinary of women, except in one respect. She has fallen down the socioeconomic ladder. Her attitude at this point is that little, if anything, worse can happen to her. She has touched bottom. What makes her different from other girls is that instead of laughing at Carl Denham's crackpot offer she eagerly ac-

cepts it. This decision is focal: all things come from it. It is a decision that reflects deeply on her character. However, this decision is also the beginning of a series of false states of mind. For at the moment Fay Wray decides in favor of Denham's proposal, she thinks that she is rising from the bottom. In fact, the bottom has just dropped, and she is falling further. She reaches the new bottom when the island savages seize her (we shall examine this in detail later). For now we can say that once more Fay Wray thinks nothing could be worse, but in fact the bottom has again dropped and she is falling. (It is part of Fay's destiny always to have her worst expectations exceeded.) She reaches a new low when, tied to the stake outside the savages' protective barrier, she hears and then sees King Kong for the first time. At this point, being down and out in a waterfront café must seem like heaven to her. Although she is conscious here of things being worse than they were with the savages, she knows that they are probably going to get still worse when Kong actually reaches her. Death, of course, will be the absolute bottom, and she cannot face it; she faints. When she comes to, she realizes that Kong perhaps has other ideas, and once more the bottom has dropped: she now faces a fate worse than death.* She exists in this extreme anxiety until she is rescued. Again the feeling of rising from the bottom. Then Kong returns for her (some brief anxiety), is subdued by Denham, and carried to the New World. Fay Wray has, apparently, reached *the* bottom and come back to tell the tale. Although she must undoubtedly be psychologically wary, she is relieved, she relaxes, she feels it is all over. She is about to resume her former life, but on a higher socioeconomic plane. And then the bottom drops again: Kong escapes, finds her, and takes her to the top of the Empire State Building.

Kong and the Empire State Building: the meeting of two giants. (Which one will get Fay?) Kong is on the verge of a great symbolic act. He will ram the Empire State into Fay as if it were (as in a sense it is) his very own. It is a desperate, noble, futile, tragic attempt on a par with Ahab's defiance of his finitude. But Ahab's attempt, while broadly human, is entirely personal (monomaniacal, as his first mate realizes). Kong's attempt is personal, yet, but it is also grandly humanitarian, an attempt to reunite two worlds God

---

* Or, to be more correct, cf. E. R. Burroughs' *Tarzan of the Apes*, Chapter XIX, when Terkoz, the deposed ape leader, bends Jane Porter to his "awful fangs": "But ere they touched that fair skin another mood claimed the anthropoid. The tribe had kept his women. He must find others to replace them. This hairless white ape would be the first of his new household, and so he threw her roughly across his broad hairy shoulders and leaped back into the trees, bearing Jane Porter away toward *a fate a thousand times worse than death.*" [my italics]

127

never meant to be separate. However, it is too late. Any progeny of such a union could be only monstrous (or totally holy, which would be monstrous). The distance is too great; time has become too irrevocable. Here Kong seems not so much apelike as he does innocent. Here we take him most to our hearts. He is, like Prometheus, Satan, and Faust, one of myth's great losers. (Or, in more recent times, winners.) For raising the specter of what has been so poignantly lost (and forgotten), he must be viciously cut down. Civilization has too much riding on its Empire State to give it up.

It is entirely to Fay Wray's credit that at the end, she has an inkling on some level of the nobility of Kong (he is not called King for nothing), and of the tragedy of his fall. At any point in this odyssey Fay Wray could, of course, have gone mad. And she has that option now. I obviously do not think she exercises it. The Kong experience has, let me repeat, consistently destroyed her notions of what the worst could possibly be. Its effect has been to instill the idea that things coud always be worse, that the bottom could (is) always open. For most people, the idea of an absolute bottom is necessary; the idea of a continually receding bottom is too great an anxiety. But it may well be the beginning of true wisdom. When Kong finally lies dead (Question: Will—can—Kong ever die?) on the pavement, it would be easy for Fay Wray to think, "It's over at last," and go about her business. I do not believe that is her thought. If it were, she would still be a very ordinary girl. But she is much more pensive. True, Kong is (seems) dead. It (the nightmare) is (seems) over. But she looks at him more like a lover. Not a lover in flesh any longer: a lover in spirit. Somehow, she senses, Kong's death is tragic. And part of its tragic quality is that Kong, in addition to being her lover, has been her teacher—but an unearthly, transcendental, metaphysical teacher. He has exploded her forever out of all possible human complacency, and there at the extreme of anxiety she has found peace, a peace that removes her from the ken of almost all other humans. Kong is dead, but Kong lives in Fay Wray. And if one does not know this, one does not know Fay Wray.

THE EXAMINATION

Before Fay Wray is offered to Kong, the savages ascertain that she is a virgin and therefore worthy of being offered. This is done by an examination. The examination is conducted by the chief, the elders, and the midwives of the tribe. It is even conceivable that the entire tribe is witness. At any rate, Fay Wray is stripped and laid bare on a (bamboo?) platform in a fire-lit hut. Her legs are forced apart, and black fingers

probe, pull, and manipulate her. God only knows what she imagines is going to happen. No doubt she yearns for the good old days on the waterfront. The savages are curious about her in general, and in spite of the business at hand they must be oohing and ahing over peripheral matters like her pale nipples (are they erect?), her skin, and her corn-silk pubic hairs, some of which they pluck (why?). Fay Wray has never been so naked, so exposed, so manhandled in her life. Being lower class she has never even had a gynecological examination. She is, in spite of herself of course, phantasmagorically titillated.

Two important things are happening here. The first is that Fay Wray is feeling totally abandoned by her world. She could not, at that moment, be further away from it. Nothing in her experience has prepared her for this. Dialogue, for example, is impossible. Imagine, if you will, the total inefficacy of, say, "What are you doing?" or "Please, you're hurting me." Not even the females look familiar to her or reachable. Everything is strange. Her thoughts, her sensations, are new. Needless to say, she also feels existentially abandoned, by her god. Where can God be if there are black fingers in her private parts? This aspect of her experience is to be repeated in the jungle with Kong (during, in effect, their honeymoon) when Kong battles prehistoric creatures (How does one react to real pterodactyls trying to eat one up?) An interesting juxtaposition for her must be the occasion when Kong and her first-rate lover are present and a Tyrannosaurus rex attacks. How ineffective and remote must seem the strengths and values of her society then. It is Kong who saves her by killing the lizard.*

The second important function of this episode is that by deranging her from the usual and the known it is preparing her for Kong, a still further derangement. Her despair becomes manageable in part by its gradual escalation. Nevertheless, one must see that in the end Fay has been staggeringly prepared. It is difficult to say whether Fay knows how much depends on her being a virgin. Had she been an experienced woman, the savages might simply have eaten her outright. In this one respect, her American upbringing has saved her for the greater experience of Kong. As low as she had fallen in America, she had not fallen so low as to sell the precious jewel of herself (eloquent testimony to America's higher standards of living). Poor but pure is an adequate description of the Fay that Carl Denham propositions for Kong.

---

* It is interesting, by way of comparison, to note that when Tarzan rescues the prim and proper Jane Porter by killing the concupiscent ape Terkoz, she springs forward, suddenly the primeval woman, and embraces and kisses him with panting lips. (Tarzan of the Apes, Chapter XIX) Fay has no such reversion.

FAY AND KONG'S PENIS

Fay's attitude toward Kong's penis is a ticklish problem. On the one hand there is the purely bestial part of it (the lesser part, we might say). On the other, there are the several metaphorical tensions. Let us take them in order. Fay, the rather ordinary virgin of the masses, is terrified of Kong's penis, which is huge. No normal girl wants to make love with a giant gorilla. (Yet, how often will a woman describe her lover affectionately as a "big gorilla" or a "hairy ape"?) But Fay, the woman of wisdom through nightmare, is aware that the loss of Kong's penis, although it would probably have killed her as it thrilled her, is tragic. It is a loss that will haunt her all her life. She grows from one woman into the other as she sees Kong change from monster supreme to victim supreme. Kong begins as horror and ends as martyr, and in the process his penis is humanized (tenderized). The impossible union between Fay and Kong is symbolic of mankind's fatal *impasse*, the dream of paradise lost irrevocably.* However, this particular symbolic inference is complicated by several other factors, notably the idea that Kong is the black man violating American womanhood and the idea that Kong is the emerging (and rampant) Third World nations. With the first we suffer from colossal penis envy and ego collapse, for we sense Fay's attraction in spite of herself. In the latter, we have violated Kong's sanctuary and brought him back for profit and display, and now he threatens (literally) to screw us. Kong is the classic myth of racist and imperialist repression and anxiety. Carl Denham is the white entrepreneur *par excellence*. Like Rappaccini in his noxious garden, he fosters evil into being. His manipulation of Fay and Kong for sideshow profit and fame is instinctive. He is also stupid. Confronted with tragedy of epic magnitude, he mutters nasally that Beauty killed the Beast. Kong's sex organ (seen, dreamed, inferred, or guessed at) is indicative of our fear of his creative energy. Our destruction of him is confession of our limited imagination. His death will weigh on us more heavily than his life, and it is part of his power that he will be continuously resurrected (by us, in fact).

Fay has come to this knowledge, and it is only in her faith in Kong and his memory that there is any hope for all of us. In these respects, we can say that Kong leaps sexually erect into New York City's streets directly from our nightmares of guilt. We have created him and can no longer awaken from him. Denham is our blundering and loud middleman. And Fay is our

vulnerability in a nutshell. Her yielding to Kong, spiritually if not physically, is felt as a betrayal. But a betrayal we ourselves *will*. (We *are* ambivalent about her and Kong.) Hence a frequently suicidal madness that engulfs us. Given time, Fay in her understanding might well have come to love Kong physically, might well have accommodated herself (as the sex books tell us) to Kong's penis. But there is no time. Kong is killed and split into millions of Kongs. And they are coming at us without quarter.

The idea of Kong leading a rat charge on New York City is entirely reasonable. For Americans, rats and cockroaches and bedbugs (vermin) are the living presence of the dark-skinned hordes, the *teeming* masses which spread themselves like crud over the face of the earth. Which is why, of course, the lower we go on the socio-ethno-economic ladder, the less we worry about them (i.e., vermin): they *belong*. A recent eruption of rats on Park Avenue caused matrons to pee in their pants and call the police. The mayor of New York peed in *his* pants when it was discovered that welfare people (epi-vermin) were living in the Waldorf Astoria (something like finding a rat using your toothbrush). By the same token, our hygienic mode is an attempt to keep America safe (pure). If ever the cockroaches and their brethren get out of hand, the *others* will not be far behind. But spick-and-span as our bathrooms are, we can never lose the awareness of all that dank plumbing in the cellar. Where *do* the pipes (finally) go? What conspiracy is happening down there in the sewers? We can never totally lose our anxiety about sitting on the toilet because when the invasion comes, there is where we are vulnerable: a black hand reaching up from the toilet bowl and grabbing our testicles when we are most unprepared. Our behaviorists, meanwhile, allay our fears by telling us all rats can be taught to drink tea. They literally have rats on the brain. Behavioral psychology is the last refuge of the imperialist.

KONG AS TOAD

And now we come to the fairy-tale aspects of the Kong legend. There is, of course, a great deal of charm in the Kong-Fay Wray romance. Consider, for example, the vapidity of Fay Wray before her discovery of Kong. She swallows Denham's tale whole and fantasizes on the purely meretricious glory that will be hers. Any girl with half a brain would have sent Denham packing. But through Kong, Fay Wray becomes a *woman* (*King Kong* is in many ways a *portrait*). She develops a depth of understanding about the nature of life that comes close to being wisdom. Her silences are no longer blank. She is *transformed*, though not at

---
* I think that somewhere in the Kong story (I am not sure where) there is a moment (but only a moment) when all *does* seem possible, even Paradise. (Cf. the double vision of America at the end of *The Great Gatsby*.)

all in the way she first envisioned. We tend to lose sight of this change in her because of all the *noise* (violence) and Kong's dramatic end. But if we concentrate on other aspects of the Kong story, we can begin to see these other possibilties.

For example, his *playfulness*. Even when Kong kills, there is often an element of playfulness in it. He seems more a petulant child than a savage beast. When in the beginning he clutches a writhing Fay Wray in his fist and she is screaming, he cocks his head and looks puzzled, as if to say, "Now what the devil is the matter with this funny little mouse?" When he plucks the screaming woman from her bed and drops her to the street, he is the child who is dropping his toy because it is the wrong one. Even when he is enraged by the sperm bullets the planes shoot into him at the end, he is the child who doesn't understand *why* he is being abused, *why* he is feeling pain. There is more puzzlement than animosity in him.

What I am saying here is that there is a colossal innocence in Kong that exists ostensibly in the midst of much evil: Kong has no awareness of doing bad things. We must learn to see and understand that. In this respect his inarticulateness is a reinforcement: Kong cannot speak because he is *too young*. But it is even more than that. The words *too young* do not mean, or say, enough. They only shadow, are emblematic. Kong is, in a sense, pre-experience; he is *prior* to experience and the consciousness that it implies. Articulation is the (deceiving) tool of civilization. Further, Kong very often seems on the *edge of articulation*. He seems often about to *tumble* into speech. But he does not. And he does not because he is *imprisoned*. With his arms, especially with his eyes, he reaches out constantly. His eyes are, in fact, the eyes of the lifelong prisoner. They plead, they cry, they scream—but they do not speak.

And the question for us is, first, who is behind those eyes? who is imprisoned within Kong? And second, what is it that will free him? (Perhaps there is a third: *should* he be freed?) The second is, I think, best answered first, because it is very easy to answer. In the familiar story, the princess kisses the frog and he becomes a handsome prince. The kiss I think we may understand to be merely symbolic. In the Kong epic, the kiss would be insignificant. Fay Wray's head would easily fit in Kong's mouth. None of the film's anxieties relate to kissing. No, what is needed to free Kong is for Fay Wray to give herself sexually to Kong out of love and trust. That alone would allow Kong to break through. That she does not do it is part of the tragedy of the story. Although Fay Wray does arrive at a deepness of womanhood at the end, it is a deepness with nowhere to go. She *understands* but now there is no application possible. She is the living memorial of the tragedy of loss. But just what would Kong have been freed into? *Who* is imprisoned within Kong?

That is a difficult question. It is obvious that no mere beast provoked such a depth of response in Fay and others, but rather the *intimations of something other*, within, something frightening, incredible, even transcendent. Otherwise we should not weep for Kong, as we do; his death would not be tragic, as it is. Perhaps Kong is twice or even thrice enchanted, that is, sexual union with Fay would only turn him into a frog, so to speak, leaving her with another ordeal, or several. (Could faith be more severely tried?) For all the change that her encounter with Kong has provoked, Fay has, in one sense, only been *prepared* for the real change, which can come only as the result of one thing. Kong's death leaves her imprisoned as well as him—but with a deep awareness of the change she can now never experience. I don't think that Kong would turn into a handsome prince as a result of union with Fay. Nor do I think that he would turn into, say, a dwarf or a pumpkin, though the ramifications are increasing. Perhaps he would just expire beautifully, or disappear, and it would all be with the seed (so large) he would leave in Fay. Jesus, son of Kong! Or something like. Fay, then, would become the bearer of mankind's redemption. A chance to regain Paradise. For surely Adam in the Garden is *not* so remote from Kong. Would not he, too, have been inarticulate with confusion and rage in the New World? Would not he, too, have been cornered atop the Empire State Building for daring to walk the streets with his penis erect? His affront to civilization would never have been tolerated. Sometimes I think that Kong should be opera. What grand arias Kong would have. But even opera is not *big* enough. Who, in voice, could project the edifice of Kong's gigantic penis? And what a stage would be needed. Alas, in our heads the drama remains. Kong *is* godlike in his unprogenitured existence. That jungle has *always* known Kong. We cannot say Kong, son of. We can only say Kong *is* and Kong *was*. And therein lie much history and sorrow.

AFTER KING KONG FELL*

Philip José Farmer

The first half of the movie was grim and gray and somewhat tedious. Mr. Howller did not mind. That was, after all, realism. Those times had been grim and gray. Moreover, behind the tediousness was the promise of something vast and horrifying. The creeping pace and the measured ritualistic movements of the actors gave intimations of the workings of the gods. Unhurriedly, but with utmost confidence, the gods were directing events toward the climax.

Mr. Howller had felt that at the age of fifteen, and he felt it now while watching the show on TV at the age of fifty-five. Of course, when he first saw it in 1933, he had known what was coming. Hadn't he lived through some of the events only two years before that?

The old freighter, the *Wanderer*, was nosing blindly through the fog toward the surflike roar of the natives' drums. And then: the commercial. Mr. Howller rose and stepped into the hall and called down the steps loudly enough for Jill to hear him on the front porch. He thought, commercials could be a blessing. They give us time to get into the bathroom or the kitchen, or time to light up a cigarette and decide about continuing to watch this show or go on to that show.

And why couldn't real life have its commercials?

Wouldn't it be something to be grateful for if reality stopped in mid-course while the Big Salesman made His pitch? The car about to smash into you, the bullet on its way to your brain, the first cancer cell about to break loose, the boss reaching for the phone to call you in so he can fire you, the spermatozoon about to be launched toward the ovum, the final insult about to be hurled at the once, and perhaps still, beloved, the final drink of alcohol which would rupture the abused blood vessel, the decision which would lead to the light that would surely fail?

If only you could step out while the commercial interrupted these, think about it, talk about it, and then, returning to the set, switch it to another channel.

But that one is having technical difficulties, and the one after that is a talk show whose guest is the archangel Gabriel himself and after some urging by the host he agrees to blow his trumpet, and . . .

Jill entered, sat down, and began to munch the cookies and drink the lemonade he had prepared for her. Jill was six and a half years old and beautiful, but then what granddaughter wasn't beautiful? Jill was also unhappy because she had just quarreled with her best friend, Amy, who had stalked off with threats never to see Jill again. Mr. Howller reminded her that this had happened before and that Amy always came back the next day, if not sooner. To take her mind off Amy, Mr. Howller gave her a brief outline of what had happened in the movie. Jill listened without enthusiasm, but she became excited enough once the movie had resumed. And when Kong was feeling over the edge of the abyss for John Driscoll, played by Bruce Cabot, she got into her grandfather's lap. She gave a little scream and put her hands over her eyes when Kong carried Ann Darrow into the jungle (Ann played by Fay Wray).

But by the time Kong lay dead on Fifth Avenue, she was rooting for him, as millions had before her. Mr. Howller squeezed her and kissed her and said, "When your mother was about your age, I took her to see this. And when it was over, she was crying, too."

Jill sniffled and let him dry the tears with his handkerchief. When the Roadrunner cartoon came on, she got off his lap and went back to her cookie-munching. After a while she said, "Grandpa, the coyote falls off the cliff so far you can't even see him. When he hits, the whole earth shakes. But he always comes back, good as new. Why can he fall so far and not get hurt? Why couldn't King Kong fall and be just like new?"

Her grandparents and her mother have explained many times the distinction between a "live" and a "taped" show. It did not seem to make any difference how many times they explained. Somehow, in the years of watching TV, she had gotten the fixed idea that people in "live" shows actually suffered pain, sorrow, and death. The only shows she could endure seeing were those that her elders labeled as "taped."

This worried Mr. Howller more than he admitted to his wife and daughter. Jill was a very bright child, but what if too many TV shows at too early an age had done her some irreparable harm? What if, a few years from now, she could easily see, and even define, the distinction between reality and unreality on the screen but deep down in her there was a child that still could not distinguish?

"You know that the Roadrunner is a series of pictures that move. People draw pictures, and people can do anything with pictures. So the Roadrunner is drawn again and again, and he's back in the next show with his wounds all healed and he's ready to make a jackass of himself again."

"A jackass? But he's a coyote."

"Now . . ."

Mr. Howller stopped. Jill was grinning.

"O.K., now you're pulling my leg."

"But is King Kong alive or is he taped?"

"Taped. Like the Disney I took you to see last week. *Bedknobs and Broomsticks.*"

"Then *King Kong* didn't happen?"

"Oh, yes, it really happened. But this is a movie they made about King Kong after what really happened was all over. So it's not exactly like it really was, and actors took the parts of Ann Darrow and Carl Denham and all the others. Except King Kong himself. He was a toy model."

Jill was silent for a minute and then she said, "You mean, there really *was* a King Kong? How do you know, Grandpa?"

"Because I was there in New York when Kong went on his rampage. I was in the theater when he broke loose, and I was in the crowd that gathered around Kong's body after he fell off the Empire State Building. I was thirteen then, just seven years older than you are now. I was with my parents, and they were visiting my Aunt Thea. She was beautiful, and she had golden hair just like Fay Wray's—I mean, Ann Darrow's. She'd married a very rich man, and they had a big apartment high up in the clouds. In the Empire State Building itself."

"High up in the clouds! That must've been fun, Grandpa!"

It would have been, he thought, if there had not been so much tension in that apartment. Uncle Nate and Aunt Thea should have been happy because they were so rich and lived in such a swell place. But they weren't. No one said anything to young Tim Howller, but he felt the suppressed anger, heard the bite of tone, and saw the tightening lips. His aunt and uncle were having trouble of some sort, and his parents were upset by it. But they all tried to pretend everything was as sweet as honey when he was around.

Young Howller had been eager to accept the pretense. He didn't like to think that anybody could be mad at his tall, blonde, and beautiful aunt. He was passionately in love with her; he ached for her in the daytime; at nights he had fantasies about her of which he was ashamed when he awoke. But not for long. She was a thousand times more desirable than Fay Wray or Claudette Colbert or Elissa Landi.

But that night, when they were all going to see the première of *The Eighth Wonder of the World*, King Kong himself, young Howller had managed to ignore whatever it was that was bugging his elders. And even they seemed to be having a good time. Uncle Nate, over his parents' weak protests, had purchased orchestra seats for them. These were twenty dollars apiece, big money in Depression days, enough to feed a family for a month. Everybody got all dressed up, and Aunt Thea looked too beautiful to be real. Young Howller was so excited that he thought his heart was going to climb up and out through his throat. For days the newspapers had been full of stories about King Kong—speculations, rather, since Carl Denham wasn't telling them much. And he, Tim Howller, would be one of the lucky few to see the monster first.

Boy, wait until he got back to the kids in seventh grade at Bucyrus, Illinois! Would their eyes ever pop when he told them all about it!

But his happiness was too good to last. Aunt Thea suddenly said she had a headache and couldn't possibly go. Then she and Uncle Nate went into their bedroom, and even in the front room, three rooms and a hallway distant, young Tim could hear their voices. After a while Uncle Nate, slamming doors behind him, came out. He was red-faced and scowling, but he wasn't going to call the party off. All four of them, very uncomfortable and silent, rode in a taxi to the theater on Times Square. But when they got inside, even Uncle Nate forgot the quarrel or at least he seemed to. There was the big stage with its towering silvery curtains and through the curtains came a vibration of excitement and of delicious danger. And even through the curtains the hot hairy ape-stink filled the theater.

"Did King Kong get loose just like in the movie?" Jill said.

Mr. Howller started. "What? Oh, yes, he sure did. Just like in the movie."

"Were you scared, Grandpa? Did you run away like everybody else?"

He hesitated. Jill's image of her grandfather had been cast in a heroic mold. To her he was a giant of Herculean strength and perfect courage, her defender and champion. So far he had managed to live up to the image, mainly because the demands she made were not too much for him. In time she would see the cracks and the sawdust oozing out. But she was too young to disillusion now.

"No, I didn't run," he said. "I waited until the theater was cleared of the crowd.

This was true. The big man who'd been sitting in the seat before him had leaped up yelling as Kong began tearing the bars out of his cage, had whirled and jumped over the back of his seat, and his knee had hit young Howller on the jaw. And so young Howller had been stretched out senseless on the floor under the seats while the mob screamed and tore each other and trampled the fallen.

Later he was glad that he had been knocked out. It gave him a good excuse for not keeping cool, for not acting heroically in the situation. He knew that if he had not been unconscious, he would have been as frenzied as the others, and he would have abandoned his parents, thinking only in his terror of his own salvation. Of course, his parents had deserted him, though they claimed that they had been swept away from him by the mob. This *could* be true; maybe his folks *had* actually tried to get to him. But he had not really thought they had, and for years he had looked down on them because of their flight. When he got older, he realized that he would have done the same thing, and he knew that his contempt for them was really a disguised contempt for himself.

He had awakened with a sore jaw and a headache. The police and the ambulance men were there and starting to take care of the hurt and to haul away the dead. He staggered past them out into the lobby and, not seeing his parents there, went outside. The sidewalks and the streets were plugged with thousands of men, women, and children, on foot and in cars, fleeing northward.

He had not known where Kong was. He should have been able to figure it out, since the frantic mob was leaving the midtown part of Manhattan. But he could think of only two things. Where were his parents? And was Aunt Thea safe? And then he had a third thing to consider. He discovered that he had wet his pants. When he had seen the great ape burst loose, he had wet his pants.

Under the circumstances, he should have paid no attention to this. Certainly no one else did. But he was a very sensitive and shy boy of thirteen, and, for some reason, the need for getting dry underwear and trousers seemed even more important than finding his parents. In retrospect he would tell himself that he would have gone south anyway. But he knew deep down that if his pants had not been wet he might not have dared return to the Empire State Building.

It was impossible to buck the flow of the thousands moving like lava up Broadway. He went east on 43rd Street until he came to Fifth Avenue, where he started southward. There was a crowd to fight against here, too, but it was much smaller than that on Broadway. He was able to thread his way through it, though he often had to go out into the street and dodge the cars. These, fortunately, were not able to move faster than about three miles an hour.

"Many people got impatient because the cars wouldn't go faster," he told Jill, "and they just abandoned them and struck out on foot."

"Wasn't it noisy, Grandpa?"

"Noisy? I've never heard such noise. I think that everyone in Manhattan, except those hiding under the beds, was yelling or talking. And every driver in Manhattan was blowing his car's horn. And then there were the sirens of the fire trucks and police cars and ambulances. Yes, it was noisy."

Several times he tried to stop a fugitive so he could find out what was going on. But even when he did succeed in halting someone for a few seconds, he couldn't make himself heard. By then, as he found out later, the radio had broadcast the news. Kong had chased John Driscoll and Ann Darrow out of the theater and across the street to their hotel. They had gone up to Driscoll's room, where they thought they were safe. But Kong had climbed up, using windows as ladder steps, reaching into the room, knocked Driscoll out, grabbed Ann, and then leaped away with her. He had headed, as Carl Denham figured he would, toward the tallest structure on the island. On King Kong's own island, he lived on the highest point, Skull Mountain, where he was truly monarch of all he surveyed. Here he would climb to the top of the Empire State Building, Manhattan's Skull Mountain.

Tim Howller had not known this, but he was able to infer that Kong had traveled down Fifth Avenue from 38th Street on. He passed a dozen cars with their tops flattened down by the ape's fist or turned over on their sides or tops. He saw three sheet-covered bodies on the sidewalks, and he overheard a policeman telling a reporter that Kong had climbed up several buildings on his way south and reached into windows and pulled people out and thrown them down onto the pavement.

"But you said King Kong was carrying Ann Darrow in the crook of his arm, Grandpa," Jill said. "He only had one arm to climb with, Grandpa, so . . . so wouldn't he fall off the building when he reached in to grab those poor people?"

"A very shrewd observation, my little chickadee," Mr. Howller said, using the W. C. Fields voice that usually sent her into giggles. "But his arms were long enough for him to drape Ann Darrow over the arm he used to hang on with while he reached in with the other. And to forestall your next question, even if you had not thought of it, he could turn over an automobile with only one hand."

"But . . . but why'd he take time out to do that if he wanted to get to the top of the Empire State Building?"

"I don't know why *people* often do the things they do," Mr. Howller said. "So how would I know why an ape does the things he does?"

When he was a block away from the Empire State, a plane crashed onto the middle of the avenue two blocks behind him and burned furiously. Tim Howller watched it for a few minutes, then he looked upward and saw the red and green lights of the five planes and the silvery bodies slipping in and out of the searchlights.

"Five airplanes, Grandpa? But the movie . . ."

"Yes, I know. The movie showed about fourteen or fifteen. But the book says that there were six to begin with, and the book is much more accurate. The movie also shows King Kong's last stand taking place in the daylight. But it didn't; it was still nighttime."

The Army Air Force plane must have been going at least 250 mph as it dived down toward the giant ape standing on the top of the observation tower. Kong had put Ann Darrow by his feet so he could hang on to the tower with one hand and grab out with the other at the planes. One had come too close, and he had seized the left biplane structure and ripped it off. Given the energy of the plane, his hand should have been torn off, too, or at least he should have been pulled loose from his hold on the tower and gone down with the plane. But he hadn't let loose, and that told something of the enormous strength of that towering body. It also told something of the relative fragility of the biplane.

Young Howller had watched the efforts of the firemen to extinguish the fire and then he had turned back toward the Empire State Building. By then it was all over. All over for King Kong, anyway. It was, in after years, one of Mr. Howller's greatest regrets that he had not seen the monstrous dark body falling through the beams of the searchlights—blackness, then the flash of blackness through the whiteness of the highest beam, blackness, the flash through the next beam, blackness, the flash through the lowest beam. Dot, dash, dot, dash, Mr. Howller was to think afterward. A code transmitted unconsciously by the great ape and received unconsciously by those who witnessed the fall. Or by those who would hear of it and think about it. Or was he going too far in conceiving this? Wasn't he always looking for codes? And, when he found them, unable to decipher them?

Since he had been thirteen, he had been trying to equate the great falls in man's myths and legends and to find some sort of intelligence in them. The fall of the tower of Babel, of Lucifer, of Vulcan, of Icarus, and, finally, of King Kong. But he wasn't equal to the task; he didn't have the genius to perceive what the falls meant, he couldn't screen out the—to use an electronic term—the "noise." All he could come up with were folk adages. What goes up must come down. The bigger they are, the harder they fall.

"What'd you say, Grandpa?"

"I was thinking out loud, if you can call that thinking," Mr. Howller said.

Young Howller had been one of the first on the scene, and so he got a place in the front of the crowd. He had not completely forgotten his parents or Aunt Thea, but the danger was over, and he could not make himself leave to search for them. And he had even forgotten about his soaked pants. The body was only about thirty feet from him. It lay on its back on the sidewalk, just as in the movie. But the dead Kong did not look as big or as dignified as in the movie. He was spread out more like an apeskin rug than a body, and blood and bowels and their contents had splashed out around him.

After a while Carl Denham, the man responsible for capturing Kong and bringing him to New York, appeared. As in the movie, Denham spoke his classical lines by the body: "It was Beauty. As always, Beauty killed the Beast."

This was the most appropriately dramatic place for the lines to be spoken, of course, and the proper place to end the movie.

But the book had Denham speaking these lines as he leaned over the parapet of the observation tower to look down at Kong on the sidewalk. His only audience was a police sergeant.

Both the book and the movie were true. Or half true. Denham did speak those lines way up on the 102nd floor of the tower. But, showman that he was, he also spoke them when he got down to the sidewalk, where the newsmen could hear them.

Young Howller didn't hear Denham's remarks. He was too far away. Besides, at that moment he felt a tap on his shoulder and heard a man say, "Hey, kid, there's somebody trying to get your attention!"

Young Howller went into his mother's arms and wept for at least a minute. His father reached past his mother and touched him briefly on the forehead, as if blessing him, and then gave his shoulder a squeeze. When he was able to talk, Tim Howller asked his mother what had happened to them. They, as near as they could remember, had been pushed out by the crowd, though they had fought to get to him, and had run up Broadway after they found themselves in the street because King Kong had appeared. They had managed to get back to the theater, had not been able to locate Tim, and had walked back to the Empire State Building.

"What happened to Uncle Nate?" Tim said.

Uncle Nate, his mother said, had caught up with them on Fifth Avenue and just now was trying to get past the police cordon into the building so he could check on Aunt Thea.

"She must be all right!" young Howller said. "The ape climbed up her side of the building, but she could easily get away from him, her apartment's so big!"

"Well, yes," his father had said. "But if she went to bed with her headache, she would've been right next to the window. But don't worry. If she'd been hurt, we'd know it. And maybe she wasn't even home."

Young Tim had asked him what he meant by that, but his father had only shrugged.

The three of them stood in the front line of the crowd, waiting for Uncle Nate to bring news of Aunt Thea, even though they weren't really worried about her, and waiting to see what happened to Kong. Mayor Jimmy Walker showed up and conferred with the officials. Then the governor himself, Franklin Delano Roosevelt, arrived with much noise of siren and motorcycle. A minute later a big black limousine with flashing red lights and a siren pulled up. Standing on the runningboard was a giant with bronze hair and strange-looking gold-flecked eyes. He jumped off the runningboard and strode up to the mayor, governor, and police commissioner and talked briefly with them. Tim Howller asked the man next to him what the giant's name was, but the man replied that he didn't know because he was from out of town also. The giant finished talking and strode up to the crowd, which opened for him as if it were the Red Sea and he were Moses, and he had no trouble at all getting through the police cordon. Tim then asked the man on the right of his parents if he knew the yellow-eyed giant's name. This man, tall and thin, was with a beautiful woman dressed up in an evening gown and a mink coat. He turned his head when Tim called to him and presented a hawklike face and eyes that burned so brightly that Tim wondered if he took dope. Those eyes also told him that here was a man who asked questions, not one who gave answers. Tim didn't repeat his question, and a moment later the man said, in a whispering voice that still carried a long distance, "Come on, Margo. I've work to do." And the two melted into the crowd.

Mr. Howller told Jill about the two men, and she said, "What about them, Grandpa?"

"I don't really know," he said. "Often I've won-dered . . . Well, never mind. Whoever they were, they're irrelevant to what happened to King Kong. But I'll say one thing about New York—you sure see a lot of strange characters there."

Young Howller had expected that the mess would quickly be cleaned up. And it was true that the sanitation department had sent a big truck with a big crane and a number of men with hoses, scoop shovels, and brooms. But a dozen people at least stopped the cleanup almost before it began. Carl Denham wanted no one to touch the body except the taxidermists he had called in. If he couldn't exhibit a live Kong, he would exhibit a dead one. A colonel from Roosevelt Field claimed the body and, when asked why the Air Force wanted it, could not give an explanation. Rather, he refused to give one, and it was not until an hour later that a phone call from the White House forced him to reveal the real reason. A general wanted the skin for a trophy because Kong was the only ape ever shot down in aerial combat.

A lawyer for the owners of the Empire State Building appeared with a claim for possession of the body. His clients wanted reimbursement for the damage done to the building.

A representative of the transit system wanted Kong's body so it could be sold to help pay for the damage the ape had done to the Sixth Avenue Elevated.

The owner of the theater from which Kong had escaped arrived with his lawyer and announced he intended to sue Denham for an amount which would cover the sums he would have to pay to those who were inevitably going to sue him.

The police ordered the body seized as evidence in the trial for involuntary manslaughter and criminal negligence in which Denham and the theater owner would be defendants in due process.

The manslaughter charges were later dropped, but Denham did serve a year before being paroled. On being released, he was killed by a religious fanatic, a native brought back by the second expedition to Kong's island. He was, in fact, the witch doctor. He had murdered Denham because Denham had abducted and slain his god, Kong.

His Majesty's New York consul showed up with papers which proved that Kong's island was in British waters. Therefore, Denham had no right to anything removed from the island without permission of His Majesty's government.

Denham was in a lot of trouble. But the worst blow of all was to come next day. He would be handed notification that he was being sued by Ann Darrow. She wanted compensation to the tune of ten million dollars for various physical indignities and injuries suffered during her two abductions by the ape, plus the mental anguish these had caused her. Unfortunately for her, Denham went to prison without a penny in his pocket, and she dropped the suit. Thus, the public never found out exactly what the "physical indignities and injuries" were, but this did not keep it from making many speculations. Ann Darrow also sued John Driscoll, though for a different reason. She claimed breach of promise. Driscoll, interviewed by newsmen, made his famous remark that she should have been suing Kong, not him. This convinced most of the public that what it had suspected had indeed happened. Just how it could have been done was difficult to explain, but the public had never lacked wiseacres who would not only attempt the difficult but would not draw back even at the impossible.

Actually, Mr. Howller thought, the deed was not beyond possibility. Take an adult male gorilla who stood six feet high and weighed 350 pounds. According to Swiss zoo director Ernst Lang, he would have a full erection only two inches long. How did Professor Lang know this? Did he enter the cage during a mating and measure the phallus? Not very likely. Even the timid and amiable gorilla would scarcely submit to this type of handling in that kind of situation. Never mind. Professor Lang said it was so, and so it must be. Perhaps he used a telescope with gradations across the lens like those on a submarine's periscope. In any event, until someone entered the cage and slapped down a ruler during the action, Professor Lang's word would have to be taken as the last word.

By mathematical extrapolation, using the square-cube law, a gorilla twenty feet tall would have an erect penis about twenty-one inches long. What the diameter would be was another guess and perhaps a vital one, for Ann Darrow anyway. Whatever anyone else thought about the possibility, Kong must have decided that he would never know unless he tried. Just how well he succeeded, only he and his victim knew, since the attempt would have taken place before Driscoll and Denham got to the observation tower and before the searchlight beams centered on their target.

But Ann Darrow must have told her lover, John Driscoll, the truth, and he turned out not to be such a strong man after all.

"What're you thinking about, Grandpa?"

Mr. Howller looked at the screen. The Roadrunner had been succeeded by the Pink Panther, who was enduring as much pain and violence as the poor old coyote.

"Nothing," he said. "I'm just watching the Pink Panther with you."

"But you didn't say what happened to King Kong," she said.

"Oh," he said, "we stood around until dawn, and then the big shots finally came to some sort of agreement. The body just couldn't be left there much longer, if for no other reason than that it was blocking traffic. Blocking traffic meant that business would be held up. And lots of people would lose lots of money. And so Kong's body was taken away by the Police Department, though it used the Sanitation Department's crane, and it was kept in an icehouse until its ownership could be thrashed out."

"Poor Kong."

"No," he said, "not poor Kong. He was dead and out of it."

"He went to heaven?"

"As much as anybody," Mr. Howller said.

"But he killed a lot of people, and he carried off that nice girl. Wasn't he bad?"

"No, he wasn't bad. He was an animal, and he didn't know the difference between good and evil. Anyway, even if he'd been human, he would've been doing what any human would have done."

"What do you mean, Grandpa?"

"Well, if you were captured by people only a foot tall and carried off to a far place and put in a cage, wouldn't you try to escape? And if these people tried to put you back in, or got so scared that they tried to kill you right now, wouldn't you step on them?"

"Sure, I'd step on them, Grandpa."

"You'd be justified, too. And King Kong was justified. He was only acting according to the dictates of his instincts."

"What?"

"He was an animal, and so he can't be blamed, no matter what he did. He wasn't evil. It was what happened around Kong that was evil."

"What do you mean?" Jill said.

"He brought out the bad and the good in the people."

But mostly bad, he thought, and he encouraged Jill to forget about Kong and concentrate on the Pink Panther. And as he looked at the screen, he saw it through tears. Even after forty-two years, he thought, tears. This was what the fall of Kong had meant to him.

The crane had hooked the corpse and lifted it up. And there were two flattened-out bodies under Kong; he must have dropped them onto the sidewalk on his way up and then fallen on them from the tower. But how explain the nakedness of the corpses of the man and the woman?

The hair of the woman was long and, in a small area not covered by blood, yellow. And part of her face was recognizable.

Young Tim had not known until then that Uncle Nate

had returned from looking for Aunt Thea. Uncle Nate gave a long wailing cry that sounded as if he, too, were falling from the top of the Empire State Building.

A second later young Tim Howller was wailing. But where Uncle Nate's was the cry of betrayal and perhaps of revenge satisfied, Tim's was both of betrayal and of grief for the death of one he had passionately loved with a thirteen-year-old's love, for one whom the thirteen-year-old in him still loved.

"Grandpa, are there any more King Kongs?"

"No," Mr. Howller said. To say yes would force him to try to explain something that she could not understand. When she got older, she would know that every dawn saw the death of the old Kong and the birth of the new.

Introductory Note

The following illustrations are (with the exception of the single frame blow-up), photographs taken during the making of *King Kong*. The first group of publicity stills shows various members of the production team of directors and actors. The second group are production stills—photographs made with a still camera of "set-ups"—which were also used for promotional purposes. The so-called "censored" footage—about one minute in all—was removed from prints soon after the movie was released. In general this footage shows Kong behaving violently—stomping and chomping the natives on Skull Island—or those on Manhattan Island. Two other scenes show him acting in what might be called a "sexually charged" manner. In the first he partially disrobes Ann Darrow in his mountain lair and then sniffs his finger in baffled curiosity; in the second scene he responds to a familiar scream just after he breaks loose in New York, then reaches into an upper-story window, inspects a woman by holding her upside-down, and drops her to the ground when he determines she is not his beloved. The effect of all these scenes is to make Kong a less sympathetic figure. We have not been able to determine when or why the footage was removed or who was responsible for its removal. (See *Esquire* Sept. 1971 for additional frame blow-ups of this material.)

Publicity Still *Courtesy RKO*. Merian C. Cooper
(left), Ernest Schoedsack (right)

Publicity Still *Courtesy RKO*

Publicity Still
Courtesy RKO

Publicity Stills *Courtesy RKO*

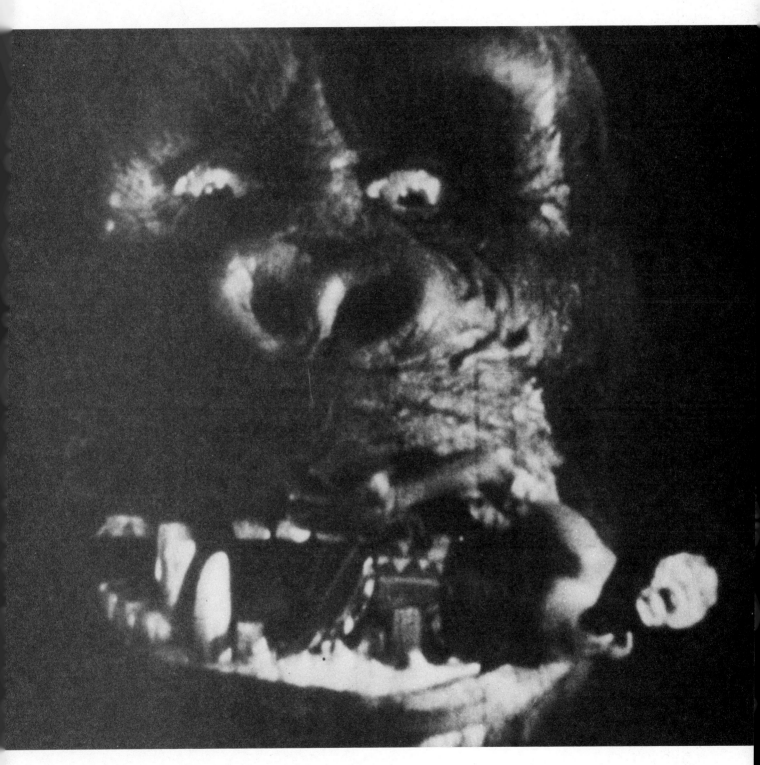

Publicity Still *Courtesy RKO*

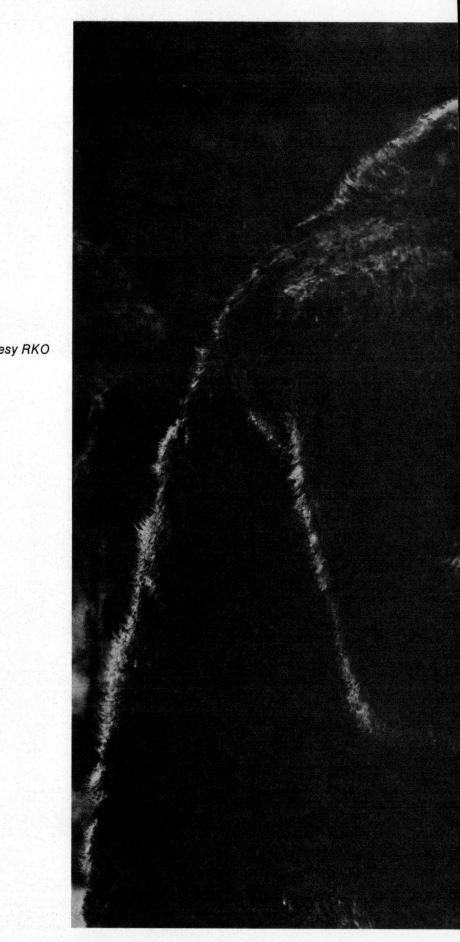

Publicity Still *Courtesy RKO*

Publicity Still *Courtesy RKO*

Publicity Still *Courtesy RKO*

Publicity Still *Courtesy RKO*

Publicity Still *Courtesy RKO*

PART IV
ARTISTS AND MODELS

KING KONG:
THE MAKING OF A CLASSIC FILM

Jimmy A. Harmon

Perhaps the greatest compliment that can be paid to a motion picture is to inspire innumerable imitations. Hence the widespread praise for *King Kong* (released by RKO in 1933), the brilliant precursor of countless "monster on the loose" films. Similar in some ways to the silent version of *The Lost World* of eight years earlier, *King Kong* differed mainly in that it centered around a major character and had a developed story line—qualities that elevated it far above its predecessor. The film's cardinal merits lie in its stunning visual effects which are still discussed, admired and "imitated." Although no Academy Awards were given for special effects in the early thirties, RKO received a special Oscar for progress in developing a reliable rear-process screen system: the one used in making *King Kong*. Thus, in a sense, *King Kong* earned an Oscar for special effects at a time when there was no such award in that category.

In 1931, David O. Selznick, vice president in charge of production at RKO Studios, had his friend Merian C. Cooper brought in to help reorganize the almost bankrupt company. His job was to re-evaluate properties planned for and then in production.

Prior to this, Cooper had been pondering the idea of shooting a story about a giant gorilla taken out of his jungle habitat where he had battled the environment and fought giant lizards. Brought back to New York, the gorilla escaped, wreaking havoc until he was finally killed atop the Empire State Building. At this time, Cooper had been trying to sell the story to producers in both Hollywood and New York. It was proposed to use live gorillas and lizards in making the film—until Cooper met Willis O'Brien on the set of *Creation*, then being filmed at RKO. The basic story of this film concerned a group of men descending into an extinct volanco and finding prehistoric life still thriving there. Miniature work on *Creation* was in progress behind the major soundstages in a slightly smaller building at the end of the RKO lot, and even after cancellation of that project, the studio area now assigned for use in making the new picture continued

to be referred to by RKO employees as the "*Creation* stage." For almost a year O'Brien had been working on *Creation*. Assisting him were Mario Larrinaga and Byron Crabbe, two RKO studio artists. After making sketches with O'Brien, Larrinaga and Crabbe had painted many glass mattes and backgrounds for prehistoric settings. Marcel Delgado, who had come to RKO along with O'Brien, was constructing a number of models of prehistoric animals representative of the dinosaur and mammal eras. Together they prepared one test reel of animation for Cooper's consideration. Cooper immediately expressed his admiration for the brilliant technical and artistic work that had gone into shooting that footage, but he was not impressed with the script of *Creation*.

O'Brien, realizing that the *Creation* project was about to be shelved, convinced Cooper that the latter's story, *King Kong*, could be made at RKO using stop-motion models rather than directing actual live anthropoids and lizards. This, he pointed out, would look much better to prospective producers (who might be persuaded to back the project) and would also cut down the cost of location shooting and animal training.

Cooper thereupon drafted a letter to Selznick, trying to convey what he wanted to achieve in the finished film and emphasizing the use of models and effects techniques that were readily available at RKO. His letter was aimed mainly at getting permission to shoot a test reel for the *Kong* project. Along with his letter, Cooper sent some drawings by O'Brien, Crabbe and Larrinaga and the reel of animation footage that had been shot for *Creation*. This footage included an allosaurus-stegosaurus battle in front of some "Yucatan" type ruins in which the allosaurus emerged the victor. Other scenes included the brontosaurus in the swamp sequence, which appears in *King Kong*, and a triceratops chasing a man. Selznick was sold on the idea almost immediately and promptly directed Cooper to prepare a scene for *King Kong* to try to convince the RKO executives of the project's merit.

Cooper and O'Brien decided to film the "log at the ravine" segment and the ensuing "allosaurus battle" as their showcase for the RKO executives. This test reel would also include the footage at the bottom of the ravine where giant spiders and lizards devoured the men who fell in. Prior to putting this scene on film, O'Brien and the *Creation* technicians made hundreds of story-board drawings depicting various parts of the proposed film. Fay Wray, Bruce Cabot and Robert Armstrong were cast as the leading characters. The Empire State Building was included from the outset, but many of the other scenes involving special effects work were still undecided.

Marcel Delgado started constructing the gorilla model, providing it with appropriate human and anthropoid qualities. In fashioning Kong and the other models, he showed considerable technical progress beyond the models he had constructed for *The Lost World.* After sculpting in clay what the finished model would look like, Delgado tooled the armature after O'Brien's design for it. He applied cotton and other stuffing around the armature, building up toward the final shape. During the final stages of his work, Delgado, using foam rubber and cotton, shaped the muscles until the model literally looked like an animal that had been skinned. In essence it was just that. The muscles would actually flex when the arms, legs and other movable parts of the anatomy were manipulated. Next Delgado applied latex rubber, layer by layer, meanwhile working in details on the skin to the exact likeness of the clay model. His final detailing involved the painting or applying of hair. For the Kong models, which stood about 20" high, Delgado used rabbit pelts cut into strips and glued onto the built-up muscles. Once in place, the fur was smoothed down by applications of glycerine. According to Delgado, only two finished models of Kong were constructed for animating. Some of his earlier designs reached completed model form but these mostly appeared too human in facial construction and were consequently changed. Minor alterations continued while the film was in production, and on occasion, Delgado tore down the models almost completely to undertake repairs. In rebuilding the models, slight changes, especially in the facial area, probably occurred. The size of the model's brows is one detectable difference. In some of the later scenes, they are almost twice as large as in some of the earlier ones. The most likely explanation for this is that the brows were often moved and so Delgado had to repair them just as frequently. This evidently necessitated the building up of more latex to hide the brow wires that wore through.

Among the models Delgado completed for the *Creation* project were those of the allosaurus, triceratops, brontosaurus, stegosaurus, a species of monoclonius and a prehistoric mammal called esocerium. Excellent in design and construction and unsurpassed until recent years, these models earned for Marcel Delgado the reputation of the cinema's leading creator of miniatures. Despite the great skill and artistry with which they were made, few of his models for *Creation* were to appear in the final edited version of *King Kong.* At the onset of production for the latter film, much of the *Creation* footage was to be incorporated. For *King Kong*, Delgado was to construct new models of the stegosaurus and allosaurus as well as models of a pteranodon, a styracosaurus, a plesiosaurus, three giant spiders, several Pterodactyls, and numerous other smaller prehistoric reptiles.

The models used in *Kong* were some of the largest ever built for table-top animation. Most averaged two and half to three feet in length. The stegosaurus model's larger back plates, which were carved out of wood, were over four inches long! Delgado himself has said that the models need not have been that large—in fact, he would have preferred building them to a smaller scale. But he followed the plans that O'Brien gave him—so it must be assumed that O'Brien liked working on this scale. Another reason that may have determined their size was the old claim that "the larger the miniature the better the illusion of reality." Actually, it has always been Hollywood practice to build miniatures as large as materials, space and budget would allow. The size of the models used in making *Kong* also contributed to the solving of the problems of minute focusing. It was possible to place the animation camera a fair distance from the set, thereby allowing for a greater depth of field. This was of considerable importance when taking into account the speed of the Eastman negative stock in which *King Kong* was shot as well as the speed of the lenses that would be used to control perspective. The matching of live action footage with miniatures and models was accomplished by four basic optical methods: The Dunning matte process, original negative splits, glass mattes, and real "background" process projection. The last-mentioned process had been used in earlier films, but it was not until the making of *Kong* that it became a well-established process. Miniature rear-process work, where the actors function in front of a large projected image, was also used for the film. (The footage of the Kong-allosaurus battle, contained in the test reel, was the first scene ever done in rear process, shooting with synchronized sound. The technique of rear process was an innovation in so far as it had only recently been perfected to professional standards; it would immediately eclipse the

Dunning matte process which had been used in innumerable silent films.) Most of the credit for the process work can be attributed to Vernon C. Walker, one of RKO's resident technicians. It was through his experience and efforts that the process work for *King Kong* was of such a high order.

Before the test reel was completed, Cooper and Edgar Wallace had drafted the film's script. Wallace died of pneumonia while helping Cooper, and so most of the work on the screenplay should be attributed to Cooper. With this newly-completed script, the test reel and drawings by O'Brien and his staff for the major special effects scenes, Cooper was able to confront the RKO executives in late 1931. This one meeting would determine whether one of the greatest films of all time would be made. After viewing the footage, the RKO executives were enthusiastic and immediately gave clearance to undertake the project for the quickest possible release date. Jubilantly, Cooper turned to his task. Coproducing with him would be Ernest B. Schoedsack with whom he had worked on three silent films: *Grass* (1926), *Chang* (1927) and *The Four Feathers* (1929).

Willis O'Brien was now faced with the greatest undertaking of his career, but working with him would be his talented crew of technicians from *Creation*: Larrinaga, Crabbe, and Delgado, as well as E. B. Gibson and Carroll Shepphird, a young man who had transferred from the RKO art department. Fred Reefe and Orville Goldner would also help out with such technical apparatus as lights and process projectors.

E. "Buss" Gibson assisted O'Brien in the setting up of the table animation sequences. Carroll Shepphird was responsible for such matters as preparing and executing tests to check alignment of glass mattes, bi-pack camera mattes and the like (to insure that the separate elements of each scene would combine), and arranging exposure data so that film plates could be matched perfectly with the original negative splits, Dunning process mattes and bi-pack mattes. Much of the film's optical realism depended upon Shepphird's skill. Orville Goldner was concerned with preparing the miniature trees, rocks, and other jungle and mountainous terrain for the animation sets.

Nearly five months after the test reel had been shot, Cooper rehired Robert Armstrong, Bruce Cabot, Fay Wray and other principal players to start filming the live action segments. Max Steiner, contracted to RKO during *King Kong*'s production, saw in this film his opportunity to write the kind of adventure music for which he later would become famous. Completing the score in only two weeks and deriving the basic theme from three notes, Steiner provided one of his greatest

compositions for *King Kong*. Several of Steiner's pieces for *Kong* weren't used, however. These consisted of different variations on the natives, jungle and swamp themes as well as music that was intended to be incorporated into scenes where destruction by Kong was prominent. The excluded pieces were more mellow than the music actually used.

King Kong was edited by Ted Cheesman, one of RKO's top feature editors. He is remembered by his lifelong friend Les Millbrook who, in the 1930s was, an assistant editor in the same studio: "I was working on short subjects for RKO at the time—in my little room. Each editor has his own little stall. Ted would peek in the door on his way by each day. I went through some 6,000 feet of film a day on those comedy shorts and here's Ted holding five feet of film in his hand and explaining 'Here's today's dailies'!"

No time was wasted by O'Brien and his crew. Crabbe and Larrinaga proceeded by painting a number of mattes based on O'Brien's sketches and Delgado was ready to animate a number of the models. Before the final screenplay had been written by James Creelman and Ruth Rose (Mrs. Ernest B. Schoedsack), animation had started on some of the scenes. Creelman was mainly concerned with continuity whereas Rose wrote most of the dialogue. As with so many films, the final shooting script was shorter than the first draft; also scenes were shot that would never find their way into final release prints.

One such excluded scene involved Kong coming upon a triceratops and her offspring. This sequence was supposed to appear just before Kong reached the log at the ravine. (The triceratops, in an instinctively protective manner, prepares to attack when Kong ventures too close. In one of his more human moments, Kong, deciding against a brute attack, pulls up slabs of solid pitch and hurls them at the charging triceratops. The slabs, hitting their target, force the creature to retreat, its horns having been broken above the eyes.) Other cuts eliminated most of the *Creation* footage originally supposed to be incorporated into the script. A scene in which a triceratops chases a man, another piece of completed *Creation* footage, would see treatment later—in *Son of Kong* (1933).

The table animation and live-action shooting schedules had to proceed simultaneously; if one fell behind, the other was held up. For some of the table animation, live action was shot for placement in small process screens within the sets. In turn, some of the live action required animation sequences shot for larger process screens in front of which the actors would perform or react. This process work was among the first attempted at RKO and the trial and error method was used to correct the system. Here again, Carroll Shepphird, assisted by Vernon Walker, directed the technical work.

Most of the film was shot in or around the RKO studios at Grower Street and Culver City where RKO had their back lot. Here Cooper renovated the mammoth wall and gate that had previously been used in Cecil B. DeMille's independent production of 1925, *The King of Kings*. A jungle appearance was given to the wall's surroundings and a native village was constructed in front of it. Exteriors—for the opening scenes showing the tramp steamer in New York harbor—were shot at San Pedro harbor in California; the interiors were shot in the RKO studios.

The Most Dangerous Game, based on Richard Connell's short story, was also being filmed at RKO by Cooper and Schoedsack contemporaneously with the production of *King Kong*. Accordingly, it was both natural and economical that the same studio jungle props and settings were used for both films. Some of *Kong*'s mattes were also employed for the other movie, most notably those for the scenes showing the log over the ravine, and the waterfall. But slightly different surroundings were used for *The Most Dangerous Game*.

In these mattes we can trace the source of *Kong*'s admirable atmospheric qualities. No natural location shooting could have improved upon the stylistic beauty of the Crabbe-Larrinaga glass matte paintings which abound in the film. Blending impeccably with the sound stage jungles, the miniature sets and the outdoor locales, these mattes symbolize all that is best about this masterly technical and aesthetic achievement.

The final screenplay had the film story open in New York the night before Carl Denham (Robert Armstrong) is to sail for Skull Island. Cooper fought the RKO executives for permission to start the narrative here. Most of the executives wanted the film to begin with Denham already arrived at Skull Island. Having convinced them of the dramatic value of the slow buildup to Kong's entrance, Cooper opened the story in New York harbor on Captain Englehorn's (Frank Reicher's) ship, *Venture*, preparing to take Denham and crew to a place where no white man had ever been before. The film proceeds by drawing its audience into a story as mysterious as the harbor fog that enshrouds the tramp steamer.

Kong's last conflict with mankind—at the end of the movie—transpires on the Empire State Building, man's greatest technical achievement of that period. Of this building, only the uppermost stories and spire are seen—with Kong defiantly aloft on its apex. Kong turns to see an airplane winging over the city in the distance behind him. In the cockpit the pilot points out Kong, and with the gunner behind him discusses how they will attack. This pilot and gunner were played by Merian C. Cooper and Ernest B. Schoedsack respectively. The background for the sequence, a photo blowup taken from atop the Empire State Building, was retouched by Crabbe and Larrinaga. This last and most famous scene was brilliantly executed technically. The footage of the actual aircraft was cut between scenes of miniatures flying at and around Kong. In all setups where planes were in the same frame with Kong, miniatures were used; no process or matte shots were employed. The miniature planes, which match the real ones very well—with only minor differences detectable in the shape of the rudder—perform their aerial maneuvers quite satisfactorily. Only in a few tight turns do the miniatures seem to lose their soaring gracefulness and symmetrical beauty.

RKO gambled about $600,000 on the production of *King Kong*. The film proved to be a triumphant success; it actually saved the company from bankruptcy during the Depression. Moreover, in repeated re-releases until 1956, just before it was sold to television, it continued to make money, turning over its original investment many times. Unlike Kong himself at the end of the picture, *King Kong* remains, without challengers, the most successful film of its genre.

KING KONG AND ME

Marcel Delgado

In the spring of 1923 I enrolled to study art at the Otis Art Institute in Los Angeles. All my life I had wanted to be an artist. Not having the means for an art education, I managed to get my tuition free for acting as a monitor at the school, three nights a week from 7:30 to 9:30. My duties were to open the school, on class nights, and call the roll of the different art classes and see that everything was in order and, when all classes were over, lock all the doors. I was doing this at the time that I met Mr. Willis O'Brien. He was in the "Still Life" class. However, Mr. O'Brien was already an artist and had done some art work and sculpture in San Francisco.

While I was calling the roll, many times I saw some of the beginners' drawings that were out of proportion and I would stop and try to correct their mistakes, even though I was not the teacher. This I did on my own. Somehow they were pleased with my criticism. One day, after I had helped a student, I passed close to Mr. O'Brien. He stopped me and said to me, "How come I don't get my drawings criticized?" I just laughed and told him, "Why, you are already a good artist. You should criticize *my* work instead of me criticizing yours." So we laughed it off. Soon we became well acquainted.

It wasn't long after that encounter when he asked me if I wanted to go to work with him at First National Studios in Hollywood. He told me he was starting Sir Arthur Conan Doyle's *The Lost World*. I told him I already had a job and, besides, this offered me the opportunity to attend school at night and I was very happy about it. I thanked him for the offer and dismissed it from my mind. Thereafter, every time he saw me he mentioned my going to work for him. After many times, I asked him what the salary would be. He told me he would pay me $75.00 a week. This (in 1923) was unbelievable to me. The sum was fantastic, but I still refused to go to work for him, though I was working for $14.00 a week at the time. Finally, on a Friday night, he said, "Tomorrow is Saturday. What will you be doing tomorrow?" My answer was that I would be going to work at the grocery store. "Well," he said, "why don't you take the day off and come and visit me at the

studio? Perhaps you will enjoy watching them shoot pictures." I had never been to a motion picture studio.

I had turned down the offer of a job, but I couldn't turn down the offer to see pictures being filmed. He said that he would leave a pass at the gate for me. That night I hardly slept for thinking about my visiting a studio. I was there promptly at 9 o'clock the next morning. I asked the gateman for Mr. O'Brien and he escorted me to his office. Mr. O'Brien was very glad to receive me and took me to the stage where they were filming pictures. All of this was of extreme interest to me. Finally, after the tour of the different sets, he took me to a room, where, evidently, he had created a studio with models of dinosaurs and pictures of dinosaurs by Charles Knight, from the Metropolitan Museum in New York. Standing in the center of this room, almost as if in a trance, seeing all the models and wonderful drawings, I couldn't believe it was true. Mr. O'Brien must have seen how thrilled I was, so he said, "Well, Marcel, how do you like your studio?" Stupefied as I was, I said, "What studio?" He said, "The one you are standing in. It is all yours. That is, if you want it." I really didn't know what to say. I had been taken completely by surprise. "O'Bie" had finally won. So he said, "Well, when are you going to start?" "Right now," I replied. He took me to the office and signed me up, and I started to work that day.

As stated before, Mr. O'Brien was starting work on *The Lost World*. As this was a new project combining stop-motion animation with real people and miniatures, we worked behind locked doors. Only the "top" stars and officials were allowed to visit our department. Among the "Greats" was Milton Sills, who had formerly been a college professor. He talked to me for hours about dinosaurs and prehistoric animals, which helped me a great deal in my work. I also had the great privilege of meeting Greta Nisson, Nita Naldi, Colleen Moore, Bessie Love, Rudolph Valentino, Lewis Stone, Wallace Berry, and many others. These people were all very gracious to me, but I was to find that after *The Lost World* was finished and I had to seek employment in the regular miniature department of the studio, I was treated with disrespect and discriminated against because of my Mexican heritage. I realize now that it was a mistake for me to have taken work in the regular department but I felt that it was necessary in order for me to continue my work along that line. Seven years went by before I got the call from Mr. O'Brien to work on *Creation* and several more before we started *King Kong*.

I made the two full body models used in *King Kong*. Both models were eighteen inches high, which is three-quarter inch to the foot. The full-sized limbs used in certain scenes were made separately and I do not know the dimensions or to what scale they were made for the different shots. I do not know who made them nor who designated the scale for them. The skeletons of the limbs were made in the studio machine shops and I covered them with muscles and fur. The full-sized arm and hand had to be large enough to hold Fay Wray and the full-sized foot had to be large enough to crush the body of a native into the muddy ground of the village.

I did not design the huge bust that was exhibited in front of Grauman's Chinese Theatre for the premiere. All I did was the fabrication on the outside. As I recall, it took about three or four men inside to work the mechanical jaws and eyes, but I have no idea what the dimensions were. I believe they would be for a creature between twenty-five and thirty feet high, although in the picture Kong appeared to be anywhere from twenty to forty feet high. But the story moved so rapidly that most of the audience did not seem to notice these discrepancies. The prehistoric animals were all three-quarters of an inch to the foot scale, and the miniature people were made one inch to the foot scale.

Occasionally I dropped in on the sets during the shooting or while Mr. O'Brien was animating the models. I was always busy trying to keep the models repaired as they would deteriorate or break. Many times I worked all night or on holidays in order to have them ready for use when needed. Many times

I had to tear them down and build them over again because the rubber and muscles deteriorated from the heat of the lights and the constant movement of the animation. Of course, they had to match the ones used previously as nearly as possible. The work had to be done by one person; therefore, I had no help.

I really did not get to know Edgar Wallace and Max Steiner personally, although I saw them many times. But they were busy with their own problems. Occasionally I saw the "rushes," and Mr. Steiner would also be among the viewers, in order to see what action would be interpreted by his musical score. We spoke a few words to each other but I was never formally introduced to him.

As I recall, everyone seemed very happy in their work and there was great cooperation and teamwork. Each one had his task to do, but no one realized that the picture *King Kong* would become a classic.

To settle a question as to whether there were two models of King Kong—yes, there were. It was a daily task for me to tighten the screws in the joints and groom the model for the next day of shooting. If one model was being repaired, the other one had to be ready. One of the armatures* (the skeleton) of Kong is at Movie World, in Buena Park, California, where it is displayed alongside a covered model.

After *King Kong*, I worked with Mr. O'Brien on *Son of Kong, Last Days of Pompeii, Gawangi* (which was stopped after the first sequence), then *War Eagles* (which was also stopped after a sequence), then *Mighty Joe Young* and finally, *Mad, Mad, Mad World* at Film Effects Studio in Hollywood. Mr. O'Brien passed away working on this job.

My career ended with work on *Fantastic Voyage* at Fox Studio. I retired in 1966. I might add that, with Mr. O'Brien's death, came recognition for both of us because the younger generation realized that *King Kong* was a fantastic creation that will probably never be duplicated nor surpassed.

---

* The other is owned by Clark Wilkinson of Baraboo, Wisconsin. Eds.

MINIATURE EFFECTS SHOTS

Willis O'Brien

In previous articles there has been so much misinformation presented relative to the methods used in obtaining effects shots (which do add immeasurably to the scope and general possibilities of the motion picture), that I believe a short description of the work as it is actually carried on might prove of interest.

The completed shot represents a combination of applied talents creating an ultimate picture or impression that, when well done is beautiful and conclusive. The dramatic value of the setting—its lighting and construction—are all necessary elements that must be studied and worked out prior to the consideration of the mechanical agencies to be applied.

A scene that flashes before your eyes on the screen for a few seconds may have required several weeks of concentrated preparation and work. Often a day's work of twenty-five feet of finished film is shown in about one-third of a minute on the screen. In the making of *King Kong* a detailed sketch was made for each set. The artist created a picture or illustration of that certain bit of action. This sketch would necessarily have to be complete in all detail—the comparative sizes of people and animals, their actions, the dramatic value of the setting and its lighting.

Each scene was planned as a single picture—a dramatic conception in black and white. Continuity sketches were made combining these larger sketches in their correct sequence, so that the protraction of the story would be kept, the whole, as well as details, receiving an infinite amount of study and research.

Then the best or necessary means to duplicate this conception was worked out. It might be a miniature set with the characters or people being projected into a part of it. The practical requirements necessary for the working of miniature animals might be necessary to consider. The advisability of using glass paintings, or, perhaps matting the lower part of the set so as to use conventionally photographed foreground must be taken into account. All these and many more possible requirements must be considered.

After deciding the means to be used, the layout or construction plans were drawn and detailed, even to the exact position of the camera and the placing of people and animals. This work is done by Caroll Shepphird. If people were to be projected or matted in the set, a complete drawing for that part of the set would be necessary, so that they would take their place in the miniature in the correct perspective and create a convincing picture. In many instances of a composite shot, a full-size set with people would be shot a month or so before the miniature of which it would become a part, thus necessitating exacting layouts and camera setups.

The layouts are conceived entirely from the sketch so that the shot would be an exact reproduction of the artist's conception. *Much research was necessary so as to obtain correct reproductions of every detail.*

When the plans were ready the set or sets were put into work. Expert craftsmen carefully built the necessary units. It might be a combination miniature set with glass paintings and projected images, the sketch artists painting the glasses and backings themselves, and in many instances having the original sketch projected on the glass to serve as a guide for the glass artist. When the set is finished the cameraman and electrician light the set from the sketch.

Then tests were made until the required and desired results were obtained, the final picture being a practical setting and exact reproduction of the artist's conception.

From the foregoing it can easily be seen that the miniature technician cannot bring his set to the screen single-handed. It is fundamentally an artist's conception but requires the united efforts of many craftsman, its success depending entirely upon the combination of artistic, photographic and mechanical effects, each person being a specialist in his field but also having a general knowledge of the whole.

When making *King Kong* it was necessary to have a large staff of experienced men to carry on the work. A group of men were kept busy building and repairing the animals or executing any mechanical necessity that was required. Another group built the miniatures, which included a New York Elevated Railway recreated in detail, and jungle settings on a tropical island. Mario Larrinaga and Byron Crabbe made the sketches and later painted the backings and glasses for the sets after the miniatures were drawn up and put to work. Besides these men, others were necessary for the actual working of the miniatures.

Experience is the only teacher of the various treatments required to obtain the desired effects. Each new set is an individual problem and requires separate treatment. There is no set rule or method by which you can classify all miniatures. The scale and size must be individually determined.

The miniature of today is a much more convincing and effective medium than it was a few years ago. The introduction of real people into the miniature (by process, matte or projection) and the addition of sound have all helped considerably. Many people pride themselves on being able to tell a minature shot on the screen. A well-executed miniature cannot be detected, except by the expert himself. Miniatures are very often shot at high speed, that is from four to eight times normal speed. This is always done when shooting water, as the scale and illusion cannot be brought about except by the use of the high-speed camera.

Miniatures and so-called trick shots are not a medium used to fool the public, but rather a means of obtaining a better or otherwise impossible angle to further the completeness of the story and often are used as the only possible solution to get the desired effect. The average picture has a few. The *Hollywood Herald* called *King Kong* "the most sensational exhibition of camera tricks in the history of motion pictures." It was probably the extreme case because of its impossibility without them. New ideas and new combinations of older processes were used. Miniature animals, combined with the projection of people on the miniature set, created a scene that was convincing, not for the purpose of fooling the picture-goer, but to give something new and formerly impossible. I believe the public has come to realize and appreciate the true creative ability required in the conception and execution of these shots so as to obtain the maximum in artistic and realistic effects.

DRAMATIC PRINCIPLES IN STOP-MOTION*

David Allen

The widely acknowledged "classic" quality of *King Kong* is generally explained in terms of its originality at the time coupled, of course, with the high quality of its special visual effects. Yet, neither of these two elements, strictly considered, offer today's filmmaker concrete guidance in recapturing the spirit of expression that gave *Kong* immortality.

Though it is always difficult, and often dangerous to dissect the elements of an entire quantity (evidenced by the inferior nature of all the variously disguised *Kong* imitations), it is *possible,* I believe, to identify the factors in the film that seem valuable for study.

FAIRY TALE AND MYTHIC ELEMENTS—Perhaps the most basic ingredient of the film. Fairy tales probably contain elements that are indigenous to the culture which produces and maintains them. One need consider only the ingredients of horror within a moral system that the typical fairy story affords to see a relationship to *Kong.* Fairy tales of the gothic school, in particular, rely on the shock value of the grotesque for effect. That *Kong* follows the tradition of mystic adventure can also be shown. This is true not only of the classical tragic elements (Kong could be compared to Prometheus—"neither beast nor man"), but of the sequential construction of the events, a formula that has worked since Homer.

KONG AS PROTAGONIST—Strongly connected to this point is the relationship which Kong as a character has to the definition of a tragic protagonist. To anyone unfamiliar with Aristotle's *Poetics,* this work, which contains the basic outline of western drama, explains the traits which the tragic figure must have to evoke sympathy and identification. To illustrate, the tragic character must be a larger-than-life personality, usually a ruler or a great hero. Kong is, of course, an ape; but he is sufficiently humanized to stand up to this requirement. Further, he displays the characteristic "tragic flaw" in an otherwise proud and secure personality—his weakness for beauty. A hopeless infatuation for beauty by the grotesque is a very strong

* Reprinted from PHOTON Magazine, copyright © 1972 by Mark Frank.

stimulus for sympathy in fiction. Here, Kong compares to the Frankenstein monster or Quasimodo or the Phantom of the Opera. My feeling is that there is something very elemental in our identification with a character who, against a known capacity for violence and revenge, is then shown to have the same possibilities for tenderness and sacrifice as we.

AN INTEGRATING MOTIVE—There is something else that is very important about the implicit conflict in the plot of Kong; something that has not been sufficiently credited. Kong and the other major characters have one identical and overlapping motivation: the possession of the girl! It is this organizing principle which binds the suspense, the struggles and the characters to each other, preventing Kong from ever becoming remote from the human actors in the film. It is the absence of this element—a shared and conflicting motivation across the line between character animation and live action—which is the consistent flaw in films of this type. The lesson to the scriptwriter is this: Kong is the hero of the story, not Denham nor Driscoll. He is not only the center of the actions, but the subject of the theme (beauty and the beast). This is the most basic and overlooked fact behind the attraction of the film.

THE IMPORTANCE OF THE ANTI-HERO—Most of us would agree that roles such as Sokurah the magician of *Sinbad,* or James Mason as Captain Nemo, often provide us with characters far more interesting than the leading roles opposite them. This is probably because the hero or heroine become stereotyped in a fantasy film and are not permitted the relative range of complexity that a villain, or anti-hero, is allowed. Carl Denham is an anti-hero, with something of the tenacity and aggressiveness of a Captain Ahab as he challenges Kong for supremacy. Nowadays, with our modern suspicion of dominative chauvinism and material exploitation, Denham appears less sympathetic as he plows resolutely and somewhat unfeelingly toward his goal. Yet, for all this, he remains the most interesting human character, with a very nostalgically American style.

THE CONCEPT—After forty years, during which

many films of the day have deteriorated and become forgotten, it is easier to give *Kong* perhaps too much credit for story originality. Of course, parallels to *The Lost World* come to mind but, after that, it should be mentioned that a part of Hollywood had just gone through a "jungle film" phase, probably reinvigorated after talkies with the highly promoted *Trader Horn* (with its blonde jungle heroine). There was even one such film, *Ingagi*, predating *Kong* which showed a man in a gorilla suit carrying off a black girl sacrifice (see: Rudy Behlmer, *Jungle Tales of the Cinema*). Cooper and Schoedsack had themselves been involved in on-location jungle films of this type with *Chang*. Looked at in this way, *Kong* can be seen more naturally as the product of a line of developing inspiration. However, this should not be taken to detract from the credit which is due to Cooper, Edgar Wallace and the perfect coalition of talent that came together at RKO. The record shows that Cooper had to argue for his vision of what he knew from the beginning would be a stunningly unique motion picture.

NOSTALGIA—This may or may not add to one's appreciation of *Kong*, but the fact is that the film has now lived so long that it is a veritable costume-period picture. This quality is accented by the photography, the acting, the dialogue and, to a much lesser extent, the direction. Any attempt to remake *Kong* would have to consider the qualities which the production gained by being filmed in 1932.

THE MUSIC—Max Steiner's score for Kong was, in his opinion, one of his three best. It is romantic and melodramatic in the grand manner, yet always sublimated to and harmonious with the total effect. This technique, the translation of emotion into musical terms, reached its full development in the operas of Wagner and Strauss, and it was inevitable that in their public accessibility, the conventions of romantic music would reach Hollywood. Later, such music would turn saccharine in the presence of hundreds of studio weepers, but in 1933, the results that Steiner achieved with an under-built orchestra of day-labor musicians were a sensation. One need only recall the musicianship of the native celebrations, the crescendos moving behind the escaped Kong, or the overture, with its ingenious repeated motifs, to have the suspicion that the romantic score may someday return to a place of honor in films.

SOUND EFFECTS—Beside the visual effects, it is easy to overlook the contribution which the sound effects of Murray Spivack and his crew made to the production. When one considers how new sound itself was to film, the accomplishment is even more impressive. Of particular interest is the careful relationship between the musical score and the sound effects. Not only do the sounds not clash with the music, they often slide in and out of the score with the effect of another instrument in Steiner's orchestra.

SPECIAL EFFECTS—Although the animation in *The Lost World* is often strangely superior technically to *Kong*, it is certainly less robust and demanding. All things considered, the general improvement seen over the six or seven years between the two films is astonishing. Those that consider *King Kong* as good "in its time" or "for its day" should question whether the qualities that have made it last are factors almost exclusive to "its time." It is often said that *Kong* might be improved today with our newer and more efficient technical apparatus. Possibly, but the effect, the mood of Kong, which is no more or less than its style, owes much to the fact that the *absence* of such technical apparatus often forced the greater burden upon *artisans*, who had to substitute art for technique simply because no other means existed! Thus, the deficiencies of miniature background projection meant that no real jungle could be projected behind the puppet characters, therefore the jungle was *designed*, painted and built by hand with an atmospheric flourish that no real jungle could offer. The situation is analogous to the regret we attach to products where the machine has displaced the craftsman in its manufacture. We may admit a newer, but not necessarily higher efficiency, and detect that the God of progress is not quality, but expediency. It should also be warned that with technique, almost invariably comes formula. This lack of a formula, of a pre-established *system* approach, gave an exploratory character to all phases of the film, In the effects, the result was that each shot, each animation set-up, was a new challenge that had to be dealt with individually. Somewhat unintentionally, I suspect, this made the finished sequences far more filmic and vital than usually seems possible today. Every known trick of the time was stretched to its furthest limits—for the sake of the desired "look." This sort of "effects license" is almost nonexistent today, because effects work tends to be chiefly augmentive in nature, and is thus forced to cut realistically with the whole. *Kong* is rescued from this modern sterilizing tendency by the fact that, until the New York scenes, it rarely has a realistic backdrop for comparison.

Remarks as extended as these should include at least some negative criticism of the picture. Although such things as fluctuations in the size of Kong, or handling marks on the fur, seem less important to me now than they did years ago (I never minded—even preferred—the "jerky" aspect of stop-motion), I must concede to the realist that they are there, and can be distracting. One of the things that does occasionally annoy me today is the generally careless attitude about much of the animation itself. There is enough good work in the film to show that they could have had better overall quality in the stop-motion. Secondly, I have been slightly disappointed in some of the contents of the "censored" scenes that have just resurfaced. The overdone people-chewing scenes diminish our sympathy for Kong, and the animation is worse than usual in most of the shots. Further, I admit that much of the sympathy accrues to Kong from the nature of the story itself, and is often not sensitively reinforced at crucial times. These things, however, I consider very minor in comparison to what was achieved, and against the vitality, the recklessness and the pervading informality of *Kong*, there is no film of the type which compares equally.

PREHISTORIC MONSTERS ROAR AND HISS FOR THE SOUND FILM*

Andrew R. Boone

From the slime of tropical mud flats, the ghost voices of prehistoric monsters have reached the screen. Hisses and grunts of the pterodactyl and brontosaurus; roars from a tyrannosaurus, largest of the dinosaur family; groans and roars of an imaginary giant ape are reproduced by mechanical contrivances.

Kong, the ape, crashed through the heavy growth of an unknown forest, uttering fierce growls and beating his breast in rage. As the scene unfolded in silence before a small group of us in a tiny projection room, the studio sound experts discussed ways and means of re-creating his awful voice and the solid thumps of clenched hands against the massive chest.

An hour later we assembled in the scoring room, with a half-dozen contrivances at hand. Some of these, it was hoped, would turn the trick.

"Gentlemen," said Murray Spivack, sound supervisor, "this is our most important noise in *King Kong*. If it's okay, the rest of our problems will be simple. The ape must beat his breast and growl."

Spivack took his place for the first recording at a kettle drum. The instrument was covered with a heavy board, a cloth stretched tightly across its face instead of the customary skin. In his hand he held two padded drum sticks.

"Bong—Bong—Bong." He struck the board lightly. The room filled with the resonant tone, but the depth and solid, fleshy sound one would expect to hear could not be made.

"Too hollow for Kong," said Walter G. Elliot, specialist in sound effects for the studio. "Let's try the floor."

Spivack turned from the drum to a nearby chair. Again simple implements began to play their parts in the filming of this imaginary tale of an unknown world. An assistant held the microphone's delicate diaphragm an inch above the floor. Meantime the chair had been placed on a soft fibrous padding. As a bell outside the thick door rang warning that sound recording was about to begin, Spivack began to beat the cane bottom of the chair with the drum mallet.

The beats gave a solider sound. I thought they resembled those one would expect to hear from the pounding of a great animal beast; but the loudspeaker slung near the ceiling said, "no good." Sound technicians sitting in the tiny glass-windowed control booth had been hearing these synthetic ape sounds through the transmitting system, exactly as a theater audience would have heard them. "Not fleshy," was the cryptic comment.

Spivack still had another method to try before turning to his sound library for further suggestions. "If wood will not take the place of flesh," he said, "let's use flesh."

Accordingly three men stepped within range of the mircophone. An aide held the delicate recording apparatus against Elliott's back. Spivack began tapping Elliott's chest, first lightly, then with stronger blows, as he observed the sound men within the little room. At last one nodded and the speaker boomed, "Okay. We pick up the resonance. That gives us plenty of lows." Which, translated, meant the metal ear had picked up the low notes with clarity and transmitted the body blows with considerable volume to their loud speaker.

"Strange as it may seem," Elliott remarked, "this breast-beating business has given us more concern than the vocal sounds these ancient brutes uttered. Now I'll show you how we think they talked."

In a moment the room was plunged into inky blackness and as we found seats around the walls the picture of the ape filled the screen. He appeared to be some seven times taller than a man as he stood erect on the domed top of New York's Empire State Building, battling with his gnarled, hairy hands an entire squadron of Uncle Sam's army pursuit planes. He alternately roared venom at his aerial enemies and uttered deep-throated love notes over the form of a girlish figure that lay perilously near the edge of a cornice far above the street.

"How," I asked, after the sequence had run its course, "did you achieve such a deep roar? No animal living today sounds in the least like that."

"That roar," Spivack explained, "provided a difficult problem, but old sound tracks finally solved it for us. You see, we have a half-million feet of animal sounds in the library—leopards, lions, tigers, elephants; every animal, in fact, we would be apt to use in pictures.

"We took one of these stock roars, ran the sound track backward at a slow speed through the projector, lowered the sound one octave and re-recorded it. From this we took the high spots, the loud peaks, and pieced them together. After we had shortened the roars in this manner, it left us with a sound track too short to fit the ape, for his mouth was still open after the roar had ended. So we pieced four of these combined roars together to keep the roar sustained, then put a sound tail on the end so it would die down naturally instead of stopping abruptly—and we had the awe-inspiring sounds you have heard."

"But why," I asked, "wouldn't some living animal's roar have done the trick? A lion, for instance?"

"The trouble with the roars of living animals," Spivack said, "lies in the fact that audiences recognize them. Even the most terrifying notes would be recognized. Also, the majority of roars are too short. The elephant, with the longest roar of which I know, sustains the sound only eight or nine seconds. Kong's longest continues for thirty seconds, including six peaks and a three-second tail."

When Kong fought to the death with a tyrannosaurus, a metal and rubber and fur reproduction of those tiny-brained giants that a million years ago roamed the region of what today is Montana, the ape barked, uttered guttural growls and breathed low, heavy gusts before breaking the tyrannosaurus' neck.

As I looked at the giant ape head used for the close-ups. I saw a mechanical creature that outdoes nature at its best. Thirty bearskins formed the hide. The rubber nose and rubber lips dilated and grinned and the large glass eyes rolled in their sockets as six men, hidden within the recesses of the skull, turned handles to provide the necessary movement. One specialist even pumped a blood-like liquid from a tank at the base of the throat into the mouth for an added touch of realism when Kong finally vanquished his mighty antagonist.

All sounds were added after the scenes were filmed. For the anthropoid's breathing, Spivack ran an old tiger sound track backward, lowering the tone an octave. This produced a low, snarly, guttural combination of growl and breath which starts low and climbs to a high peak, giving a sound entirely different from the animal sounds one hears today. The growl alone consists of a sharp bark, with the peak of a particularly loud blast used to tie the bark to a roar and a piece of breathing tied to that to tail the entire sound off into nothingness.

But the love notes! There were no scientific data to guide the movie makers in reproducing any of these sounds. When asked for aid in this direction, J. W. Lytle, vertebrate paleontologist of the Los Angeles Museum, replied, "for the dinosauria I would suggest that you reproduce various degrees of hissing sounds and for the mammals an admixture of grunts and groans."

As anyone knows, not even a wild animal makes love by groaning and hissing. So Spivack stepped before the microphone with only a megaphone to utter deep "r-r-r-ump," "r-r-r-ump," "r-r-r-ump" in long and short grunts, thereby establishing for all time the love call of the prehistoric ape.

The tyrannosaurus—the largest animal ever known to exist—sixty feet long and with a three-foot skull—hisses and roars his vocal contributions to the battles and his mystical contact with man. But these two sounds, when produced with the necessary low tones, offered too little contrast.

During a battle with the ape, the voices of the two animals not only must be distinguishable, but the lows must blend. That was a poser! As the scene developed on the projection room screen, I heard what sounded remotely like the hissing of steam and a panther's purr.

Spivack had mixed an old puma sound track with the steam-like noise from a compressed air machine and added a few screeches from his own throat, uttered a few inches from a microphone in the soundproof room. Exactly in what proportions they were blended I cannot say, for each sequence demands many trials before the mixed noises come through the loud speaker in such volume and of such quality that the small audience of men expert in diagnosing sound declare, "Kong and the tyrannosaurus must have sounded like that."

Now the brontosaurus, one of the best known of the prehistoric quadrupeds, once lived in the Wyoming-Colorado region. Little did he think that one day his guttural croaks and hisses would reach the movie screen. But Elliot has gone the anthropologists one better; not only does he declare the brontosaurus croaked and hissed, but with dramatic license he inserts one croak after every four hisses.

The triceratops resembles an enlarged boar or a rhinoceros; more like a boar, perhaps, because of the three large horns protruding from his head. This little fellow measures only twenty-five feet long, yet in the picture he bellows like a bull, gores a man and tosses him into some long-forgotten bush—to the accompaniment of a reversed and lengthened elephant roar.

Some of the miscellaneous sounds were created with the simple instruments one would find in any studio sound laboratory. One hour Elliot was grunting into a hollow double gourd with a microphone conveniently placed to pick up deep growls and grunts of the triceratops; later in the morning he was half-reclined on the floor, grunting through a water-filled mouth into a megaphone, thus producing the animal's death gurgles.

When Kong went prowling down a river bed, Spivack squatted close by the ever-present mike, pounding with two enlarged plumbers' friends on a gravel-filled pad.

For two years the movie makers have had this fantastic picture in preparation. Technically, it has proved the most difficult idea to put into a motion picture that has ever been attempted. Readers of POPULAR SCIENCE MONTHLY already are familiar with the technique of animating mechanical animals for the movies. For such pictures only one-sixteenth of a foot of film can be exposed on a given scene and never more than twenty feet may be completed during a working day.

Many of the scenes, particularly that in which the ape fights a squadron of pursuit planes while straddling the tower of the Empire State Building, are made up of four distinct shots merged into a composite timed to a split second. The mechanical monsters move with apparent ease, but each was created on skeletons of metal duplicating those to be seen in various museums.

But the problem was only half solved with perfect animation. In order to reproduce the ape's jaw movements, as the six men hidden inside the massive head operated levers controlling the movements, it was necessary to expose 238 frames, each measuring one-sixteenth of an inch.

It would have been impossible a few years ago to film such a story. It might have been told in the form of drawings, yet the movies would not have touched the weird tale. But the technical growth of motion pictures is astounding.

As the sound in *King Kong* demonstrates, the rapid development of electrical recording equipment during the last two years has made obsolete many devices previously used to manufacture synthetic noises for talking pictures. Fully three-fourths of these sound effects instruments have been discarded during the last year.

Some mechanically-produced noises sound more like the genuine sound than the original itself. One of these is wind. Another is thunder. Thunder is so expensive to record, so many takes being required at different times and locations to record one peal successfully, that most of the thunder you hear is synthetic.

But the majority of animal sounds you hear are natural. Their recording is made possible through use of an immense electric ear, as large as a door, which picks up distant sounds and concentrates them at a small microphone placed in the center. This giant mike is able to hear hoofbeats before they become audible to the human ear, record them as their volume builds up and permit them to fade naturally into the distance as the horse canters by.

Frequently natural noises are mixed, several sound tracks being run simultaneously in order to re-record them on a single track. With these, many tricks may be played, such as running one backward, another forward at an accelerated speed, or lowering the tone an octave. Some of the results would chill your backbone were you to hear them at night.

KING KONG: MUSIC BY MAX STEINER

Robert Fiedel

It is perhaps futile to attempt to determine the exact value and significance of the contribution of a musical score to any given film. Such an appraisal will always be relative to the critic's aesthetic criteria, musical knowledge, and personal taste. It is valid, though, to state that a good musical score is likely to be more essential to the success of a *fantasy* film than to a film belonging to any other genre. The prime factor in determining the effectiveness of a fantasy film is its ability, and the degree of this ability, to suspend the disbelief of an audience in regard to the incredibility of its subject matter. The musical score thus gains added importance in the fantasy film because it is one of the most powerful forces in the suspension of disbelief.

As one of (if not *the*) most important cinematic excursions into the realm of fantasy, *King Kong* certainly demands its share of an audience's suspension of disbelief. This is accomplished—principally by the outstanding special photographic effects, animation, and sound effects work, for which the film is best known. Certainly it is through technical wizardry that the film immediately demolishes audience incredulity in the situation. But these visual and aural images, as convincing as they may be, are only capable of suspending our disbelief superficially, momentarily, appealing most immediately to the relatively shallow consciousness of an audience. There remains a nagging subconscious, however, which insists that despite what these things *seem* to be, they *must*, in fact, be the products of technical invention. This all-important suspension of disbelief to the subconscious is accomplished in *King Kong* by the supplement of Max Steiner's stunning musical score. It is Steiner's score, which, by the very nature of music, reaches our innermost feelings making us aware of Kong's soul, and thereby generates the great sympathy and audience identification which sets *King Kong* apart from the long legacy of prehistoric monster films. The score, in essence, "believes" in the screen narrative and conveys this "belief" immediately to our own subconscious despite our intellectual objections. The score, then, is a highly manipulative device used to control audience reaction to the film.

It would be foolish, though, to dismiss the score as relevant only to the subconscious. There is, of course, a certain degree of audience consciousness of the score, as music, and especially in the moments when it almost becomes one of the sound effects as, for example, during the scene in which Kong battles and kills the serpentlike creature by smashing its head against some rocks—each "smash" accompanied by a staccato orchestral outburst. But in *King Kong* (and, for that matter, in all of film), the visual element is the primary focal point of attention. Unless making a specific effort to direct its attention elsewhere, the average audience is, for the most part, oblivious to the score. This especially holds true for those experiencing their first viewing of a film—when only an overall impression is registered.

Viennese-born Maximilian Raoul Steiner arrived in Hollywood in 1929, securing employment at RKO-Radio Pictures as an arranger in its newly established music department. In 1930, Steiner was appointed head of this same department, and composed his first original film score for Wesley Ruggles' *Cimarron* (1931). Other notable original Steiner scores from this early period include Gregory La Cava's *A Symphony of Six Million* (1932), King Vidor's *Bird of Paradise* (1932), George Cukor's *A Bill of Divorcement* (1932), and Ernest B. Schoedsack and Irving Pichel's *The Most Dangerous Game* (1932). At this early period in sound cinema, the art of original film music composition was just beginning to develop. Many early "talkie" musical scores consisted merely of arrangements of famous classical pieces or "moods," arranged in a manner so as to complement the mood of the film. Other functions of film music were usually left relatively unexplored. Occasionally one of the few original film scores received limited acclaim, but for the most part, the music in the background of so many early sound films went unheralded by the critics and public alike.

Early in 1933, RKO was wrapping up production on the film that was either to make or break the studio, Merian C. Cooper and Ernest B. Schoedsack's *King Kong*. RKO executives were reluctant to spend any additional funds for the composition of an original musical score for the film. So much capital had already been invested in the film's production (most of it tied up in the special process work) that it was thought unwise to put any more money into what might conceivably be a tremendous box-office failure. Accordingly, Steiner was instructed by RKO executives to score the film using stock material from the RKO music library and earlier films. However, Merian C. Cooper had a great deal of faith in his new production (quite rightly so!) and insisted that Steiner compose an original score which he would agree to finance out of his own pocket if need be. Artistic creativity would be permitted to triumph over the inhibitive Hollywood studio system!

Steiner composed the score to *King Kong* in eight weeks and recorded it with the then unheard-of complement of an eighty-piece orchestra, at a cost of $50,000. The resulting score, due to its originality of form and content, received great acclaim as a milestone in the development of the art of film music composition. Never before had the full potential of an original musical score for a film been so brilliantly realized. Consequently, Steiner's *King Kong* music marks the first major aesthetic step in the development of scoring for the sound film.

King Kong's score relies heavily on the use of the Wagnerian *leitmotif*. Lush themes in a late Romantic style are used to identify and suggest characters, moods, and settings. There are individual motifs for Kong and Ann Darrow as well as themes for the native tribe, a native ceremonial dance, Skull Island, the jungle odyssey of the ship's crew, mystery and perplexity, a theater overture, and even a theme to identify the ill-fated elevated train. Steiner expertly weaves all of these themes and motifs together, developing and expanding them as the narrative unfolds, to create an explicit narrative for orchestra. This musical narrative complements the screen narrative so precisely that the score ceases to be merely an extraneous element, but is, rather, a crucial, integral element of the film. The extent of this integration is so great, that to imagine *King Kong* without its score is inconceivable.

The score makes an immediate impression from the very start of the film, beginning with the main title and opening credits. The first sounds we hear are those of the famous three-note descending "Kong" motif played boldly by the brass and without harmonic accompaniment. As such, it is a statement of power and brute force, void of any greater depth of character. A brief transition leads into the exposition of the "Ann Darrow" motif which is also based on a descending scale. Next follows the wild and frenetic "Native" theme, building up to the overpowering catharsis of a

blaring dissonant chord which accompanies the screen credit, "King Kong—The Eighth Wonder Of The World." Hold on to your seat! Kong's screen credit yields to the famous "Old Arabian Proverb."

Steiner accompanies this title with a haunting variation and development of the "Kong" motif played passionately in the lower string register, revealing quite a different aspect of Kong's character from that stated initially. The descending "Kong" motif as stated and developed here and in other portions of the film, suggests the passionate yearning of Kong for the object of his infatuation which will always be beyond his reach. As the developed motif climbs and ultimately descends, so it expresses Kong's vain unrequited passion, failure, and ultimate destruction. By the very nature of Kong's motif, we are made aware at this early stage, of his inevitable doom; thus he is immediately established as a great tragic figure in the classic tradition.

After this brief prelude, the score ceases for approximately twenty minutes of the film's running time. This early section of the film concerns itself with the exposition of the narrative and introduction and development of the various "human" characters. Being aware of when *not* to use music in a film is almost as great a concern to the composer as the actual composition and "placing" of the music itself. Steiner was obviously aware that a film like *King Kong* would require a great deal of music to sustain the all-important suspension of disbelief its incredible situations would require. Since it is known that an excess of music can become quite tedious and detrimental to a film's success, (that is, at least, known by Steiner!), he wisely decided to refrain from scoring scenes which did not absolutely require musical support. Since—relatively speaking—nothing really out of the ordinary occurs during these first twenty-odd minutes of the film compared to the events which follow, it was thought best to limit the music.

The score resumes on the morning of the ship's arrival at Skull Island. An ominous and brooding theme accompanied by native tom-toms is heard as Skull Island is first sighted by Denham and Captain Englehorn. As the ship's crew lands on the shore and begins to venture into the native village, this "Skull Island" theme continues, anticipating the horrors to come. While Denham and party cautiously approach the native village, the "Skull Island" theme gradually yields to the ceremonial "Native Dance." This music is wild and unrestrained, full of strident dissonances and savage rhythm. It quite effectively conveys raw, unleashed primitive excitement, as the natives, costumed in ape skins, savagely beat their breasts shouting "Kong! Kong!" accented by orchestral outbursts.

This "Native Dance" comes to a violent and abrupt conclusion when Denham and crew are spotted by the irate native chief.

Later, back on the ship, there is a love scene between Jack and Ann. Somewhat awkwardly acted (and probably directed by Schoedsack), this scene and all its naïveté are salvaged by Steiner's music. As Jack and Ann make small talk and stilted conversation ("Say, I guess I love you!"), there is a development and variation of the "Ann Darrow" motif heard earlier during the opening credits. The descending motif is developed into a typically Steineresque waltz, accompanied by a haunting and apprehensive harmony. This arrangement of the motif suggests a romantic mood while at the same time hinting at a descent into a nightmare world, subtly foreshadowing the adventures to come.

Frenzy breaks loose both visually and musically when Ann is kidnapped by the natives and offered as a sacrifice to Kong. To intensify the primitive revelry of the spectacular torch-lit sacrificial ceremony, Steiner gives us a savage and orgiastic development of the "Native" theme heard earlier during the opening credits. Crescendo follows crescendo as the hysteria mounts to a fever pitch. Woven into this musical pandemonium is a heart-pounding variation of the "Ann Darrow" motif which is heard as Ann (as seen from an overhead tracking shot) is led to the sacrificial altar. The music ceases with one final crescendo as the native chief calls for silence from his position high atop the great wall. As the huge gong is struck—a signal to Kong that his "bride" awaits—there is unbearable silence as Ann, the natives, and we, anxiously anticipate the appearance of Kong! Steiner then accents the unseen steps of the approaching Kong with musical rumblings and heavings. These musical "grunts" develop into a threatening and awesome statement of the "Kong" motif as we catch our first glimpse of him through the parting tree tops. The frightening subjective dolly shot to a tight close-up of Kong's face is accompanied by a panic-stricken statement of the "Ann Darrow" motif, tensely played in the upper string register. It immediately conveys her readily understandable terror and frenzied state of mind. Kong's important initial appearance and his first encounter with Ann have been heightened to a point of overwhelming excitement and extreme effectiveness.

As Denham and crew begin their jungle odyssey in pursuit of Kong and Ann, we hear the cautious but steady "Jungle March" played firmly by the woodwinds, suggesting the apprehensive but determined perseverance of the heroic party. The pursuers soon become the pursued as an unfriendly brontosaurus decides that the small band of men would be just the right thing for dinner. As the terrified men flee through almost impenetrable swamp and vegetation, the reserved "Jungle March" becomes an electrifying scherzo for full orchestra, pounding twice as fast as our own hearts! This frantic scherzo variation of the "Jungle March" is also used to accompany the other jungle chase scenes which follow.

There is another major section of musical silence which occurs soon after, at approximately the middle of the film. This is during the spectacular battle scene between Kong and the tyrannosaurus. One of Steiner's criteria for the use of musical silence in a film score has previously been discussed. But the musical silence during this scene is prompted by a very different theory, one which applies not only to the scoring of *King Kong*, but to the scoring of practically all sound films. As such, it is worthwhile to discuss this theory at some length.

To borrow from elementary psychological theory,[1] if two or more stimuli of equal or unequal intensities are applied to a subject simultaneously, that subject will be forced to divide his attention proportionately among them. He will therefore be unable to focus his total attention (unless previously conditioned to do so) on any *one* of the stimuli, thus experiencing each stimulus only superficially without realizing the full intensity of prolonged exposure to any individual one. Inversely, if the degree of discomfort created by any single stimulus becomes to great to endure, the subject can consciously divert his attention to another stimulus thereby preventing any single stimulus from causing too much anxiety—in effect, a "safety valve" mechanism.

Theoretically applying this concept to the sound film and specifically to the scoring of film music, we have two basic stimuli: 1) the *real* element—the physical reality and actuality of screen action and circumstance, and resultant sounds; 2) the *plastic* element—the enhancing, artificial, and manipulative devices, such as the musical score, stylized and deliberately artificial aural and visual effects, etc. When these two stimuli occur simultaneously (in any combination of the defined sub-elements), an audience is consciously and subconsciously forced to divide its attention between them. The battle between Kong and the tyrannosaurus, being the single most spectacular action sequence in the film (and rightly perceived as such by Steiner), is quite capable of generating and sustaining excitement by virtue of its *real* elements alone. These *real* elements would, to some degree, be

1 This concept of psychological perception has been greatly simplified and idealized from extensive theses on the subject, in order that it may be theoretically applied to the discussion of a film music concept. It is, on no account, to be taken as a definitive statement of psychological fact.

distracted from were there any musical accompaniment or other simultaneous *plastic* elements. Thus, as presented, we are forced to direct the whole of our attention to the *real* element without any background music to distract us and relieve the almost unbearable excitement generated. This excitement is, then, extremely intensified precisely because there is no other stimulus to serve as an emotional diversion.

It would not be feasible, however, to apply this technique of musical silence to the entire film which, it can be argued, is capable of generating and sustaining excitement throughout by virtue of its *real* elements alone. The prolonged, sustained tension which would result from the absence of a musical score would be detrimental to the dramatic structure of the film. An audience can only tolerate this intense degree of sustained anxiety for short periods segregated by relatively calm stretches of narrative. Dramatic pyrotechnics can only be fully appreciated when carefully and strategically placed. The battle-to-the-death between Kong and the tyrannosaurus is only of about five minutes' duration, yet we experience extreme tension for what seems to be an eternity. Moreover, the elimination of a musical score throughout would also entail the elimination of the all-important suspension of disbelief which we made such a fuss about earlier. Kong's battle with the tyrannosaurus can suffice without musical accompaniment because: (1) Steiner's music has, for the previous twenty-odd minutes, suspended our disbelief in Kong and company's incredibility; (2) The emotions expressed in and necessary to this scene are only those of brute force and bestial ferocity. As such, they are quite aptly conveyed by the *real* elements alone. It is when the nuances of Kong's emotional complexities are to be conveyed that the score becomes most essential.

Steiner also applies this theory of musical silence to the crucial final scene in which Kong is attacked by the airplanes atop the Empire State Building. From the moment the first airplane breaks formation and dives to attack, to the moment when Kong begins to weaken and realize that his death is impending, Steiner refrains from musical accompaniment, leaving this entire section in tense silence. The effect of this musical silence is the same as in the previously discussed battle scene. Steiner's uncanny judgment of when and when not to use musical accompaniment is one of his *King Kong* score's most outstanding assets.

To return to earlier episodes of the film, the next important musical development occurs when Kong returns with Ann to his lair and proceeds to examine his new possession more closely. This scene is probably the single most important episode in the development of the narrative, both musical and dramatic.

No other scene in the film so clearly explains and explores the very nature of Kong's infatuation with Ann and thereby justifies his later resulting actions. Until recently, this vital scene has been excised from all circulating prints of the film as the result of a typically asinine censorship decision. Thankfully, it has now been restored by enterprising business concerns, and is available for evaluation. As Kong quietly sits atop his mountain retreat, gently peeling off and inquisitively sniffing fragments of Ann's dress, Steiner musically conveys all of the hidden nuances and ambiguities of his thoughts and reactions with a four-note "Mystery and Perplexity" motif. This enigmatic motif was previously heard momentarily during the earlier "Skull Island" theme, the initial encounter between Denham and the native chief, and the "Jungle March." Here, this "musical question mark" is developed to express Kong's sympathetic perplexity and bewilderment over his new interest, while at the same time suggesting the loneliness and underlying gentleness of his character, and the intimacy of the entire profound relationship. To achieve this effect, the motif is played slowly and passionately by a solo violin, with a shimmering string accompaniment. Here the score is called upon to express the intangible—the emotions essential to the film's narrative, but unexpressed by the *real* elements alone.

Pandemonium breaks loose once again as the enraged Kong breaks through the great wall and runs amok in the native village in his frantic search for the previously rescued Ann. Steiner accents this unleashed fury with blaring dissonances, brutal variations of the "Kong" motif, and violent crescendos, all woven together to emphasize the horror of Kong's savage actions. When Kong is subdued by a well-thrown gas grenade, Denham envisions his captive's name up in lights on a Broadway theater marquee. At this point there is a dissolve to the actual marquee as it stands a few months later on the opening night of Denham's colossal attraction. A "Theater Overture" accompanies the excitement of opening night as various patrons and members of the press enter and mill about the theater, candidly conversing. The "Theater Overture" is a thrilling, rapidly paced grandscale development of a motif heard earlier in the film as Kong is seen crossing the great log over the treacherous ravine. Its syncopated rhythm conveys a feeling of jungle savagery, while a second, or "B" theme, is more in the style of conventional theater music. The overture concludes as Denham walks on stage to introduce the evening's event. As the curtain rises to reveal Kong, there is a magnificent fanfare which, in itself, has enough power to bring an audience to submission.

There are relatively less spectacular fanfares to introduce Ann and Jack.

Pandemonium breaks loose for a third and final time as Kong breaks his restraining chains, crashes out of the theater, and runs amok in the streets of New York, passionately resuming his search for his lost Ann. Steiner again accompanies the savage rampage with wild and brutal musical passages composed of variations and developments of the many previously established themes and motifs. Dominant, of course, is the "Kong" motif, heard repeatedly and threateningly throughout this final onslaught of violence and destruction. There is also a newly introduced theme for the elevated train, which is heard as it unknowingly approaches its destruction. Here, Steiner musically imitates the sound of the oncoming train with an ascending series of rhythmically arranged chords, and a musical mocking of the train's whistle.

Crescendo yields to crescendo as Kong brings terror and destruction to the panic-stricken city, with his violent actions matched every step of the way by Steiner's violent musical accompaniment. As Kong begins his legendary ascent up the face of the Empire State Building, the score spirally ascends against a dissonant harmony, conveying a feeling of vertigo emphasizing his great height.

The true genius of the *King Kong* score is nowhere in greater evidence than in Kong's final death scene. Most critics have always been at a loss to give adequate explanation for the great feeling of tragedy evoked by Kong's death. This enigmatic reaction has always been one of the film's great philosophical ambiguities. Great sympathy is generated when Kong is finally destroyed—this is a universally acknowledged fact. Yet most critics and audiences alike have traditionally been unable to pinpoint exactly whence this sympathy stems. The answer to this question lies, in fact, in the musical score, and by careful analysis of the music accompanying the death scene, we can shed some light on the mystery.

Nowhere is the score more manipulative than in the final death scene. As Kong realizes that his death is immediately impending, we hear a lamenting variation of the "Ann Darrow" motif played passionately by the strings. Somehow, as familiar as we may be with the motif at this time, his variation seems more disturbing than previous variations. The reason for this reaction is that the motif, as heard previously, has never been musically *resolved*. Its supporting harmonies have always concluded with *active* chords—chords which seek to proceed further in an attempt to be resolved by *rest* chords. In this variation of the motif, the harmonic accompaniment *is* finally resolved by rest chords, signifying the finality and resolution of the Ann Darrow character's dramatic development. Then, as Kong finally dies and loses his hold atop the Empire State Building, his motif is also resolved by rest chords (though far more spectacularly than the "Ann Darrow" motif), signifying his acceptance of defeat, and the resolution of his dramatic development. The fact of Kong's death thus makes far more than a superficial impression on us because it has musically been driven deep into our emotional psyche. Kong's actual fall is accompanied by a sustained blaring dissonant chord, and finally resolved by an orchestral outburst. It is interesting that his fall is resolved *only* by the score, and not by the visuals. This enables the actual situation to elevate itself from the harshness of reality by allowing an audience to imagine its own imagery of the inevitable crash. The score serves the vital function of resolving the tension of the actual fall, and denoting the precise moment of impact to trigger our emotional responses. The "Ann Darrow" motif is heard once again as she and Jack are reunited, this time in the same variation as heard during their earlier love scene aboard the ship. Here, the apprehensive tone of the harmony suggests not anxiety to come, but rather the recollection of the previous nightmarish experiences. As Denham muses philosophically over the body of Kong ("Oh no, it wasn't the airplanes. . . . It was beauty killed the beast!"), a celestial statement of the "Ann Darrow" motif is played in the upper string register which makes a final tragic comment on the death of Kong. A final recapitulation of the resolved "Kong" motif ensues, concluding the film on a negative, disturbing theme. Throughout this entire final death scene, the score, by virtue of the very power of music, enables the film to transcend the bounds of actuality and attain a great degree of spirituality. It is this incredible spirituality brought about by the score which suggests the "soul" of Kong, forcing our reaction to his destruction to be more than just pity over the slaughter of an animal. It is, in fact, this spirituality that we are reacting to with our watery eyes—("I know, I know. . . . You've just got something in your eye!").

One of the interesting techniques which Steiner employs in his score to *King Kong* (and, for that matter, many other film scores) is the closely synchronized accenting of physical movement with musical sounds. Three obvious examples of this technique are: (1) As the native chief slowly walks toward Denham in their initial encounter, each of his steps is musically accented; (2) In the aforementioned scene in which Kong battles the serpentlike beast, each smash of the beast's head is accented by a musical "smash"; (3) When the first of the four biplanes breaks formation and dives to attack Kong, it is accompanied by a spirally descending theme, accenting the plane's descent. This accenting technique, sneeringly referred to as "mickey mousing"[2] by certain other composers who have never been able to master its complexities, is one of the *King Kong* score's most outstanding and singular characteristics. Steiner displays a unique talent for being able to match a piece of screen action with its most appropriate musical counterpart. He is thereby able to greatly enhance the film experience by conveying musically, and heightening the undertones of, a physical gesture.

Despite the possible disadvantage of "overemphasizing" screen action which this technique, if carelessly used, may sometimes be prone to do, it is directly responsible for another closely related highly advantageous scoring technique: the precise conformation of the score to the actual edited structure of the film. This technique is effected by having the musical "cuts" (crescendos, tempo changes, theme changes, etc.) timed and perfectly synchronized to the actual shot cuts, thus serving to further integrate the score into the film and further enhancing the film experience. Three examples of this technique as applied in *King Kong* are: (1) Early in the film when Denham and crew approach the native village, we hear tribal ceremonial music originating from the center of the village. Denham parts some branches to see what is happening. As the camera cuts to reveal the thrilling ceremony he sees, Steiner also "cuts" to a powerful crescendo in the "Native Dance," which, up to this point has been heard only in the background; (2) Later, as the men are keeping watch on the great wall, pessimistically waiting the return of "Mr. Driscoll and the lady," we hear a very tranquil but attentive variation of the "Jungle March" theme. Suddenly there is a cut to the exciting head-on tracking shot of Jack and Ann fleeing through the jungle from the rapidly pursuing Kong. On this cut, Steiner also "cuts" to a frantic scherzo variation of the "Jungle March" theme; (3) As Kong climbs the face of the hotel building with a terrified Ann clutched in his paw, Steiner begins to swell to an enormous crescendo on the "Mystery and Perplexity" motif. When the film cuts to a heart-stopping medium shot of Ann in Kong's paw suspended high about the city streets, Steiner once again "cuts" to the throbbing crescendo on the anticipated "Kong" motif

variation. The excitement generated by this technique of synchronized musical "cuts" is overwhelming—another of the score's unique, outstanding characteristics.

Max Steiner's score to *King Kong* has an interesting history of "recapitulations," so to speak. Excerpts of it appear again in Schoedsack's *Son Of Kong* (1933), along with additional original music by Steiner; in the same director's *The Last Days Of Pompeii* (1935) during the climactic devastation scenes, with musical credit given to Roy Webb; and lastly, sections of it appear again in George B. Seitz' *The Last Of The Mohicans* (1936), as incorporated by Nathaniel Schilkret. (Isn't there an old adage about imitation being the sincerest form of flattery?) Also, a brief *King Kong Suite* was recorded in the mid-1950s for Decca Records by Jack Shaindlin and His Orchestra, which appeared on the LP *50 Years of Movie Music*. In recent years more recordings have been released. Selections were included in a collection of Steiner scores performed by the National Philharmonic Orchestra, conducted by Charles Gerhardt, and in 1975 LeRoy Holmes recorded the score for an entire LP.

A discussion of any film scores merits inevitably leads to the question of how well the score would fare in the concert hall, isolated from the visual element. Many film music compositions are unfortunately unsuited for the concert hall because of their lack of recognized appreciable musical form. (Sonata-allegro form, theme and variations, etc.) Film music has its own aesthetics and "forms," however these are most often incompatible with those of music composed specifically for the concert hall. Much film music is composed of fragmented themes and motifs, stated and repeated momentarily throughout a given film without regard for any coherent development and form. This does not necessarily mean to say that such a score is a *bad* score: the criterion for this judgment is only the degree of the score's ability to work with and enhance the film. But isolated from the visuals and heard in the concert hall, such a score would lack the ability to capture and sustain an audience's interest, unless, of course, specifically rearranged for the concert hall as some such scores occasionally are. An example of such an independently incoherent film score would be any one of John Barry's fine scores for the *James Bond* films.

Steiner's *King Kong* score presents an entirely different situation. The Wagnerian *leitmotifs* which he incorporates, build and develop throughout the film, bridged by interesting transitions and interludes which preserve dramatic continuity. The individual themes and motifs thus, in a sense, become *dramatis personae*

---

[2] The term "mickey mousing" as applied to film music criticism, is derived from the style of musical scoring used to accompany early animated cartoons. Such cartoons (i.e., Walt Disney's *Steamboat Willie*, 1928) employ musical sounds to accent physical movements of the characters. These accents are usually greatly exaggerated to achieve a comic effect.

in a narrative for orchestra, as they are initially stated, developed, varied, and ultimately resolved. This style of film score would most certainly be capable of capturing and sustaining an audience's attention if presented as an independent entity in the concert hall, first conceding, of course, to a few minor modifications.

We have seen how the musical score to *King Kong* plays a crucial role in the film's time-proven success by generally enhancing the film experience. Hopefully it may be realized now that Max Steiner's musical contribution to the film was as unique and significant as the more obvious visual contributions. Certainly this commentary will have succeeded if the reader has been made more aware of the technique of film music. And so, perhaps in future screenings, *King Kong* will be *heard* as well as *seen*. Who was it that asked, "Is there music in *King Kong?*"

ORPHAN IN THE STORM: *SON OF KONG**

Gerald Peary

While Franklin Roosevelt was moving into the White House in Spring 1933, Americans went in droves to see *King Kong* in its original release. The film was such an immediate financial (and also artistic) success that it became apparent that the dead would not rest. It was time for regeneration, Hollywood style: a sequel. Prodded into activity by an anxious RKO, the *King Kong* artistic crew (Merian C. Cooper, Ernest Schoedsack, Willis O'Brien, Max Steiner, and scriptwriter, Ruth Rose) went scurrying back to work.

Before any other studio could capitalize by jumping on the bandwagon of "big ape" movies, RKO did so itself, making the best of the realization that Kong's agonizing demise before the camera possessed such finality that to risk a *Return of Kong* would be rather ridiculous. The filmmakers instead restored to a simpler device of inventing an orphaned foundling child for the late monster: *The Son of Kong*. Six months after *King Kong's* release, the sequel was playing in neighborhood theaters.

Son of Kong begins imposingly enough with ominous, dramatic jungle music and a closeup of Kong himself at his ferocious best—all muscles, hair and teeth. Then the camera dollies back for a most disappointing revelation. Kong is only a picture on a poster, an inanimate artifact, hung on a wall. In place of the cosmically energized, tempestuous stomping grounds of *King Kong*, the locale introduced is the drab, confined living quarters of a cheap New York rooming house.

Who lives here? *Son of Kong* is full of surprises, for it is nobody other than Carl Denham himself, though hardly recognizable. He has fallen on terrible times in the month since Kong took blocks of New York with him to his final destiny, leaving his business manager full responsibility for his damages. "Tell the public that Carl Denham, the smart guy who was going to make a million dollars off of King Kong is flat broke," he tells a reporter. "Everyone in New York is suing me."

Denham is not only impoverished but, even less characteristic of him, penitent and remorseful about the havoc caused by Kong. "Don't you think I'm sorry for the harm?" he asks, and not without feeling. "I wish I'd left him on the island. I'm paying for what he did." Denham is now a spiritless, guilt-ridden man, hiding away in this obscure rooming house from a host of creditors, finally fleeing to safety incognito on the back of a junk wagon.

The seemingly indomitable entrepreneural spirit of dynamic Carl Denham has disappeared. Instead, Denham in *Son of Kong* is weary and helpless, the victim of impossible financial obligations. Reduced in status to a penniless Depression Everyman, his last gasps of energy and imagination are devoted not to combating the Depression but to fleeing it.

Son of Kong, then, is an escapist film, expressing through Denham's subsequent actions a wistful yearning (probably on a national level in late 1933) for a fantasy alternative to the hard times of America. Whereas *King Kong* reflects a momentary national mood of optimism, perhaps bred of Roosevelt's campaign of 1932 and the prospect of reversing the Great Depression, *Son of Kong* reveals the mood of post-inauguration despondency at the failure of this reversal to materialize.

In retrospect, *King Kong* was a pacesetter: bold of conception, unique of content, pushing its way effortlessly toward new frontiers unexplored either in reality or previously on the screen. *Son of Kong* is conservative and cautious by comparison, a movie of quiet excitements and leisurely pace; it is also predictably derivative of the filmic past. Not only are many of its scenes variations on similar sequences in the parent film, but huge chunks of its plot are lifted directly from a lost, generally unknown silent of the Tiffany Corporation called *The Enchanted Island* (1927) and probably suggested by Shakespeare's *The Tempest*.

For the record: *The Enchanted Island* concerned a man (Henry B. Walthall) and his daughter (Charlotte Stevens) stranded for fifteen years on a tropical island with only their trained animals as companions. The peace is broken in the sudden invasion of three men:

* This essay was prepared especially for this volume and is published by permission of the author.

the hero, Bob Hamilton (Pierre Gendron), the villain, "Red" Blake, and Ulysses Abraham Washington, a Negro cook. Hamilton falls in love with the young girl and teaches her about the outside world. "Red" Blake kills off the father in a quarrel, but he is in turn done in by Ulysses in a fight during a volcanic eruption. The lovers escape from the molten lava and are rescued by a cruiser.

Son of Kong retains in its script by Ruth Rose all of the plot elements listed above for *The Enchanted Island*, with some minor adjustments. A young girl, Hilda, and her alcoholic father, a refugee from the circus, have lived for years as expatriates at the port of Dakang, supporting themselves through a sideshow trained monkey act. Into this locale comes the hero, Denham, the villain, Helstrom, a Chinese cook, Charlie, and the ship's captain. Helstrom quarrels with Hilda's father and murders him. Denham becomes enamored of Hilda. Later in the movie, Helstrom is killed by a sea-monster and buried beneath a volcanic explosion. Denham and Hilda escape from both the molten lava and the island sinking into the sea. They are picked up by a cruiser and rescued.

The Dakang of *Son of Kong* is hardly, however, an idyllic, "enchanted island" setting; rather it is harshly pictured as a dank, impoverished port town, a hangout for derelicts and shiftless drifters. Denham's own rejuvenated romanticism swiftly is undercut here. He and the captain follow a sign pointing out the way to an exciting musical interlude with the mysterious "Belle Helene," a trip which ends for them on a flat bench in a tent crowded with the lowest native element. They sit in stony silence watching a monkey orchestra perform its dreadful act. The tiny animals, dressed like miniature bellhops, pound on their instruments in arythmic, atonal counterpoint, an unnerving baroque introduction to the show's main attraction.

"Belle Helene" in person proves equally unsettling. Instead of the sultry, husky-voiced continental probably anticipated, "Helene" turns out to be the inexperienced and awkwardly misplaced American, Hilda, who strums an Hawaiian guitar in a clumsy attempt to appear exotic and sings badly in a high-pitched voice, "Oh, I've got the runaway blues today . . ." Denham and friend have been taken.

It seems clear that the rich atmospheric details in this strangely compelling scene are based on the filmmakers' personal acquaintances with such locales during global travels in the 1920s. In fact, Merian C. Cooper (whose resemblance to actor Robert Armstrong is uncanny) speaks at length of exactly such an experience in his autobiographical journal, *The Sea Gypsy*, a 1924 account of an around-the-world voyage with the famed explorer, Captain Edward Salisbury.

It was a trip much like Denham makes in *Son of Kong*.

Cooper had landed in Jibuti, an Abyssinian port, and wandered with a friend into the native quarters, where they were confronted with an invitation to "See Arab dance, de Somali dance." Taylor, Cooper's companion, remarked excitedly, "Well, here's a chance to see the famous and beautiful and sensuous dances of the East." They followed their hosts through crooked streets and finally into a tiny tent where, in place of a lavish stage show, three Arab women pathetically attempted to sway their bodies in the floor space between the beds. The disenchanted Cooper wrote in his diary, "These dancers and the fly ridden café are Jibuti's only amusements. Absolutely nothing else."

In *Son of Kong*, Carl Denham, the avowed misogynist and producer of all-male adventure movies, the man who told sexy Ann Darrow in *King Kong* that their relationship would be "strictly business" and meant it, this same person is in love. The totally different, muted character of *Son of Kong* allows Denham to fall for the shy, naïve young woman, as he disregards in true romantic fashion the embarrassing inadequacy of her show-business personality. And when Hilda's father is murdered, Denham takes her willingly aboard for a return voyage to Skull Island. This bashfully grinning middle-aged courtier even finds time to flirt with Hilda under the moonlight once the ship is again at sea.

At last, with the exposition completed and romance brewing, *Son of Kong* brings its plot around to the concerns for which people presumably paid their money, the strange and fantastic doings on Skull Island. The party sails up on the beach to be greeted in warning by Willis O'Brien's eerie black apparitions floating through the air like furies. It is *King Kong* over again, including that flamboyant and chilling jungle music.

The excitement quickly passes, however, as the neighborhood seems cleaned up a bit since the last sojourn, with most of the rougher prehistoric beasts, from tyrannosaur to pterodactyl, apparently in migration (only the monstrous amphibian dinosaur from *King Kong* remains to gobble up the villain at an opportune moment, thus revenging the death of Hilda's father without need of Denham to bloody his hero hands). But all in all, the rejuvenated Skull Island isn't a bad place to bring up a kid, unless the youth happens to be the Son of Kong.

Denham and Hilda come across a most distressing sight, the titular star of the movie up to his neck in quicksand and yelping like a puppy for assistance. It is in this long-delayed, rather anticlimactic moment that the Son of Kong finally reveals himself: like Denham, he is a much-diminished thing.

This twelve-foot Kong will not trample on native villages nor rampage through the streets of New York. Moreover, the son is clearly prepubescent and shows no more interest in sexual possession of the heroine, Hilda, than in searching out his strangely nonexistent Mom, the "missing woman" of the Kong pictures. The Son of Kong is consistent with the gentle, mellow, and sexually subdued mood of this second movie.

Denham and Hilda come to the rescue. They pull little Kong out of the mire, for, as Denham later explains, "I felt I owed his family something." Kong, Jr. lumbers after them in gratitude like an overgrown child; but in this case it is the adults who require protection against the more insistently carnivorous of the neighborhood animals.

In parody imitation of the astounding Darwinian battle to the death between King Kong and the fierce tyrannosaur, little Kong takes on a nasty-tempered bear in schoolyard brawl fashion. They box, wrestle, and stumble about the terrain with more noise than with physical damage, as Denham and Hilda root on their new friend to victory in the mock heroic tussle. An admiring Denham, comments vapidly, "Gee can he scrap. Just like his old man."

Skull Island seems safe for the time being. It is the end of the day's wandering through the forest maze, and Son of Kong's heroes have found themselves conveniently separated from the other party of sojourners. As the new lovers bed down near each other for the night, with Kong, Jr. secretly keeping watch over them, (like the lion in Rousseau's painting of The Sleeping Gypsy, the movie begins to assume a tranquil beauty reminiscent of Shakespearean romance.

This feeling is reinforced by the sudden splitting of the movie into a double plot, complete with ironically paralleled events. The enchanted jungle greenery brings the romantic couple closer and closer together, a relationship further sanctified through the harmonious alliance of man, woman and beast. These three have a restful night of sleep and sanctuary from the turmoils surrounding them, followed the next day by discovery of the treasures and hidden riches of the island.

Markedly different is the nighttime fate of their three companions—the captain, the Chinese cook, and the villain, Helstrom, who have holed up for the night against their wills in a bare stone cavern. Outside a raging prehistoric behemoth pounds against the rocks trying to get at them. These three get no sleep at all, not even the chance to sit down. Perhaps they are plagued by the presence among them of a secret murderer, Helstrom, killer of Hilda's father.

Son of Kong appears at this point finally to have found itself, evolving out of its previous loose, rambling, and even haphazard form into a work of some purposeful structure. Unfortunately, everything gained is lost again in a split second, in the blowing of the wind. Literally from nowhere a mighty storm breaks on the horizon; and without warning Skull Island, its volcanoes erupting everywhere, crumbles into the sea, taking with it the last vestiges of prehistoric culture and the body of the evil Helstrom.

The virtuous protagonists—Hilda, the captain, the Chinese cook—all row away in the nick of time. (What happens to the black native populace on the other side of the island? Their plight is ignored.) And Carl Denham is plucked from Davey Jones' locker by way of the most valiant (and also contrived and sentimental) heroic sacrifice since Tale of Two Cities. Little Kong, noble savage until the end, holds Denham above the waves in his gentle fist until the rescue. Then, with Max Steiner's mournful elegy of strings soaring and moaning passionately in the background (the same music which lay King Kong to rest), this well-meaning young giant gorilla is swallowed by the ocean.

The harsh, dislocated ending to Son of Kong can not be explained in terms of this narrative logic, no matter how melodramatic. Quite clearly there were outside, nonaesthetic factors at work influencing the last of the filming. Perhaps the budget ran out. Or, more likely, RKO insisted on cutting short the shooting schedule in order to rush King Kong's sequel into the market.

Whatever the case, Son of Kong suffers to the point of near ruin in this abrupt halt to the narrative after only sixty-two minutes. The slow and deliberate development of the story for nearly an hour deserves much better than the five minutes of packaged apocalypse which is followed, in Kong Jr.'s ostensibly heroic drowning, with a few seconds of vulgar cinematic apotheosis.

Hardly more satisfactory is the concluding tag of Denham and Hilda cooing together aboard a rescue vessel, bantering in cute innuendo about an impending marriage between them. Has the hero of the movie become wiser and more perceptive from living through this harrowing adventure? "Poor Little Kong. Do you think he knew he was saving my life?" asks Denham with the most blank-faced seriousness.

Luckily this absurd inquiry is not answered, as the animated conversation turns to more important issues for Hilda and Denham at the fadeout: love, and portioning out the treasure money. Kong, Jr. becomes a forgotten memory for them, perhaps the inevitable conclusion to the adverse existence of this orphaned, then deceased gorilla giant. He was already denied artistic immortality by the callous mercenaries of RKO, who released a half-baked, virtually sabotaged movie so that it arrived in the theaters in time for the quick profits of the Christmas season.

This misfortune occurred in late 1933, yet its terrible implications stretch immutably into the cinematic future. Forty years later hardly anyone remembers that the famous King Kong had a son.

Marcel Delgado, working with Willis O'Brien and Merian C. Cooper, actually constructed the complicated models used in King Kong. The armatures or "skeletons" for these models needed to provide for refined, flexible articulation demanded by animation that would result in a satisfactory illusion of complex physical movement; the armatures also had to be durable enough to stand the punishment that the thousands of repositionings would entail.

David Allen, a young animator, had been inspired by his admiration for *King Kong* to "reconstruct" the original models. He later used the model in a one-minute television commercial for the new "big" Volkswagen. The commercial was striking and included a sequence in which Kong climbs into the driver's seat only to find Fay Wray's daughter screaming beside him. Market research revealed that audiences remembered the Kong commercial but not the product being advertised!

Willis O'Brien preparing a take from *Son of Kong*. *Photograph supplied by and used with the kind permission of Mrs. Darlyne O'Brien.*

Profile of one of the models suggesting the various moods that could be created by lighting and camera angle. *Photograph supplied by and used with the kind permission of Marcel Delgado.*

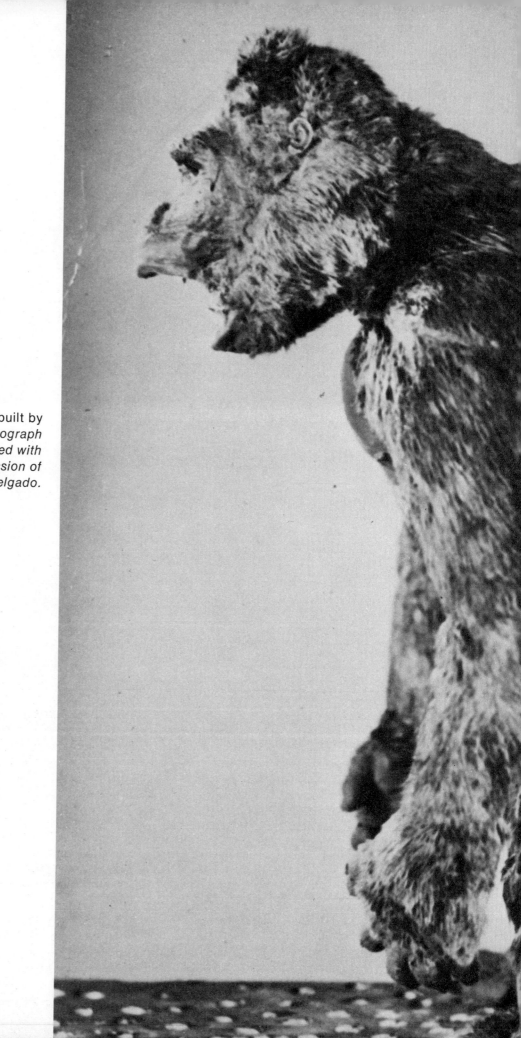

The original models built by Marcel Delgado. *Photograph supplied by and used with the kind permission of Marcel Delgado.*

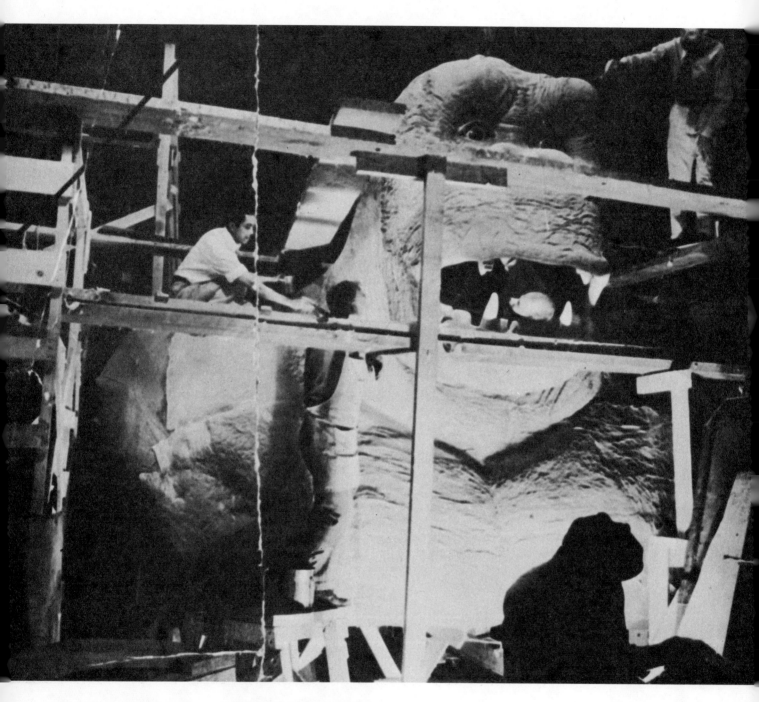

At left: *Delgado on scaffold* putting finishing touches on *Giant Bust of Kong* before covering with bearskins. It took forty bearskins to cover bust of Kong! *Photograph supplied by and used with the kind permission of Marcel Delgado.*

The giant bust of Kong fully covered. *Photograph supplied by and used with the kind permission of Marcel Delgado.*

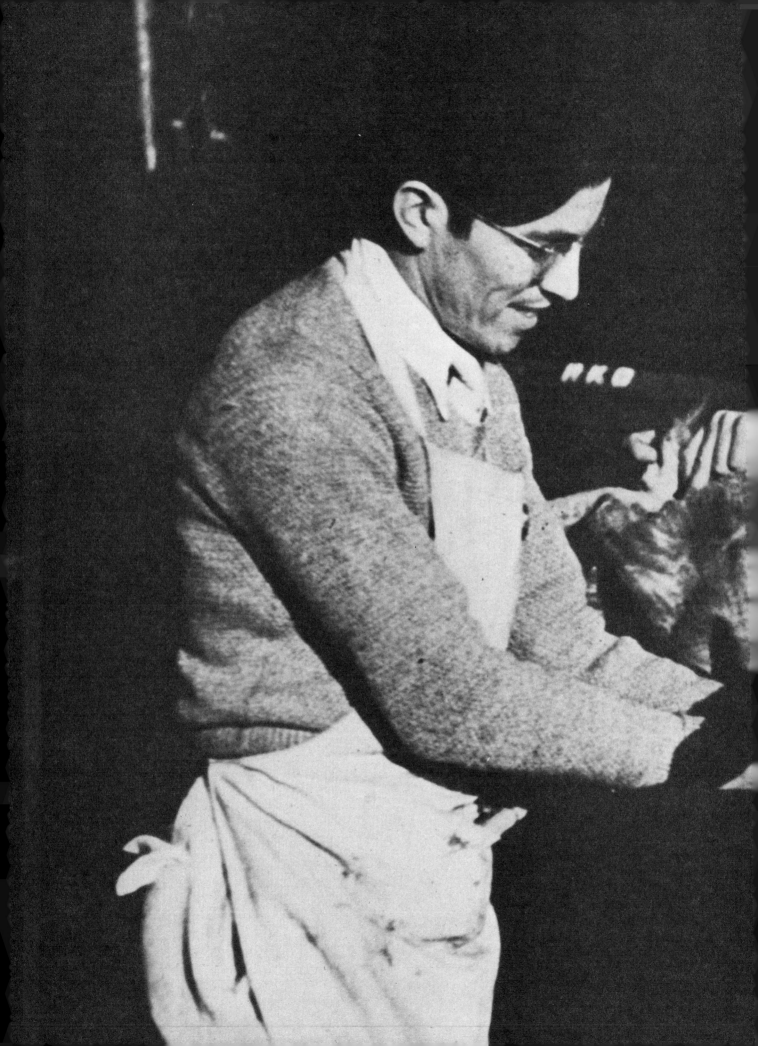

Marcel Delgado (right) and assistant working on giant hand of Kong. *Photograph supplied by and used with the kind permission of Marcel Delgado.*

Fay Wray in the giant hand. *Photograph supplied by and used with the kind permission of Marcel Delgado.*

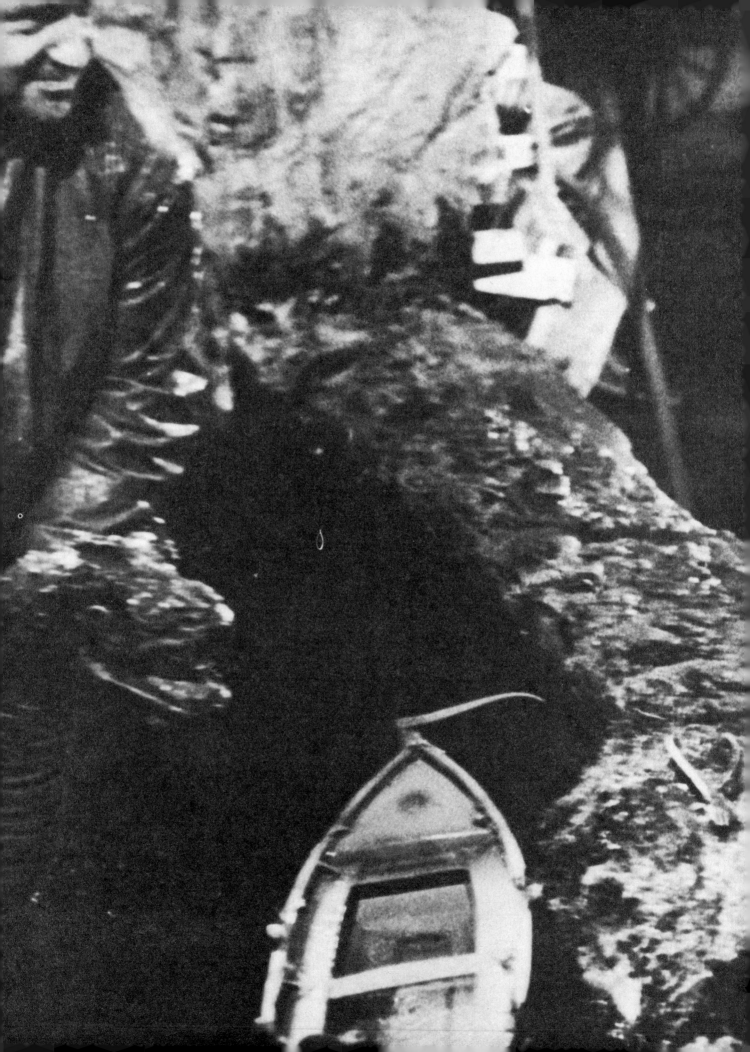

Willis O'Brien on the set of *King Kong*. Photograph supplied by and used with kind permission of Mrs. Darlyne O'Brien.

"Buster" Gibson animating Kong as he ascends Empire State Building. *Photograph supplied by and used with the kind permission of Marcel Delgado.*

David Allen's studio during the animation process for the Volkswagen television commercial. *Photograph supplied by and used with the kind permission of David Allen.*

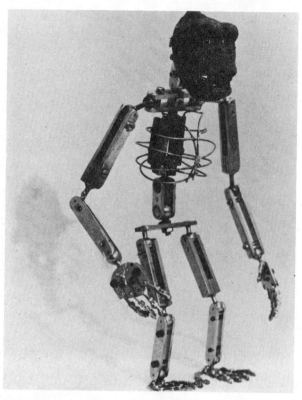

Armature for David Allen's Kong. *Photograph supplied by and used with the kind permission of David Allen.*

Partially covered armature of David Allen's Kong. *Photograph supplied and used with the kind permission of David Allen.*

A frame from the full color television commercial for Volkswagen created by David Allen. *Photograph* *supplied by David Allen and used with the kind permission of Doyle Dane Bernbach for Volkswagen.*

David Allen's studio during the animation process for the Volkswagen television commercial. *Photograph supplied by and used with the kind permission of David Allen.*

David Allen's Kong in action. *Photograph supplied by and used with the kind permission of David Allen.*

Close-up of David Allen's Kong. *Photograph supplied by and used with the kind permission of David Allen.*

PART V
INCONGRUITIES

HOW FAY MET KONG, OR THE SCREAM THAT SHOOK THE WORLD*

Fay Wray

"You will have the tallest, darkest leading man in Hollywood." Those were the first words I heard about *King Kong*. Although I knew the producer, Merian C. Cooper, was something of a practical joker, my thoughts rushed hopefully to the image of Clark Gable. Cooper, pacing up and down in his office, outlined the story to me . . . about an expedition going to some remote island where a discovery of gigantic proportions would be made. My heart raced along, waiting for the revelation. I enjoyed his mysterious tone, the gleeful look in his eyes that seemed to say "Just wait until you hear who will be playing opposite you!"

Cooper paused, picked up some poster-size sketches, then showed me my tall dark leading man. My heart stopped, then sank. An absolutely enormous gorilla was staring at me. "We're going to make him look about 50 feet high. All in animation." There were sketches of the big ape, who would be captured and brought back to civilization, alongside prehistoric animals, even alongside high buildings. Was that the Empire State Building? Cooper was delighted at my amazement, especially, I think, at the look of shock and apprehension on my face.

"Of course you'd have to be a blonde. We've got to have that contrast. We thought about Jean Harlow, then we decided you could wear a blonde wig." The "we" meant himself and his partner Ernest B. Schoedsack, who would be co-directing, and David O. Selznick, then executive head of R.K.O. Those were the salient points in that interview. I left the studio, my head spinning. How could I say yes to being in a film with an ape, however unreal he might be? But how could I say no? I had already worked with the team of Cooper and Schoedsack in *Four Feathers* and

had great regard for them. Actually, my admiration had begun earlier when I had seen their first film, *Grass*, a stunning documentary about migratory herders in Persia. Their second film, *Chang*, about a Siamese family and a horrendous elephant stampede, had been made entirely in the jungle country of Siam. These were adventurers— Cooper, the voluble visionary, Schoedsack, the self-styled "strong, silent one."

Now, for the first time, they would be adventuring within the confines of a Hollywood production lot. It was compelling to think that this newest project would have all the flavor and excitement of their personal experience. But Cooper's having called the Kong story a kind of "Beauty and the Beast" concept in no way made the thought of the ape more appealing! Although the entire country was in an economic depression and I was eager to make a movie, I wondered how I could bring myself to face such an animal. Gradually, my enthusiasm for the strangely wonderful humor, imagination and talent of the Cooper-Schoedsack team overcame the original shock. I said yes and got fitted for the wig and the dress that soon would be torn apart. Then I saw the figure of Kong. He was in a *miniature* jungle habitat, and was less than two feet tall! It was only the great furry paw, in which I would spend much of the next ten mouths, that was absolutely *enormous!*

On an average of twenty times a year, I am asked, "How was it done? Was it a real gorilla? . . . a man in a suit?" When I explain that the tall, dark leading man was, in fact about 13 inches high, a model made of something rubberish, animated by stop-motion within a proportionately miniature background, the reaction is usually "Incredible!" And it was, considering that the hand and arm in

which my close-up scenes were made was about eight feet in lengh. Inside the furry arm, there was a steel bar and the whole contraption (with me in the hand) could be raised or lowered like a crane. The fingers would be pressed around my waist while I was in a standing position. I would then be raised about ten feet into the air to be in line with an elevated camera. As I kicked and squirmed and struggled in the ape's hand, his fingers would gradually loosen and begin to open. My fear was real as I grabbed onto his wrist, his thumb, wherever I could, to keep from slipping out of that paw! When I could sense that the moment of minimum safety had arrived, I would call imploringly to the director and ask to be lowered to the floor of the stage. Happily, this was never denied for a second too long! I would have a few moments rest, be re-secured in the paw and the ordeal would begin all over again . . . a kind of pleasurable torment!

I never learned, or tried to learn, how that great arm was combined with the little Kong so that he seemed actually to be carrying me. It was too much fun to go the projection room and experience the suspense of guessing whether the three-inch figure in the hand of the animated Kong was a doll (sometimes used for long shots) or whether it was me. Watching intently, I would be sure it was the doll. Then it would move! It had life, it would kick, it would scream—it was me! To see that was a delightful puzzler and is to this day. I rather like the idea, I think, because as someone said to me only recently, "We were more naïve then and it was better for us."

Understanding the technique of the ensemble scenes was simpler. Pre-filmed animation of Kong and/or the prehistoric animals was projected from the rear onto a full-size screen or "transparency." Working in front of the large screen, we became mini-people by comparison. The fore-ground scenery at such times was fragmentary—a log, a rock, a portion of a jungle cliff, the limb of a tree. All the rest we had to imagine.

The animation expert, Willis O'Brien, had made the prehistoric animals years before for *The Lost World*, a film based on a story by Sir Arthur Conan Doyle. O'Brien brought them out of the studio storage rooms to meet his newest creation, Kong, and to do battle with the gorilla. One of these sequences, with me clutching a tree in front of the transparency screen, was photographed for a consecutive twenty-two hours. There was no Screen Actors Guild then to limit our time in the studio. I was weary, sleepy, hurting and aching! Fortunately, such intensive filming was intermittent. While the animation was being prepared, there was time off, even time enough to do other films. Two of the movies I made during the ten months that *Kong* was underway were *Doctor X* and *The Most Dangerous Game* (the latter also for my friend, Cooper). These were "horror" films, an indication of how *Kong* was already beginning to affect my career; I was fast becoming Hollywood's most victimized heroine!

All of the transparency and animation sequences were directed by Cooper. He worked the little Kong so much that O'Brien had to make six models of him. About two years ago, when Cooper and I did a television interview. I was given one of the models to hold in my lap. Then, for the first time ever, I touched the complete Kong. It was a lovely feeling to have the "upper hand," without the slightest need to scream.

Ernest Schoedsack directed the scenes with the people. When he called a first take of the movie test scene on the boat "Okay," I was delighted. I didn't want to be hollering over and over again. Sometimes people wonder if I did my own screaming. Yes. "But how could you?" I made myself believe that the nearest possible hope of rescue was at least a

mile away and my only chance of survival was to be heard loud and clear!

After all the filming was finished, we went into a sound room where I recorded an outpouring of various screams. These were cut into the picture additionally as it was edited. When the premiere night arrived at Grauman's Chinese Theater on Hollywood Boulevard, I thought the picture was overscreamed. I remember wanting, more than once, to put my hands over my ears! But then I had no idea I was seeing what would be considered one of the great successes of motion pictures, and was surprised to read the superlatives in the reviews that followed.

For a year after the release of the film, I continued to feel in the grip of the Beast. My first important role had been in *The Wedding March*, with Erich von Stroheim as writer, director and actor. The film was rich with realism, perception and sensitivity.

Naturally, I had hoped for a continuation of the particular values I found in such filmmaking. Instead, because of the enthusiastic reception given *Kong*, more horror films were offered me. By the time I had finished *The Mystery of the Wax Museum* and *The Vampire Bat*, I was desperately in need of escape and welcomed an invitation to go to England, to make pictures there. It seemed an irony to be met, upon my arrival, by a representative of the BBC who asked that I come to their studios and broadcast a sample of my scream. I didn't feel like doing that. Later, when I was walking in Hyde Park and overheard a Cockney woman threatening her tiny child with "If y' don't behive I'll 'ave Fye Wrye get King Kong arter yer!" I did feel like screaming—at that mother!

When my own children were small, I didn't want them to see *Kong*, believing that it might disturb their sleep. When it began to appear on television, they had arrived at an age of tolerance, I thought, and it turned out I was right. Their concern was not for me but for Kong who, my seven-year-old Vicki said, had no intention of hurting me but just liked me and never should have been shot at by those airplanes. That confirmed

a belief I developed during the filming and which has been reinforced as the years pass by, that *Kong* should be classed as an adventure fantasy, not as a horror film. If *Kong* were purely a horrifying and horrible fellow, the sympathy he evokes when, finally, he is struck down wouldn't exist. There is no doubt about such sympathy. Even I, seeing the film a year or so ago, felt a great lump in my throat in behalf of Kong. I've seen the film four times: at the premiere, twice at home screenings and once on television. This in no way matches the records of the *aficionados*. Letters have come to me claiming forty to fifty viewings. Recently, Rod Steiger told me he had seen it twenty-two times. I have read that in a theater in South Africa it is played perpetually, alternating every other evening with *The Mark of Zorro*, and that these two films are shown as a double feature on weekends.

Although I made perhaps a hundred pictures, *King Kong* is certainly the one most remembered. During a decade when I chose to stay at home with my family, it was *King Kong* who kept those cards and letters coming in. At the present time, when I have decided to let the acting go and write a play, it is Kong who seems to function as my Public Relations Man. I no longer make any effort to escape. When I'm in New York, I look at the Empire State Building and feel as though it belongs to me . . . or is it vice-versa? I can laugh at all the jokes and gags that have Kong as a reference point, enjoy Bob Newhart's monologue about the dilemma of the Empire State's night watchman as he watches Kong proceeding up the side of the building. I am intrigued to read, on occasion, that there are those who find sociological, even religious symbolism in the film, and some who consider Kong as being representative of Man. I am amused to hear that others look upon the film as strictly camp. I like very much reading an appreciation by Paul Johnson in *The New Statesman* recognizing Kong as ". . . more than a monster. He is a genuine character, a creature of intelligible rage, nobility of a kind and, above all, pathos. A prehistoric Lear, in a sense . . ." I am not dismayed when I observe an attractive young man wearing a lapel button with the words: King Kong Died For Our Sins. I feel tempted to read the current bestseller, "Portnoy's Complaint," when a column by Russell Baker in *The New York Times* imagines that Portnoy has a mother who imagines that it might have been she who played opposite the great gorilla.

King Kong seems always to be in the stream of contemporary goings-on, and big and powerful enough to keep himself alive and living well in an assortment of considerations and imaginings. If there is a public that is pleased to carry him about in this way, I am, at last, pleased enough that he carried *me*.

FAY WAS A DARN NICE GIRL*

Arnold M. Auerbach

Fay Wray's recent reminiscence about the filming of *King Kong* prompted this reporter to track down the rumors that Kong himself is alive and well and living quietly in a jungle hideaway. Sure enough, the erstwhile star was traced to San Simian, his secluded estate on an uncharted Indonesian island near his birthplace. Since his retirement, Mr. Kong has learned to speak and write fluent English. But he remains shy and considers himself a "loner." It was only after a lengthy correspondence that he consented to the following interview.

"Hold tight! Up we go!" With a casual swipe of his paw, King Kong hoisted the reporter 500 feet from the ground into the sumptuous living room of a luxurious villa on a rocky ledge high above the Indian Ocean. "Hope the ceiling isn't too high for you," chuckled the genial primate, as he gently plucked the visitor from his palm and set him down on a straw mat near a magnificent picture window.

Still trim at 6,370 pounds—though his fur is beginning to gray at the temples and he occasionally has to use binoculars for reading—Mr. Kong retains the fierce physiognomy and beetling brows that terrified movie-goers more than a generation ago. But behind the forbidding exterior are a surprisingly benign disposition and contemplative mind.

"What's the first thing you want to know?" he asked, making sure that the visitor was comfortable and proffering a clump of bananas. "Shoot. That is, begin."

"Well, to tell the truth, I find you much less—er—savage than I'd expected," said the reporter. "Why is that?"

Mr. Kong smiled, revealing still sound fangs in the famed prognathous profile. "The years have mellowed me, I guess. As a young actor, I was the pushy type, trying to claw my way to the top. But now I'm 4,812. And at that age, you're not as scrappy as you were at 4,776."

"You're aware that most people think you never really existed. Why did you let that story get around?"

He leaned back in his pterodactyl-hide hammock and put his paws together reflectively. "I made my picture in 1933, remember. In those Depression days, the public panicked easily. So the producers had to spread that nonsense about my being only an 18-inch miniature. If people had known there was a real King Kong, they might have gone Republican again."

"Did you really climb the Empire State Building for your famous death scene, when the airplanes shot you down?"

As it happens, that scene was faked. The thing they shot down was a miniature. It was the only time I let them use a stand-in. But by then I'd taken my money and headed home."

He stared back across the years. "The fact is, I always thought that death scene was a frightful phony." Then, thumping his chest in the familiar prideful gesture: "Believe me, son, they'll have needed more than a few puny Army planes to kill off K.K." A sardonic grin crinkled his mouth. "Besides, from what the papers say, I can still handle the Pentagon boys. Plus the C.I.A."

"What did you think of Fay Wray?"

"Fay was a darn nice girl. Frankly, that constant scream of hers got on my nerves at times, but I liked her. Off the set, we were good friends. Just actor-and-actress, of course. There never was anything between us, no matter what the columnists said."

Mr. Kong's long-time servant, an elderly orang-outang, padded in with a low-calorie snack of rare lionburger and minced rhinoceros. "Lately I've had to cut down to five meals a day," explained the host wistfully. "There aren't any weight-watching groups for chaps like me."

When the reporter, who confined himself to mango juice, commented on the servant's almost-human appearance, Mr. Kong emitted a characteristic deep-throated chuckle. "Bimbo was an assistant supervisor at RKO when I first met him. After I heard some of his suggestions at story conferences, I thought he'd be more at home in this environment. So I worked out a deal with his agent and took him away."

"Have you ever considered making a Hollywood comeback?"

Absently he plucked off the top of a nearby coconut tree and scratched his ear with it. "I have mixed feelings about Hollywood. The oldtime prehistoric crowd is pretty well thinned out these days. And now that my old friends are gone—Godzilla, Mighty Joe Young and the other boys—the evenings would be rather lonesome." He hurled the coconut tree playfully at a passing jet. "Still, with Cary Grant and Doris Day willing to face the cameras, perhaps one shouldn't be so bashful."

"You realize that you're not the easiest actor in the world to cast."

He darted the visitor a quizzical glance. "I'm well aware of my limitations. But there's one role I know I I could play—the lead in 'Gargantua and Pantagruel.' Unfortunately, producers don't seem interested." He sighed ruefully, "I'm afraid Rabelais isn't Rabelaisian enough for modern audiences."

"Do you think you've had any permanent influence on acting styles?"

"Absolutely. Look at the photos of the rock groups on today's record albums. You'll see my features, my haircut . . ." He wagged a reproving finger. "Now don't go writing that those misbegotten creatures are my litters! I'd be ashamed to have such whelps."

"Which brings up a delicate topic." The reporter hesitated, then took the plunge. "Most film buffs consider you a classic sex symbol. What's your reaction to that?"

A blush, awesome in its grandeur, slowly ascended Mr. Kong's cheeks. "Modesty forbids. Let's leave those theories to the Ph.D. boys and girls." He allowed the hint of a smile to creep above his whiskers. "But you'll remember that I pioneered in the field of frontal nudity." The smile widened. "And I daresay they'd be glad to have me in 'Oh! Calcutta!'"

He glanced at the grandfather's clock on his wrist. "Oh, dear. Nearly time for my afternoon nap."

Gently he lowered the reporter back to the outrigger canoe waiting on the beach. He stood looking down from his doorway, smiling, waving—a hulking, formidable, yet somehow touching figure.

"Goodbye! Goodbye! Come back in another eighty-five or ninety years," he called. "And give my regards to that girl Viva."

PORTNOY'S MOTHER'S COMPLAINT*

Russell Baker

Lines composed after a reading of America's best seller:

"I was a real looker once. Can you believe it, doctor? A real looker. No kidding. 'She looks just like Fay Wray with red hair,' the fellows on the drugstore corner used to say, and believe me, when they said it, they'd get that King Kong look all over their faces.

"When they'd get fresh with me, though, I knew how to shoot them off the Empire State Building because I was saving myself for a decent, hardworking insurance salesman and maybe if we were lucky and he sold enough insurance, someday we'd be able to have a little son who'd look like Bruce Cabot and we'd name him Alex and he'd get a job on the public payroll doing, you know, something vague for Mayor Lindsay and that way, I thought, maybe I'd have somebody to get me tickets to a few Broadway shows.

Fay Wray in the Kitchen

"So like a sap, what do I do until the right man comes along? While other girls are on the drugstore corner dancing the Big Apple. I'm home in the kitchen practicing making chicken soup. How am I supposed to know I'm going to have a kid who's going to hold chicken soup against me?

"If I'd known at the time, I would have practiced making vichyssoise. Frankly, I couldn't care less, but even at that time I could see that most people in the average neighborhood have chicken-soup sons. How was I supposed to know I was going

to have a vichyssoise son?

"Am I making any sense, doctor? Excuse me, I should have said *chutzpah, shikse* and *shlemiel* so we can tune in the reader that this is a very ethnic psychoanalysis. Where was I?

Mrs. Chicken Soup

"Making chicken soup. One day I'm Fay Wray making chicken soup and the next I'm 'Peaches' Portnoy, married to Portnoy the insurance salesman, one of the sweetest, handsomest guys I ever saw in my life. You know, doctor, the kind of guy who'd call his girl 'Peaches,' but never in front of his son, of course.

"To this day, it's never crossed Alex's mind that I could have been 'Peaches' to any man. To himself Alex will still be the only apple on the tree when he's seventy-five, but when he looks at me all he can see is Mrs. Chicken Soup.

"Listen, doctor, I'm not complaining about the boy. Everybody has children. What does it mean? When you want to be out doing the Big Apple, you're sitting home teaching multiplication tables.

"'How come there's never anything to eat around here?' he wants to know. So, instead of shopping around downtown to keep yourself looking like Fay Wray, you spend hours in a dull kitchen making soup. You know something? I hate the sight of chicken gizzard. If I'd started out making vichyssoise I'd hate the sight of a potato.

"All right, I'll tell you the worst thing there is about myself. About me, dreary old multiplication-table-teaching 'Peaches' Portnoy, but not 'Peaches' to her son. I'll admit it. I've got a Fay Wray complex. All my married life I've wanted Portnoy *père*

to grab me in his big hairy fist and carry me up the side of a building. Sounds sick, you think?

"Well, I'll tell you what's sicker. It's knowing you're growing older and don't look so much like Fay Wray any more, or at least not enough so that Portnoy is going to do any building-climbing with you in his fist.

"I once told the truth to Portnoy. Think of it, doctor. I told a thing like that to my own husband. And you know what he said? He said, "That's really funny, Peaches, because I never had the nerve to tell you this before, but you've always made me feel like King Kong.'

"'Well,' I asked him, 'why don't you ever let the beast in you take charge?' and he says, 'The kid never gives us a minute's privacy.'

Ubiquitous Alex

"He was right, doctor. You could count on it. As soon as I'd see the gorilla hair sprouting out on Portnoy's face—I'm speaking figuratively, mind you—in would pop Alex. 'I'm not doing so hot on my multiplication tables,' he'd whine. Or, "Why isn't there ever anything to eat around here?' For years, he's always popping in just when the gorilla hairs are sprouting on Portnoy.

"One day Portnoy told me a terrible thing. 'You don't look like Fay Wray any more,' he said. I went up to the bathroom to cry alone, but can I even cry alone in my own bathroom? No sir. It's occupied, day and night, night and day, by—do you have to guess who? Little Alex.

"I'm gray, doctor. The weight has shifted. The gorilla has died in Portnoy, and what have I got to show for it? My son? My son, the chicken-soup hater? Aaaggghhhooourrrghh. . . ."

THE NIGHT WATCHMAN*

Bob Newhart

I worked as an accountant for about two years in Chicago. I got a degree in accounting, went into the army during the Korean War. Remember that one? . . . No benefits, but I have held close to thirty separate accounting jobs in two years, which is like three weeks at each place. I found one thing is true; that they always put you through an orientation program. You spend one week learning all the problems you're going to have to face in this new job. But, invariably, after the week in orientation, the first problem you run into your first day on the job was never covered in any of the sessions. Now, with this kind of prologue, this may seem kind of a jump, my favorite movie is *King Kong*, the monster movie. This is the greatest movie ever made and the biggest scene, of course, the one you all remember from *King Kong*, is when King Kong climbs the outside of the Empire State Building. All right now, put these two thoughts together. . . . This is the night that King Kong climbs the outside of the Empire State Building, it is also the first night on the job for a new guard . . . This is his first night on the job. . . . He has gone through a week's orientation on the problems he is going to face and it happens to be the night that King Kong climbs the outside of the Empire State Building. . . .

H-Hell-Hello, uh Mr. Mr. Mr. Nelson, yes. This is Sam Hennesey, the new guard? Sir, you know I hate to bother you at home like this on my first night, but, see, something's come up sir and it's not covered under the guards manual. . . . Yes, I looked in the index, yes sir. . . . I looked under unauthorized personnel and people without passes, and apes and ape's toes. . . . Uh, apes and ape's toes, yes sir. . . . uh, there's, there's an ape's toe sticking through the window sir. . . . Well, uh, see, see, this isn't your standard ape sir. . . . he's between eighteen and nineteen stories high. . . . depending on whether there's a thirteenth floor or not.

. . . Well sir, you know, I'm sure there's a rule against apes shaking the building. . . . there is. Yes sir. So I yelled at his feet, you know, I said, uh, I said, uh, "Shoo, Ape," and, uh, . . . I'm sorry but you're going to have to leave sir. . . . and you know, I know how you like the new men to think on their feet, so I went to the broom closet and I got out a broom without, uh, without signing out a requisition on it . . . I will tomorrow, yes sir. . . . and I started hitting him on the toes with it, you see, but, uh, it didn't seem to bother him too much, see, there are these planes sir, and they're flying around shooting at him, you know, and they only seem to be bothering him a little bit, so I figure I wasn't doing too much good, uh, with a broom. . . . D-Did I try swatting his face with it? Well, I was going to take the elevator up to his head sir, but my jurisdiction only extends to his navel. . . . You don't care what I do, just get that ape off the building? Uh, this uh, this might complicate things a little. He, uh, he's carrying a woman in his hand sir. . . . no, I don't think she works in the building, no sir. . . . Well, see, as he passed by my floor, she had this kind of negligee on, you know, so I doubt very much if she was one of the cleaning women, you know. . . . Well, well sir, the first thing I did, I, uh, filled out a report on it. . . . Well, now, I don't want to give the building a bad name either sir, you know, but. . . . Well, I doubt very much if we can cover it up sir. . . . Well, you know, the planes are shooting at him and people are gonna come to work tomorrow morning and some of them are going to notice the ape in the street, you know? . . . and you know the broken window, you know. And they'll start putting two and two together, you know. . . . I think we're safe on that score, sir. I doubt very much he signed the book downstairs. . . . You don't care what I do, just get the ape off this building? Well, I came up with one idea, sir, but I'm not supposed to leave my post. . . . Well, I thought maybe I could smear the Chrysler Building with bananas.

* Available on a Warner Brothers recording, this material is used by permission of the author.

KING KONG

As it might be told by Joseph Conrad, Charlotte Bronte, Ernest Hemingway, Jonathan Swift, Samuel Richardson, and William Faulkner in a celestial story conference.

Brandon French

Part One: The Approach to the Island (Joseph Conrad)

We stood on deck, peering into the dark, ominous excrudescence of fog, linked to one another, human being to human being, by the eternal bond of the sea. "Listen," the captain whispered in a voice that struck awe into our hearts. Faces twitched, hands trembled ever so slightly, eyes forgot to blink. We heard only the heavy, ancestral beat of our blood serpenting through our opaque veins. And then, perhaps it was a moment later, the muffled thunderous crush and sigh of water breaking against some invisible, nocturnal barrier. "Drums," the captain muttered, and the word seemed to sputter in his throat like a match tossed into a muddy trough. An exuberant gloom tugged at our loins, for we were glad, don't you know, to have emerged from the recesses of nowhere into this dim, unspeakable somewhere where we might at least come to know what we had come for. "Look!" Denham cried, and we saw through the slowly dispersing density of darkness the dismal outline of the dome of the island in the shape of a human skull. Gripped by the primordial terror of unknown, unknowable demons that bump up against the soul of the adventurer in the heavy, sluggish silence of expectation, we steadied ourselves as best we could for debarkation.

Part Two: Ann is Kidnapped (Charlotte Brontë)

Both frightened and heartened was I by the gleam of exultation which I perceived in Mr. Denham's eye as our tiny bark approached the shore of the island. Jack took my little hand in his great large dark one and an icy cold shiver passed through me like a jolt of electricity. "Ann," said Jack, "I'm frightened for you." Raising my tear-dimmed eyes to his somber face, I experienced true pleasure, yet not without some pain, for Mr. Denham was my cherished benefactor and I suffered humiliation to have so utterly disregarded his behest that I not fall in love with the first mate. "Oh, Jack," I murmured loyally, "Mr. Denham has fed me, costumed me, wrenched me from the poverty of my loveless childhood and now he is going to take this dear little elfin face (this pale, tear-stained face which you love) and render it the toast of all Broadway!" With great effort, I avoided sobbing. But before Jack could utter a reply, a band of dancing natives approached our little group. How black they were! How stony their gazes! How sharp their pointed spears! How painted their faces! Dear reader, can you fathom my woe, my shock, my wretched consternation when they offered to buy me! Oh then, how fast we retreated, and how dear the little boat that had brought us to this dreadful island seemed, what a refuge and a haven from the sight and the sound of these vulturous savages!

That evening I felt strangely comforted. Calmly I stood upon the deck, filling my little lungs with chill night air. Good God! Little did I dream the fate which was in store for me, as a painted savage unseen crept up behind my straight, staunch back and (without allowing me opportunity for a single anguished cry) spirited me away into the darkness. Jack's frantic ejaculation—"Ann! Ann! Ann!"—entered my sorrowful ears a moment before the canoe in which I lay captive attained the shore. Too late! Too late! my heart cried out in response. For I (as one of the natives who spoke a smattering of English had informed me) was to be the bride of Kong!

Part Three: Capturing Kong
(Ernest Hemingway)

They dragged her screaming past the tall doors that were open now and up the stone steps of the sacrificial tower and when they had finished fastening her arms to the pillars and left her sagging in terror and closed themselves again behind the tall doors and the great wall that stretched the length of the island, the chief of the tribe gave the signal and one of the native boys sounded a gong. *Gaawong! Gaawong!* He was at the other end of the island when he heard it—*Gaawong*—but he came fast, crashing and clumsy, roaring and whinning and breaking the top off fifty-foot trees with his arms, came toward the sound—*Gaawong!*—that the man figures made on the shiny red metal sun shape, blinking when he saw what was tied to the pillars, what he had not expected to see, something small and white with narrow rivers rushing down from the eye places and sharp high noises jumping from the mouth.

He broke the strings that held the woman's arms with a finger from his hand that was larger than the body of a large man. The tribe cheered when he took her and waved their torches. He carried her soft in his hard dark half-open fist over the mountain hill and the swamp puddle and did not see the white man figures that followed him but smelled the man smell where he had never smelled it before and kept moving to move away from the smell.

Jack and Denham and twenty of the white boys from the ship followed him, afraid but not hesitating, clawing their way through the branches that tore the skin from their faces, staggering and stumbling in the bubbling soup of the soil of the island, from footprint to footprint.

At the edge of the deep swamp water they pushed together logs to make a raft and were half across when the head and neck of a brachyosaurus rose up and up and up above them cobra-like and then swooped down on the raft with its dark cave mouth open, lined with a hundred mossy spikes, then up again, the mouth filled with a man, screaming like a woman and flailing his arms and legs until they came unattached and dropped down into the water.

The men who did not die in the mouth of the brachyosaurus or drown dragged their muddy bodies out of the far side of the swamp and hid beneath heavy ferns. The brachyosaurus lumbered up onto earth, roaring and snuffling. Shreds of shirt and bloody tendon and half a man's boot were lodged between his teeth. Kong put the small white woman figure down on a cliff and went to do battle with the monster. While they were fighting, Jack brought Ann down from the cliff a thousand feet on a vine to the river that carried them back to the wall at the edge of the island.

When Kong came to the cliff and saw that the white woman figure was gone and smelled the man smell that was not her smell, he beat his blood-purpled fists from the broken dead jaws of the brachyosaurus against the mudcrusted mass of his chest and came across the island again to reclaim her, who was his now, broke the doors down and went on the other side of the wall where Denham was crouched with a 55cc. Finzi-Garnet gas bomb. He did not fear Denham or the flat silver cylinder that sailed out of Denham's hand, hitting him hard above the groin with a great *boom!* and clouds of coughing yellow smoke that burned his eyes and throat, but they made him want to lie down and forget the woman and go to sleep.

"I hit him," Denham said, watching the beast crumble like a building in a 7.2 Richter Scale earthquake.

"Yes," said Jack.

"I've got him now," said Denham. "The eighth wonder of the world."

"Yes," said Jack, "you've got what you came for." Denham looked uneasy.

"I know you're thinking of the men we lost . . ."

"Yes," said Jack.

"It couldn't be helped," said Denham, wondering how large a raft they'd have to build to take the gorilla back to the States. "Its' a damn shame even so," he added, and drew a long swallow of ten year old scotch from his canteen. "I think we ought to go light on the details with the newspapers, Jack."

"Certainly Denham. Don't give it another thought." Jack took the canteen which Denham held out to him and rubbed the opening against his sleeve to rub out where Denham's mouth had been. "I'm sure you'll find a way to make it all sound very picturesque."

Part Four: Kong Comes to America
(Jonathan Swift)

The single most pressing problem subsequent to the construction of a raft of sufficient size and strength upon which to transport Kong to America was how to care for him. It was necessary to maintain the giant gorilla in a state of unconsciousness for the entire duration of the voyage, a consequence of which was that he received no solid food and only sufficient liquid to prevent him from dying of malnutrition or dehydration. In order to administer the liquid, Mr. Denham himself descended to the raft, each morning and evening, with a hastily devised crowbar which he employed to pry open Kong's jaw, and a seven foot long, two foot diameter wooden tube, carved by the cook and sanded down by six sailors so as to prevent splinters, through which the liquid, a heavily sugared coconut broth, was administered a gallon at a time, twelve gallons per day. Upon arrival in New York harbor thirty-eight days after our departure from the island, Kong, still unconscious, was transferred by means of five cranes to a specially constructed wheeled platform and delivered by diesel trucks to the abandoned Armory on 128th Street and Lexington Avenue, wherein he was made perpetually to remain in a sitting position due to his exorbitant height of 61 feet 7 inches. This, however, complicated another problem, resulting from the fact that the diet prescribed by Dr. Herman Micklemasher in his celebrated *The Care and Feeding of Apes and Other Wild Monkeys* did not agree with Kong. Five men in gas masks had to be continually present to hose the pathetic barbarian off, and two plumbers worked on alternating twelve-hour shifts for a week constructing adequate drainage. Dr. Micklemasher himself was consulted in Somaliland by long-distance phone for an alternate diet and a prescription for a constipatory agent. But no sooner had we brought the gastrointestinal difficulty under control than it was replaced by a bronchial complaint. The chief veterinarian from the Bronx Zoo was of the opinion that the radical alteration in climate, aggravated by the protracted voyage, during which Kong lay bare to the elements, had lowered his resistance, thereby rendering him vulnerable to the pneumococcus germ. Penicillin was prescribed, and a tropical heating system and hot water heater were installed in the Armory, the latter so that Kong could be hosed off with warm water rather than cold. At the same time, potted palms and several dinosaur posters graciously lent us by the curator of the Museum of Natural History were distributed throughout the Armory in congenial arrangements to make Kong feel more at home. Mr. Denham, upon whom the financial burden for all these expenses rested, was understandably anxious to have Kong well and figuratively on his feet again so that he might begin to organize a show around him and thereby regain some of the quarter of a million dollars which he had hitherto expended. This rehabilitation was accomplished within a month, which left only the difficulty of locating someone who would instruct Kong and of discovering a dentist in the area who was willing to replace one of Kong's missing front teeth, this latter considered advisable for cosmetic reasons. Dr. Horace Poposchlachter, for a considerable fee, provided the tooth, and the former Snake Lady of Madame Huong Fu's House of Horrors became mistress of Kong's obedience school. It was therefore feasible for Mr. Denham to arrange an opening for the now well behaved, beautified, and thoroughly content Kong on December 3rd, a Saturday, at 8:30 p.m., at the Helen Hayes Theater on 44th Street off Seventh Avenue. ($25 a seat, available at the box office only.)

Part Five: Kong Escapes with Ann (Samuel Richardson)

Dearest Parents—for I call you dearest though there are none dear or dearer to me—you must forgive my miserable scribble as I am composing this letter in darkness upon nothing more substantial than my chaste (heaven forbid it should ever be otherwise) lap, reduced as I am to one wretched pen purchased in haste at the notions counter of E. J. Korvette. Why, you will ask one another, am poor I writing in darkness, and the answer, dear father and mother, is that my employer, Mr. B————, bethought himself to provide me with a ticket to the debut of a most spectacular (we are informed in the program notes) gorilla! Do not think me naughty to have accepted it nor be vexed with me for attending such a debacle unescorted, for your daughter is safer in this blackish as nightish theater than she would be in the subways or in her little garret on MacDougal Street, robbers, muggers, and rapists being unanimously disenchanted with New York's live theatrical entertainments, and therefore avoiding them like poison. O, shame; your dear silly has gabbled on so lengthily, she has neglected to inform you that the curtain has arisen to reveal—gasp not nor faint nor fear for me!—a male monster of such proportions that even now I am clinging with my free hand to the arm of the person seated next to me and squeezing it for dear life! But lest you mistake my inference, dear parents, and contemplate the offense of my feminine sensibilities, let me reassure you that while the gorilla faces front and I am beholding him even now in an upright position, he is abundantly furred and my intimation of his gender is entirely speculative! Moreover, every part of him is chained to a steel pillar against which he leans very like father against the door while he awaits you, mother, on bridge night. O, but what is this? Alas, I am struck to the heart by what I am witnessing now! A woman has appeared on the stage and the man to whom she clings (let us hope it is her husband, or not less than her fiancé) is explaining that t'was she who lured the gorilla from the jungle, for he—did you suppose it possible?—loved her more even than his own life. Yet hold—I must break off—O God protect me! The gorilla is trying to wrest himself from the chains! All about me are people screaming and arising from their seats. O, fie! I am jostled and jarred. Whoops! The pen has slipped nearly from my hand. Trample me not! say I to a man who has stepped over his seat onto my treasured lap in a vain effort to escape the gorilla's wrath. I shall not shock your ears with his vile response, nor will I delay this account to report how effectively I repaid his rudeness. Let me only repent of the pen I have virtually destroyed in doing thusly and proceed to inform you that the gorilla has snapped the chains and taken the woman up into his great hairy hand. Let God be praised he did not see me, and that he cannot properly descriminate between a bleached blonde and the genuine article, or it would surely be poor I your only issue in that hand even now. O! I durst not think such thoughts! Let me haste to remove my bruised but honest body from this frightful spectacle and flee to the nearest post office where I may purchase both refuge and a stamp, that you may have your minds eased by the knowledge of my welfare in this wicked city!

Part Six: Kong is Killed (William Faulkner)

I pick her up in my hand and smile at her. She is not glad. She does not know me. I am I, I say, so she will know me. EEEEEE! she says. No, I say, I am I who will not hurt you. EEEEEEE! she says again. The sharpness hurt me. She has gone to sleep in my hand. Good. Where is the outside? The outside is outside this wall. Wall! Wall! Wall! The wall is soft now and not a wall and the inside is outside and I am outside. It is cold. Whiteness is on the ground, soft and sharp. It stings me. Where will I go? I want to go up. I will go up to the top of a stone tree. When she stops being asleep I will tell her again that I am I and then she will not make the noises and she will be glad. This is a good tree. It goes up into the clouds. I climb the tree with one hand. The wind cuts me. The whiteness dances into my eyes. What is this whiteness? I taste it with my tongue. It is water. Good. I am thirsty. Breath hurts. I go slowly. I look down but nothing follows me. There are persons inside the tree but they do not come out. I go slowly up and my mouth is open and my tongue is out for the whiteness. Jack, she said. Jack is a person. I am I, and he is Jack, and she is she, and the whiteness is water. I am where the trees are stone and noisy animals have persons inside them. They go in and out doors. In and out. A door is like a mouth. But it has no teeth. I am at the top of the tree. The wind blows hard. I see birds flying in the sky. One, two, three, four, five birds, louder and louder. Persons are inside the birds. The birds are coughing. I reach out to catch one. Its wing is hard and sharp. It cuts my hand. I put her down on the whiteness where it is soft on the stone. Her eyes are opening. She sees me. I am I, I say, but softly. She does not make the noise. We are in a tree, I say, and show her where it is down below and where we are up here. There is red on my hand. She sees the red. I put the red behind me where she cannot see it. The birds are coming again. I put out my hand which is not cut and catch a bird and throw it down below. There is fire and black smoke where the bird is hurt and a loud boom from the place where it falls. I am I, I say to the other birds. They cough at me. Something flies into myself. I do not see it but it is there where my arm stops. I reach and feel. There is a hole in myself where it hurts and red is in my hand. The birds cough again and something I cannot see flies into my head where my ear is. I am I, I say to the birds very loud, but I am not seeing the birds anymore. I hear them coughing but I do not see them. She makes the sound. EEEEEEE! But it is not at me. It is at the birds. I look at her, but I am not seeing her anymore. And then I am hearing the birds very loud and not seeing them and hearing her make the sound and not seeing her and then not hearing the birds or her but only knowing quiet and dark and cold fast falling.

Introductory Note

Since his birth in 1933, King Kong as character, theme, and icon has pervaded both popular and serious culture. He has engendered hundreds of filmic offspring (see "Introduction," pages 19–28), and has also inspired countless parodies, advertisements, cartoons, posters, songs, jokes, toys, games, plastic models, and puzzles. King Kong is not just another terrifying face. He is instant recognition and universal currency for tens of millions of people all over the world. Although we have only suggested here some of the ways Kong has been a source for "serious" literary (see Pynchon's *Gravity's Rainbow*), plastic, graphic, and performing, artists, Kong has served élitist purposes as well. Kong, perhaps more than other single creation of this century, has fascinated and stimulated world culture at all levels and has been transformed into myth.

Two early *Son of Kong* posters. *Courtesy RKO.*

SON OF KONG

with
ROBERT ARMSTRONG
HELEN MACK · FRANK REICHER
JOHN MARSTON · VICTOR WONG
LEE KOHLMAR · ED BRADY
DIRECTED BY ERNEST B. SCHOEDSACK
MERIAN C. COOPER · Executive Producer

RKO
Radio
PICTURES

18

SON OF KONG
42-B-6

Still from
Son of Kong.
Courtesy RKO.

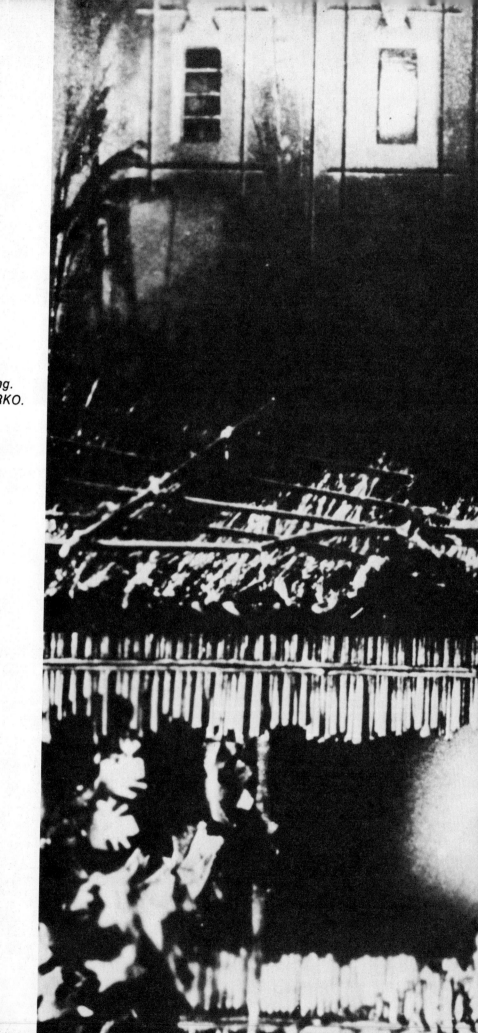

Still from
Son of Kong.
Courtesy RKO.

Publicity still from *King Kong Escapes*. Copyright © 1968 Universal Pictures.

Konga poster. *Courtesy of American International Pictures, Inc.*
© *1961 American International Pictures, Inc.*

Publicity still from *Konga*.
Courtesy of American
International Pictures, Inc.
© 1961 American Inter-
national Pictures, Inc.

Publicity still from *King Kong vs. Godzilla.* Copyright
© 1963 Universal International.

A big hand for the little
lady. But Ronrico's a rum.
Light and dry, smooth
but devastating. Often downed,
never bested. Not for 112 years.

©1970 General Wine & Spirits Co., NYC, 80 proof.

Ronrico. A rum to remember.

From the collection of Elliott Stein.

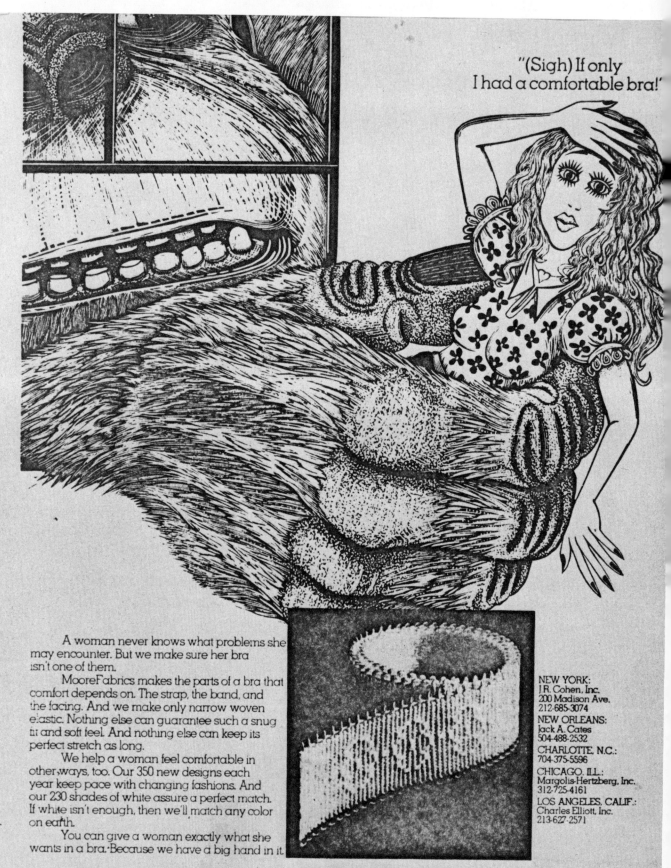

"(Sigh) If only I had a comfortable bra!"

A woman never knows what problems she may encounter. But we make sure her bra isn't one of them.

MooreFabrics makes the parts of a bra that comfort depends on. The strap, the band, and the facing. And we make only narrow woven elastic. Nothing else can guarantee such a snug fit and soft feel. And nothing else can keep its perfect stretch as long.

We help a woman feel comfortable in other ways, too. Our 350 new designs each year keep pace with changing fashions. And our 230 shades of white assure a perfect match. If white isn't enough, then we'll match any color on earth.

You can give a woman exactly what she wants in a bra. Because we have a big hand in it.

NEW YORK:
J.R. Cohen, Inc.
200 Madison Ave.
212-685-3074
NEW ORLEANS:
Jack A. Cates
504-488-2532
CHARLOTTE, N.C.:
704-375-5596
CHICAGO, ILL.:
Margolis-Hertzberg, Inc.
312-725-4161
LOS ANGELES, CALIF.:
Charles Elliott, Inc.
213-627-2571

MooreFabrics. The narrow minded people. ©MF 1971

THE NARROW ELASTIC DIVISION OF CHICOPEE MILLS, INC., 1450 BROADWAY, NEW YORK, N.Y. 10018

So he made it to the top. Where did he go from there?

Nothing demands more careful, expert guidance than success.

Artists Entertainment Complex is in the business of career management. We manage the careers of *successful* creative and performing talent in motion pictures, television, recording, personal appearances and the theater.

It is our job to direct those careers into areas of long-term growth and development.

We are extraordinarily well-equipped to do so.

Artists Entertainment Complex represents a new merger of some of the best people in career management.

People with years of experience, leverage, and reputation in the industry. We've got the personal weight, the material resources and the creative imagination.

We regard every one of our clients as unique. For each we create unique career development plans on a very personal, individual basis. Plans that look three, five, ten years into the future.

Just imagine if Mr. Kong had thought a bit about long-term goals. Maybe he'd have stayed on top.

ARTISTS ENTERTAINMENT COMPLEX, INC.

NEW YORK
641 Lexington Avenue
New York, New York 10022
(212) 421-3760

CALIFORNIA
1100 North Alta Loma Road
Los Angeles, California 90069
(213) 657-3390

**MARTIN BREGMAN
ROY GERBER
NORMAN WEISS**

**JANE GELFMAN
MICHAEL LIEBERT
DAVID YAGER**

From the collection of Elliott Stein.

Where to eat in the jungle.

Even its severest critics have to admit to one singular advantage of this jungle over any other: no matter where you are, you're seldom further than a coconut's throw from a great restaurant.

And one way to make sure you'll have a great meal is to let the American Express Money Card shield be your native guide. It'll take you to places like this:

Fraunces Tavern
Broad & Pearl Street. 269-0144. New York's oldest tavern. Serving luncheon and dinner. Noon to 8 p.m. Revolutionary War Museum. Closed weekends.

Guv'nor Steak House
303 Madison Ave. 867-0540. Four rooms with the British touch. Steaks, prime ribs and lobster tails. Try the free Muncheon Board from 5-9 p.m. 7 days.

Al Cooper's Restaurant
130 W. 36th St. CH 4-2828. Excellent service accompanies great American meals. Specialties: steaks, chops, seafood. Free valet parking after 5 p.m.

Jimmy Weston's
131 E. 54th St. 838-8384. Handsome, comfortable restaurant. Excellent cuisine specializing in steaks and chops. Music and entertainment nightly.

Christo's
143 E. 49th St. 355-2695. This intimate steak house is a favorite gathering place for celebrities. Features à la carte specialties at lunch and dinner.

Bruce Ho's Four Seas
116 E. 57th St. PL 3-2610. Excellent Cantonese cooking, with some surprises. Try sizzling worba or Oceanica. Open lunch and dinner every day except Sunday.

Swiss Center
4 W. 49th St. 247-6545. Spectacular in décor, service and cuisine. Varied Swiss dishes featuring 12 authentic fondues. Closed Sundays.

Aperitivo
29 W. 56th St. 765-5155. Gourmet Italian cuisine. Luncheon and dinner. Holiday Magazine Award for excellence. Closed Sunday.

Keewah Yen
40 West 53rd St. 246-0770. The elegant Court cuisine of China, superbly interpreted.

Proof of the Pudding
1st Ave. Betw. 63rd & 64th. 421-5440. Frank Valenza welcomes you to this excellent restaurant specializing in outstanding cuisine from seafood to steak.

The Library
2475 Broadway (92nd St.) 799-4860. Brass, wood paneling and 5,000 books create easy comfort for dining on Continental cuisine. Open from noon-1 a.m.

Old Homestead
380 Northern Blvd., Great Neck. (516) 466-0606. Early American décor. Famous for lobsters, steaks and prime ribs. Luncheons, cocktails, dinner. Free parking.

The Money Card

TODAY'S BUILDING OWNERS ARE FACING A NEW KIND OF CRISIS. LOF GLASS HELPS SOLVE IT.

If the movies are any indication, building owners in the 30's had little to worry about except for an occasional visit from wandering gorillas. Today, in some parts of the U.S., there's something tougher to wrestle with . . . an energy shortage. At Libbey-Owens-Ford, we've engineered materials to help ease this shortage.

Vari-Tran® coated reflective glass is being used in buildings around the nation to cut building construction and operating costs. It does this by reducing both the installation and operating cost of air conditioning. Its ability to significantly reduce solar heat gain also reduces the amount of energy needed to cool buildings, which, in turn, helps cool the energy crisis.

For more information on Vari-Tran and other LOF architectural glass, write for our booklet "Reach for a Rainbow," Dept. B-1173, Libbey-Owens-Ford Company, Toledo, Ohio 43695.

LOF

KING KONG

ALL PLASTIC ASSEMBLY KIT

BUILD AND PAINT YOUR MODEL ANY WAY YOU WANT, BUT FIRST READ THE GENERAL INSTRUCTIONS ON THE BACK PAGE

KING KONG

Seven million years ago a gigantic ape was born on a small island off the Malay Peninsula. While still a baby, Kong's parents were killed by a tyrannosaurus. Millions of years passed, but the island remained the same. Prehistoric monsters still roamed there. It was as if time stopped on this one small island. King Kong grew unbelievably large and strong. Savage natives invaded the island, but Kong remained absolute ruler. In desperation, the natives built an immense wall across the base of the island to keep out the prehistoric creatures and the monster, Kong. They worshipped Kong as a god and appeased his wrath by sacrificing young natives to him.

A movie producer, known for his exciting and dangerous films, acquired a crudely drawn map of Kong's island, Skull Island. He hired a tramp steamer and set sail from New York in quest of adventure. With him was a girl, an unknown whom he was going to make into a star.

As weeks passed, the crew became disturbed at the secrecy of the voyage. Only the producer knew the destination. They were also disturbed by the great quantity of ammunition and gas bombs on board, enough to launch a full scale war. Finally, the crew insisted upon knowing the destination, so the producer asked if they had ever heard of King Kong. Of course they had, since it was a Malay superstition that most sailors had heard at one time or another. He told them that it was not a superstition, that he had the only existing map of the legendary island where Kong lived. Skull Island was their destination!

Early one morning the ship became fog-bound in strange waters. Suddenly out of the mists arose a gigantic skull. On closer inspection, the crew realized that it was only a rock formation, the one for which the island was named. In fact, the whole island was surrounded by rocks except for a small sandy peninsula. From the deck they could see the enormous retaining wall. They shuddered at the horrors that lay in wait for them behind the wall.

Landing on the beach of this Lost World, they realized that a sacrificial ceremony was going on. A native spotted them and the ceremony stopped. Their witch doctor wanted the girl from the ship as a gift for Kong. The crew refused and ran for their lives.

That night a group of the natives kidnapped the girl from the ship. They tied her to a stone altar outside of the gates of the wall. She heard the sounds of some immense beast drawing closer. The natives ran in terror. Kong came out of the jungle. He approached the altar, ready to take his delicious snack. Suddenly he stopped. Never had he seen a creature like this, a girl with golden hair. He picked her up

and held her close to his hideously wrinkled face. His hot breath seared her flesh. Then he carried her off into the jungle.

By now the crew realized that the girl was gone and went in search of her. They tore open the gates in time to see Kong carry her off. The producer sent back to the ship for gas bombs. When they arrived, he and the crew plunged into the dense underbrush. Overhead they saw flying lizards, around them they heard weird noises. From a thicket a gigantic spiked-tailed monster charged at them. Bullets would not stop it. Luckily, the gas bombs did, and the beast fell to the ground, stunned. Now they were able to kill the beast at close range.

Then the girl was sighted high on a ledge. A plan of rescue was decided upon. The crew would divert the ape while the first mate climbed onto the ledge to bring her down. It worked, but now they had to get back to the wall. They scattered, each taking a different path so Kong would be unable to follow them too easily.

Once inside the gates, the producer decided to bring King Kong back to civilization rather than to film him. Using the girl as a lure, they got Kong inside the gates where they used gas bombs to subdue him. Then, heavily chained, they loaded the unconscious Kong onto the ship.

Back in New York, King Kong was to go on display in the city's largest theater. Crowds gathered at the entrance. When the last person had been admitted, the lights grew dim. The building was silent with expectation. At last the curtain went up. There, behind bars was the mighty Kong. The crowd grew noisy in their fear and amazement. The noise so enraged Kong that with his tremendous strength he broke through the bars which imprisoned him. Frightened people scattered in all directions.

Kong got loose on the street. Helicopters followed his path of destruction. Buildings toppled. He crushed the elevated trains with one powerful blow from his mighty fist. At the Empire State Building Kong found what he was searching for, the girl from the voyage. He snatched her up and began climbing the side of the building. Fighter planes were called out. Kong set the girl on a ledge and began swatting at the planes as if they were flies. Finally, one plane got in range and mortally wounded Kong. He came crashing down the side of the building to the street beneath.

When the people realized that the monster, Kong, eighth wonder of the world, was killed, they breathed a sigh of relief. But, what of the rumors that Kong had a son? Is it merely legend — or is it fact?

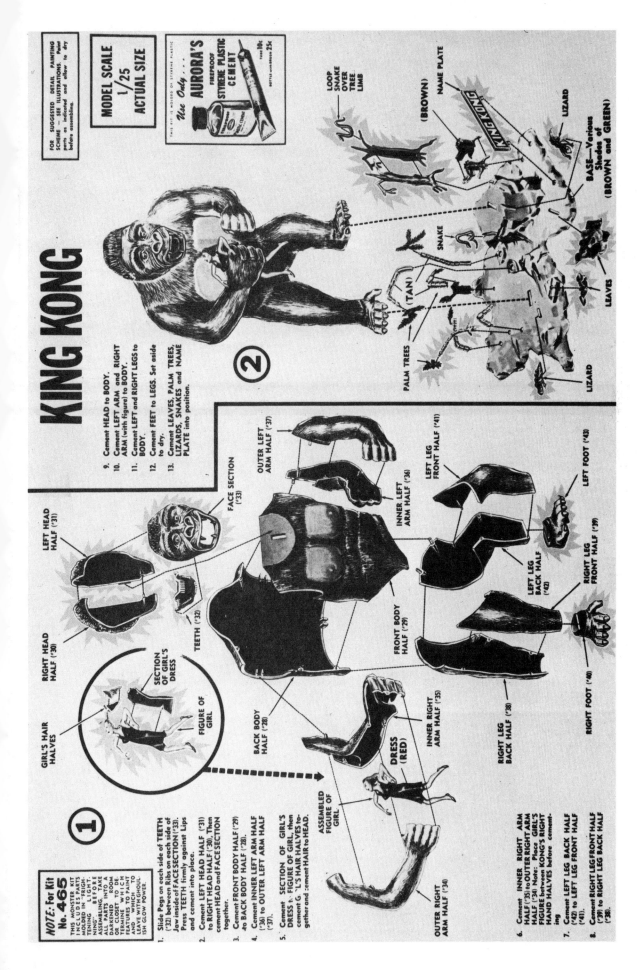

KING KONG

MODEL SCALE 1/25 ACTUAL SIZE

FOR SUGGESTED DETAIL PAINTING SCHEME — SEE ILLUSTRATIONS. Paint parts as indicated and allow to dry before assembling.

Use Only... AURORA'S FIREPROOF STYRENE PLASTIC CEMENT

THIS KIT IS MOLDED OF STYRENE PLASTIC

①

NOTE: For Kit No. **465**

THIS MONSTER KIT INCLUDES PARTS MOLDED IN "FRIGHTENING LIGHTNING". BEFORE ASSEMBLING, TAKE ALL PARTS INTO A DARKENED ROOM OR CLOSET TO DETERMINE WHICH FEATURES YOU WANT TO LEAVE WITH GHOULISH GLOW POWER.

1. Slide Pegs on each side of TEETH ('32) between Ribs on each side of Jaw inside of FACE SECTION ('33). Press TEETH firmly against Lips and cement into place.

2. Cement LEFT HEAD HALF ('31) to RIGHT HEAD HALF ('30). Then cement HEAD and FACE SECTION together.

3. Cement FRONT BODY HALF ('29) to BACK BODY HALF ('28).

4. Cement INNER LEFT ARM HALF ('36) to OUTER LEFT ARM HALF ('37).

5. Cement SECTION of GIRL'S DRESS to FIGURE of GIRL, then cement G. 'L'S HAIR HALVES together and cement HAIR to HEAD.

6. Cement INNER RIGHT ARM HALF ('35) to OUTER RIGHT ARM HALF ('34) Note: Place GIRL'S FIGURE between KONG'S RIGHT HAND HALVES before cementing

7. Cement LEFT LEG BACK HALF ('42) to LEFT LEG FRONT HALF ('41)

8. Cement RIGHT LEG FRONT HALF ('39) to RIGHT LEG BACK HALF ('38).

9. Cement HEAD to BODY.

10. Cement LEFT ARM and RIGHT ARM (with figure) to BODY.

11. Cement LEFT and RIGHT LEGS to BODY.

12. Cement FEET to LEGS. Set aside to dry.

13. Cement LEAVES, PALM TREES, LIZARDS, SNAKES and NAME PLATE into position.

②

LEFT HEAD HALF ('31)

RIGHT HEAD HALF ('30)

FACE SECTION ('33)

TEETH ('32)

GIRL'S HAIR HALVES

SECTION OF GIRL'S DRESS

FIGURE OF GIRL

OUTER LEFT ARM HALF ('37)

INNER LEFT ARM HALF ('36)

FRONT BODY HALF ('29)

BACK BODY HALF ('28)

ASSEMBLED FIGURE OF GIRL

DRESS (RED)

INNER RIGHT ARM HALF ('35)

OUTER RIGHT ARM HALF ('34)

LEFT LEG FRONT HALF ('41)

LEFT LEG BACK HALF ('42)

LEFT FOOT ('43)

RIGHT LEG FRONT HALF ('39)

RIGHT LEG BACK HALF ('38)

RIGHT FOOT ('40)

LOOP SNAKE OVER TREE LIMB

(BROWN)

NAME PLATE

KING KONG

LIZARD

BASE—Various Shades of (BROWN and GREEN)

SNAKE

(TAN)

LEAVES

LIZARD

PALM TREES

Amusement Park, New Jersey. Courtesy Steve Vertlieb.

Courtesy Punch

"*Frankly, I never dreamed the World Trade Center would get finished so quickly and without incident.*"

• • •

"... and then I got an idea. If only one could train him to become a window cleaner ..."

"*It looks like
an urban gorilla.*"

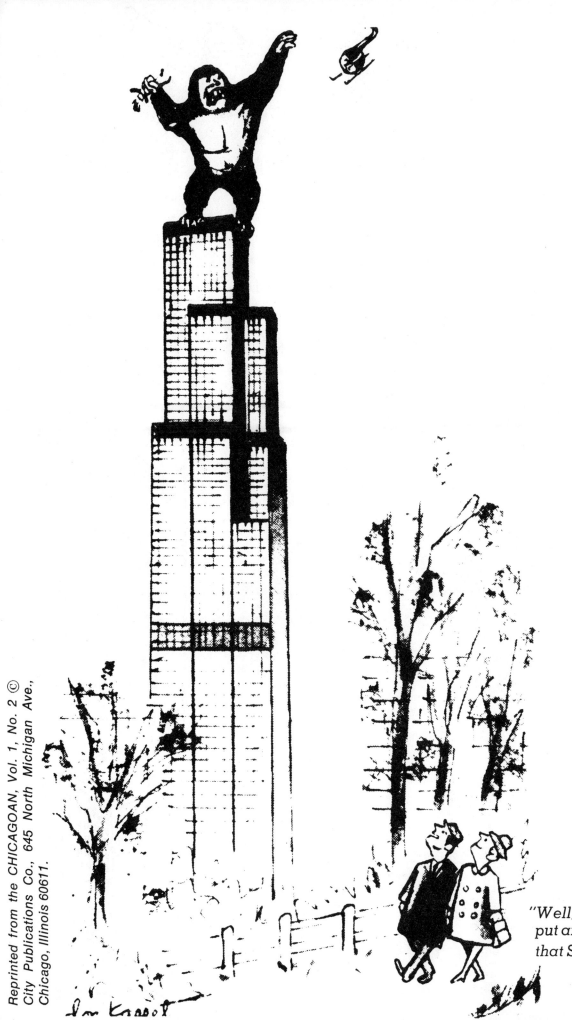

"Well, that should
put an end to all
that Second City talk."

From the collection of Elliott Stein.

Aragonés

"*No one, but no one, is safe on New York's streets these days!*"

BROOM-HILDA

SON OF MIGHTY JOE KONG

STARRING:

JAMES GARNER
as
Robert Headstrong

DORIS DAY
as
Rae Faye

DICK VAN DYKE
as
Bruce Cabbage

and **RICHARD BURTON** in his greatest character role as the

SON OF
MIGHTY JOE KONG

Illustrated by Mort Drucker   Written by Dick De Bartolo

YOU'LL GO "APE" OVER THIS ISSUE OF
MAD
IND
OUR PRICE 25¢ CHEAP
No. 94
April '65
NAM

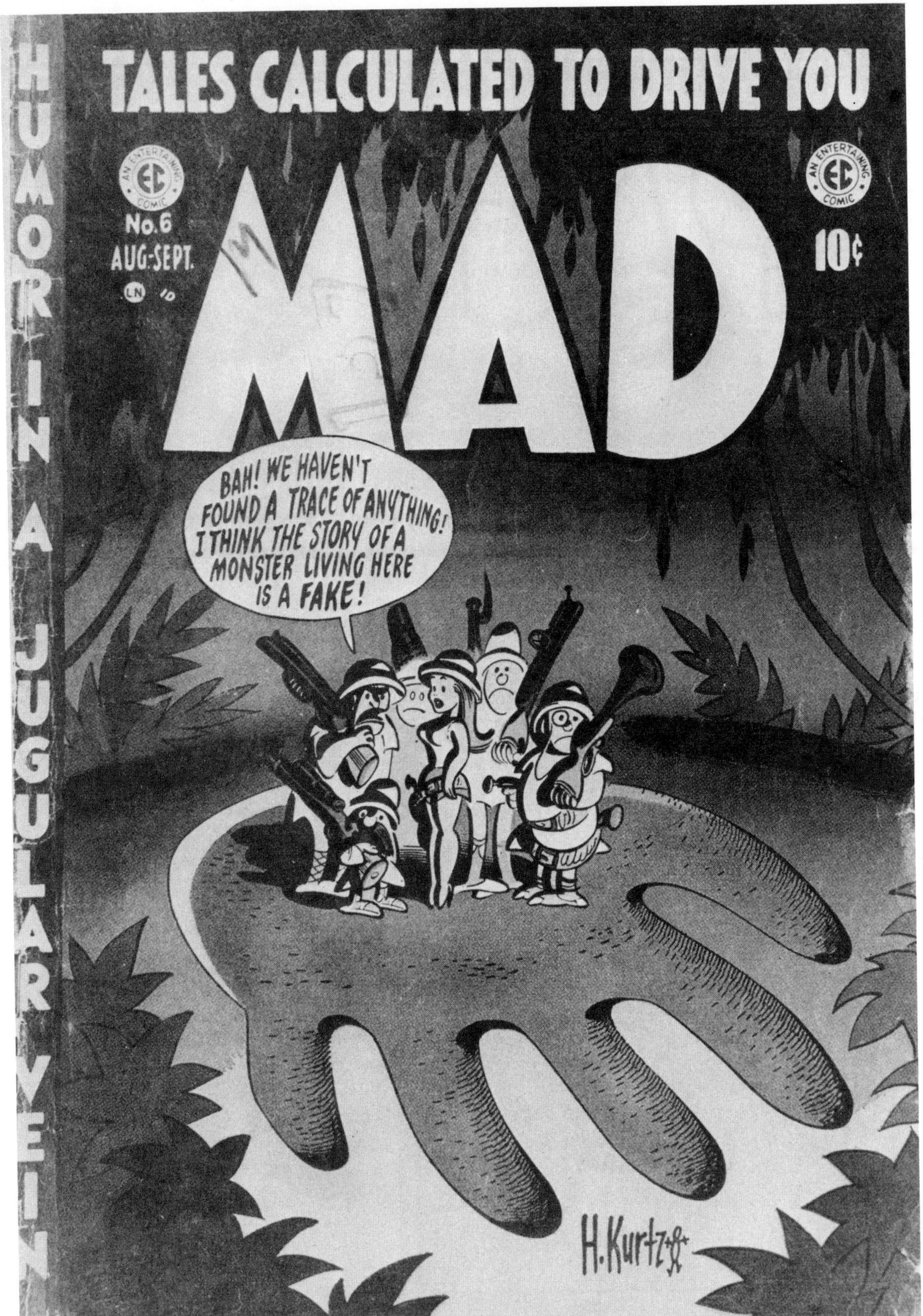
TALES CALCULATED TO DRIVE YOU
MAD
AN ENTERTAINING EC COMIC
No.6
AUG-SEPT.
10¢
HUMOR IN A JUGULAR VEIN
BAH! WE HAVEN'T FOUND A TRACE OF ANYTHING! I THINK THE STORY OF A MONSTER LIVING HERE IS A FAKE!
H. Kurtz

PING PONG!

THE TROPICS!...SOMEWHERE IN THE LATITUDES, SOUTH OF THE SARGOSSA SEA, A PEA-SOUP FOG...SO THICK YOU COULD CUT IT WITH A KNIFE... HUGS THE OCEAN!

AND INSIDE THE FOG...A SHIP RIDES LIKE A GHOST...A BLACK SHIP WITH A GRIM-FACED FEARLESS CREW OF MEN...RIDING TO ITS DESTINY...WITH *DEATH*...WITH *PONG!*

Cosmopolitan Parody   Women's Lib Pinups

NATIONAL LAMPOON

Jan. 1971 the Humor Magazine 75 Cents

Women

Special Would You Want Your Brother to Marry One? Issue

PRICE $1
SEPTEMBER 1971

THE MAGAZINE FOR MEN

Lt. Calley on Mylai 4
Gay Talese on Joe Bonanno
Kenneth Tynan on Roman Polanski
Malcolm Muggeridge's autobiography
New Fiction by
    William Styron
    John Updike
    Vladimir Nabokov
    F. Scott Fitzgerald
Rex Reed on Tennessee Williams
William Burroughs Jr. on his father
Graham Greene on his childhood
College preview '71-'72

Robert Alan Aurthur on Harry S Truman
James Dickey on Vince Lombardi

Censored scenes from King Kong and....
        Germaine Greer
            on Norman Mailer!

From the collection of Elliott Stein.

King Kong Memorial. *Courtesy Erik Forrest.*